RELIGION, SPIRITUALITY AND THE SOCIAL SCIENCES

Challenging marginalisation

Edited by Basia Spalek and Alia Imtoual

This edition published in Great Britain in 2008 by

The Policy Press
University of Bristol
Fourth Floor
Beacon House
Queen's Road
Bristol BS8 1QU
UK

Tel +44 (0)117 331 4054
Fax +44 (0)117 331 4093
e-mail tpp-info@bristol.ac.uk
www.policypress.org.uk

British Library Cataloguing in Publication Data
A catalogue record for this book is available from the British Library.

Library of Congress Cataloging-in-Publication Data
A catalog record for this book has been requested.

ISBN 978 1 84742 041 1 hardcover

Cover design by The Policy Press.
Front cover: image kindly supplied by Michael Chambers.
Printed and bound in Great Britain by MPG Books, Bodmin.

Contents

List of tables

Foreword

James A. Beckford, Professor Emeritus, University of Warwick

For much of the 20th century journalists and programme makers in the mainstream media of advanced industrial societies showed relatively little interest in stories about religion. 'The religion beat' and the 'god slot' tended to be among the least prestigious areas of the media in which to work – with some honourable exceptions such as the *New York Times* and *Le Monde*. The place of religion in the graphic and performing arts was also a faint echo of the prominence that it had enjoyed in previous centuries. But this changed in the 1990s when the public profile of religion began to increase. Not only did the news value of religious groups go up, but public curiosity about aspects of religion also heightened. The reasons for – and the timing of – these changes make the chapters in this edited collection particularly opportune and helpful in explaining the balance between continuity and change in spirituality and religion. The point about continuity is important, for public interest and involvement in religion had never declined in some regions of the world, including significant sections of technologically sophisticated societies.

There is no point in looking for a single event or factor that kick-started the revival of public interest in religion towards the end of the 20th century. It was more a question of separate developments that have criss-crossed in some complicated ways. Let me take the example of the regimes in Central and Eastern Europe that underwent rapid – if uneven – transformation in the early 1990s in the wake of the Soviet Union's collapse and the removal of the most repressive parts of the apparatus that had previously excluded religions from the public sphere. Various Orthodox churches and the Roman Catholic church were among those that regained control over their own activities and resources. As a result, levels of participation in religious activities and rates of professed beliefs increased sharply, ensuring that religious voices were once again heard in public life. The public profile of religion increased dramatically in a few years.

What is even more interesting from my point of view, however, is that many Evangelical and Pentecostal churches also took advantage of the relatively free market for religions at that time and launched recruitment campaigns in all the formerly state socialist countries. These churches were joined by large numbers of new religious movements, some of which deployed sophisticated marketing operations in countries where the level of religious diversity had previously been low. The resulting collision between, on the one hand, the mainstream churches that saw themselves as the natural guardians of religious and national identity and, on the other, the religious 'upstarts' in the region continues to be noisy and contentious. Constitutional changes and the work of constitutional courts have so far failed to resolve the tensions and conflicts between the formerly suppressed churches of the majorities and the recently mobilised churches and movements of the minorities – including the sizeable Muslim populations of the former Yugoslavia, Bulgaria, Albania and Russia. In other words, religion suddenly became a matter of contentious and high-profile dispute throughout Central and Eastern Europe in the early 1990s. The ramifications have been felt in other regions of the world where, for example, Muslim refugees and asylum seekers from the violence in the former Yugoslavia have settled. International debates about the freedom of religion have also been triggered, in part, by the reluctance of political authorities in Russia to accept the legality of religious movements as diverse as Jehovah's Witnesses, the Salvation Army and the Church of Scientology. Finally, it remains to be seen how far the influx of Polish migrants into the UK in the early 21st century will affect other Roman Catholics in their leaving and receiving parishes.

The UK provides a second example of the heightening of the public profile of religion since the 1990s. The process began with preparations for the millennium celebrations and was boosted by the personal interest that the then Prime Minister Tony Blair and some of his government ministers displayed in matters of faith. After much wrangling, the Millennium Dome in London was equipped with a faith zone and chaplains. But the most interesting developments occurred after 2000 when it was decided to place on a permanent footing the consultative arrangements through which the British government had worked with various faith communities and the UK Inter-Faith Network in preparing the millennium celebrations. This eventually led to the establishment of protocols covering regular consultations with representatives of faith communities in virtually all government departments and at the level of local government as well. In addition, many of the government policies that were aimed at achieving 'sustainable communities' and 'urban regeneration' contained provisions for working with faith communities and faith-based organisations as valued partners of central and local government. Official encouragement of 'faith schools' has been another manifestation of support for policies that give a higher profile to religion in the public sphere.

A further boost to the newly acquired significance that the British government attached to religion was the appointment of the first full-time Muslim Adviser to the Prison Service of England and Wales in 1999 and the expansion of the Faith Communities Unit at the Home Office. The government's response to the attacks on the US in September 2001 and the bombings in London in July 2005 included massive investment of resources in programmes to monitor Muslim groups, to combat ideological extremism among young Muslims and to foster the closer integration of Muslims in civil society in the UK. The background to these eye-catching developments is the much less spectacular – but in the long term more important – rise in the salience of religion in discussions of multiculturalism. British discourses about visible minorities initially centred on notions of race and racism but slowly made way for discourse about ethnicity. More recently, however, increasing importance has been accorded to questions of religious differences and to policies that promote religious diversity as a value in itself as well as a part of the overall vision of British society as a 'community of communities'. By contrast, French governments have consistently asserted the principle of *laïcité* or republican secularism in order to oppose practices that might seem to acknowledge the value of religious 'communal' identities in the public sphere.

In addition to these particular reasons for the heightened public profile of religion in the supposedly secular continent of Europe, there are many other factors that have pushed or pulled religion higher up the public agenda in most regions of the world. They include a wide range of developments in science and technology that have elicited strongly religious and anti-religious responses. Bioethical issues concerning reproductive rights, genetic manipulation, cloning, stem cell cultivation and alternative therapies are especially controversial in the perspective of some faith traditions. The religious stakes are also high in relation to the environment, warfare, torture, racism, sexism, human rights, poverty and justice.

In short, religion and spirituality now demand serious attention for a wide variety of reasons. One of the great merits of the contributions to this volume is that they grapple directly with the theoretical, conceptual and methodological challenges presented to social scientists by the upsurge of public interest in religion. The authors are self-reflexive and critical about the need for a social scientific study of religion that is well equipped to investigate not only the changes that have occurred in the meanings of religion and spirituality but also the contexts in which religion and spirituality are practised. Politics, gender, the media and the law are four particularly important contexts. The interplay between empirical and theoretical arguments is another feature of many chapters.

This collection is also distinctive for including chapters about a variety of different countries and religious traditions. This degree of inclusiveness is increasingly necessary in a world where the forces of globalisation are refracted through regional, national and local lenses. Unusually, several chapters also examine the changing forms of secularism at a time when religion's place in the public sphere has become simultaneously more contested and more visible.

Finally, readers will appreciate the slightly subversive or iconoclastic spirit with which the chapters challenge the rigidities that have characterised some social scientific approaches to understanding religion and spirituality. The intention is clearly to gain fresh insights by crossing boundaries and provoking debate about shibboleths and received wisdom. This breath of fresh air will inspire new thinking and exciting research in the future.

Acknowledgements

Basia Spalek and Alia Imtoual would like to thank the following:

The Creator
The Merciful
The All-Knowing,

our families in various parts of the world,

the Institute of Applied Social Studies, The University of Birmingham (UK),

the School of Education, Flinders University (Australia),

colleagues and friends who provided critique and encouragement,

Philip de Bary, Emily Watt and the team at The Policy Press for believing in the book,

the late Jo Campling for getting us started,

and, of course, all the contributors who made this book possible. Without their wonderful work this book would be still just an idea.

List of contributors

John D'Arcy May, Professor, Irish School of Ecumenics, Trinity College Dublin, Ireland.

Miguel Farias, Research Associate, Ian Ramsey Centre, Theology Faculty, University of Oxford, UK; Psychology and Religion Research Group, Faculty of Divinity, University of Cambridge, UK; Númena – Research Centre of Human and Social Sciences, Portugal.

Maria Frahm–Arp, Research Fellow, Wits Institute for Social and Economic Research (WISER), Wits University, South Africa.

Leslie Francis, Professor of Religions and Education, University of Warwick, UK; Canon Theologian, Bangor Cathedral, UK.

Maree Gruppetta, Lecturer, School of Education, University of Western Sydney, Australia.

Elisabeth Hense, Assistant Professor, Faculty of Theology and Religious Studies, Radboud University, Nijmegen, the Netherlands.

Caroline Humphrey, Senior Lecturer in Social Work, Department of Social Sciences/Centre for Spirituality Studies, University of Hull, UK.

Alia Imtoual, Lecturer, School of Education, Flinders University, Australia.

Ursula King, Professor Emerita of Theology and Religious Studies and Senior Research Fellow, Institute of Advanced Studies, University of Bristol, UK; Professional Research Fellow, Centre for Gender and Religious Research, School of Oriental and African Studies, University of London, UK.

Gordon Lynch, Director of the Centre for Religion and Contemporary Society, Birkbeck, University of London, UK.

Tariq Modood, Professor of Sociology, Politics and Public Policy, Centre for the Study of Ethnicity and Citizenship, University of Bristol, UK.

Lareen Newman, Research Fellow, Department of Public Health, Flinders University, Australia.

Adam Possamai, Associate Professor of Sociology, University of Western Sydney, Australia.

Muzammil Quraishi, Lecturer in Criminology, School of English, Sociology, Politics and Contemporary History, University of Salford, UK.

Holly Randell–Moon, Doctorial candidate, Macquarie University, Australia.

Natassja Smiljanic, Visiting Lecturer, University of Birmingham, UK.

Basia Spalek, Senior Lecturer in Criminology and Criminal Justice Studies, Institute of Applied Social Science, University of Birmingham, UK.

Introduction

Alia Imtoual and Basia Spalek

Religion, spirituality and the social sciences is an international, edited collection of work, consisting of contributions from key academics in the fields of religious studies, cultural studies, political science, criminology, sociology, health and social policy. It is part of a growing body of social science research that is increasingly including, and engaging with, issues of religion and spirituality. As such, this book is very much a product of contemporary theorising and debate around religion and spirituality, which, despite the effects of the Enlightenment and modernisation, are generating considerable and ever-expanding discussion, controversy, policy making and research.

For contributors such as John D'Arcy May, the engagement must commence with the various disciplines beginning to have dialogue with one another on questions of religiosity and spirituality so as to break down some of the artificial and unhelpful borders that have been placed around knowledge. A number of other contributors, such as Lareen Newman, Maria Frahm-Arp and Leslie J. Francis, argue that quantitative social science across a number of disciplines has ignored religion and faith identities as an important variable in data collection. They demonstrate that the marginalisation of such factors has been to the detriment of understandings about the social worlds we inhabit. Other contributions argue that the deep embedding of secularism within contemporary social science approaches has imposed rigid borders on knowledge and understandings of the experiences of people who hold faith identities. Work by Maree Gruppetta, Muzammil Quraishi, and Natassja Smiljanic demonstrates that secularism in the social sciences has operated as an oppressive structure which de-legitimises research that values faith perspectives.

This edited collection is divided into three parts. Each part brings together a series of contributions that focuses on a particular theme.

Part 1: Key debates on secularism and society

In this section contributions argue that secularism is a powerful, if largely invisible, framework of understanding. While scholars have critiqued similar frameworks over the years (for example, patriarchy, capitalism, hetero-normativity), secularism has been overlooked despite also being a framework that imposes borders on knowledge and understanding about the social world. Contributions to this section of the volume map the early engagements with religion in the social sciences and the subsequent banishment of religion and spirituality to specialist studies. They argue that religion and spirituality pose significant challenges for social scientific research as it has developed in the Western tradition. The emergence of social science disciplines can be closely linked to ideas of modernity, when scientific rationale (secular rationalism) increasingly came to replace doctrinal outlooks and perceptions, and religion and spirituality were marginalised as parochial and unscientific. Contributions to this section also examine the ways in which discourses of secularism and religiosity are played out in particular social arenas. This creates the context for later contributions in the volume examining the ways in which the social sciences have engaged with these practices.

John D'Arcy May's chapter (Chapter One) places this historical trajectory in the context of the division of disciplines within the social sciences. He argues that only through an explicit engagement with religions can the disciplines of social science overcome the restrictions placed around them by hegemonic secularism. He also argues powerfully that if the social sciences wish to remain pertinent in commenting and critiquing social practices and events, they need to be better prepared to engage with faith perspectives than current hegemonic epistemologies and methodologies allow for.

For Adam Possamai in Chapter Two, the hegemony of secularism and the process of secularisation are being undermined by the gradual (what he terms 'shy') re-introduction of the religious into the social fabric of Australian society, particularly in its political manifestations.

Tariq Modood's contribution (Chapter Three) uses Islam as a case study by which to examine European secular states' abilities to interact with overt religious identities and politicised religious communities. He argues that a certain understanding of secularism which would oppose the inclusion of such communities into the functioning of the state is less helpful in building tolerant societies than more 'evolving interpretations' allow.

Focusing again on Australia as a case study is Holly Randell-Moon's chapter (Chapter Four), which argues that although Australia sees itself as secular in nature there is an implicit and unacknowledged relationship between certain forms of religious expression and the Australian secular state. For both Possamai and Randell-Moon, the deployment of particular discourses of secularity poses a major problem for multi-faith, pluralistic societies. Their work demonstrates that only through the existence of critical social science research in which religion and spirituality are valued and respected can these issues be examined and addressed.

For Gordon Lynch in Chapter Five, understandings of the 'secular' and 'religious' or 'spiritual' are problematised in the context of contemporary forms of media. He argues that the popularity of 'lifestyle' magazines, television shows and so on operate as a re-visioning and re-inscription of religiosity and spirituality in a secular society. He argues that the presence of 'invisible religion' poses significant challenges to the hegemony of discourses of secularism both in society and in the social sciences.

Part 2: Marginalisation of religious and spiritual issues

This section of the volume focuses on the growing body of social science research that is challenging the marginalisation of issues of religion and spirituality. Many of these challenges come from new and emerging scholars who are increasingly less content to accept hegemonic social science approaches. Coming from a diverse range of disciplinary traditions, these writers have presented powerful and transformative engagements with their respective disciplinary frameworks such as Natassja Smiljanic's futures-oriented envisioning of legal theory and judgement (Chapter Ten) and Lareen Newman's critique of quantitative demography's marginalisation of religion as a variable in fertility research (Chapter Seven). Some of the contributions focus on issues specific to their disciplinary tradition while others engage with broader questions such as: 'are social science practices that emerge from "Western" traditions, including an engagement with Western Christianity, useful for analysing non-Western contexts, particularly when non-Western religions are a factor?', and 'is it possible for a research practice that values "secularity" and "rationality" to genuinely and respectfully analyse discourses of faith and spirituality?'.

Many of the contributions argue that current and hegemonic social science discourses and practices are unable to allow researchers to fully engage with issues of religion and spirituality so long as contemporary notions of secularism remain a part of them.

For Maria Frahm-Arp (Chapter Six) and Lareen Newman (Chapter Seven), their respective contributions argue that social science research has not only failed to successfully engage with the potential of faith perspectives for methodology but has also ignored the importance of these perspectives for data collection and analysis. Their critiques of existing approaches indicate the shortsightedness of the hegemony of secularist discourses for nuanced and complex research with communities, including faith perspectives.

Caroline Humphrey (Chapter Eight) proposes quite a radical alternative to current practices in her contribution. She argues that spirituality and faith-based world-views should be embraced as part of the repertoire of social science analyses. Humphrey terms this 'turning the world upside down' whereby researchers and caring professionals are encouraged to explore faith-based world-views as tools of social analysis.

Ursula King's contribution to this volume (Chapter Nine) offers a unique critique of feminist research that has not kept pace with the increasing number of feminist movements identifying with spirituality and faith perspectives. She argues that secular feminist approaches predominate in social science research and are unable to recognise or engage with spiritual-feminisms. She argues that this needs to be challenged.

In the final contribution to this section, Natassja Smiljanic (Chapter Ten) similarly argues that legal theorisations have become so devoid of connections to the lived worlds of those they affect that they are no longer able to meet the needs of complex, multi-faith societies. She conceptualises a deeper and more spiritual approach to understanding the law and its applications and argues powerfully that this approach would produce more nuanced, and ultimately more just, legal understandings.

Part 3: Reflections on social science research methodologies

Contributions to this section reflect on the social scientific tools of analysis that are used to document, explore, reflect, critique and acknowledge the religious and spiritual dimensions to individuals' lives and communities. Both quantitative (for example, Leslie J. Francis, Chapter Eleven) and qualitative (for example, Muzammil Quraishi, Chapter Thirteen) researchers have brought their own perspectives and experiences to bear on the processes and methodologies used. One common and key argument made in many of the contributions is that the methodologies developed within the secular social sciences are unable to fully embrace faith perspectives and are thus inappropriate for analysing many aspects of religion, spirituality and how these intersect with individuals' lives.

Leslie J. Francis (Chapter Eleven) engages with the notion of the 'slipperiness' of definitions of religion and spirituality in his contribution when he reflects on the ways religion has been used in quantitative studies. He argues that the marginalisation of self-assigned religious affiliation as an indicator of religious behaviour and belief has been to the detriment of the literature because without it, the nuances of lived belief and faith are unable to be fully captured by quantitative data.

In their contribution, Miguel Farias and Elisabeth Hense (Chapter Twelve) engage with the construction of spirituality as a marginalised aspect of religiosity. They argue that the social sciences need to be more accepting of researcher engagements with spirituality and non-mainstream faith perspectives because they argue that these can offer new insights into a range of social factors.

For instance, Muzammil Quraishi (Chapter Thirteen) argues that notions of 'insider' and 'outsider' are often complex and difficult to untangle when placed in the context of shared faith perspectives. He argues that particular disciplines, such as criminology, have only recognised religion as a factor to be 'studied' rather than as an integral part of the complexities of real-world research. His chapter posits that such markers of identity are legitimate factors in shaping the research interaction and that the social sciences need to accept faith-based perspectives and religious affiliation as important to the research process and relationships.

Maree Gruppetta's chapter (Chapter Fourteen) reflects on the lived results of working within a disciplinary tradition that marginalises religious knowledge. For her, this lack of knowledge when interacting with research participants who hold faith perspectives, even when the research did not involve a study of religious belief, was a major factor in shaping the subsequent interactions. Gruppetta argues that a researcher who holds little theological knowledge of a particular religion will encounter significant difficulties when trying to understand individuals' interpretations of their religion and their belief systems. At the same time, the complexity and fluidity of a term such as 'spiritual', and the difficulty of applying scientific techniques to its measurement and exploration, poses some difficult research questions.

Religion, spirituality and the social sciences is engagingly written, providing an invaluable resource for social science students, educators and researchers who are interested in issues relating to religion and spirituality in the context of the strong influence of secularism in most Western societies. In a time when, despite the centrality of secularist attitudes, a growing number of individuals are claiming or reclaiming a religious or spiritual identity for themselves, social science researchers must engage with this seeming incompatibility if they are to conduct ethical, respectful and accurate research. In order for this to occur social science researchers must engage with the implications of a religious/spiritual identity on social science methodologies that arise from a largely secularist intellectual tradition. The contributions in this book begin this engagement.

Part I
Key debates on secularism and society

In this Part, John D'Arcy May (Chapter One) argues that secularisation occurs differently depending on context but that a process of political secularisation is not necessarily concomitant with a decline in religiosity among the population. This leads him to ask whether or not religion can, or should, be allowed a role in the politics of an otherwise 'secular' state. Also dealing with the process of secularisation is Adam Possamai, in Chapter Two, which critiques the boundaries and categories social researchers have developed around issues of secularisation and religiosity.

Tariq Modood in Chapter Three explores political multiculturalism, and the kinds of specific policy demands that are being made by, or on behalf of, religious groups, and Muslim identity politics, in particular. For Modood, the inclusion of Islam as an organised religion and of Muslim identity as a public identity are necessary to integrate Muslims and to pursue religious equality. Furthermore, he argues that although such inclusion might run against certain interpretations of secularism, it is not inconsistent with what secularism means in practice in Europe. For Modood, an evolving, moderate secularism that can support compromise should be developed and encouraged, rather than an ideological secularism that is being reasserted which opposes Islam – this needing to be resisted no less than the radical anti-secularism of some Islamists.

Holly Randell-Moon focuses her chapter (Chapter Four) on the representation of secularism in Australian constitutional and lego-political discourse. Specifically, she argues that hegemonic constructions of both modernity and secularism have allowed for the strategic deployment of such terms to marginalise minority religious groups in Australia. Gordon Lynch's chapter (Chapter Five) explores the theoretical implications of the intersection between religion and 'secular' lifestyle media. Lynch argues that secular contemporary lifestyle media might be viewed as being an example of the 'invisible religion' of late modern Western society. In this chapter, Lynch considers the concept of 'invisible religion' and its implications for the study of religion and the sacred in contemporary culture.

ONE

Political religion: secularity and the study of religion in global civil society

John D'Arcy May

Introduction

The former German Chancellor Helmut Schmidt, himself a committed Christian, remarked in the late 1970s: "You can't run a country by the Sermon on the Mount." Yet, referring to the fraught situation in the Middle East, with its continual demonisation of the enemy and endless tit-for-tat killings, my German colleague Heinz-Günther Stobbe observed around the same time: "The Sermon on the Mount is the most realistic text in the New Testament." The two comments neatly sum up the dilemma of religions in the public arena: the case could be made that their idealism, their promise of transforming society by transcending it, is indispensable to public morality and good government. Yet when such aspirations are turned into a programme, suspicions arise: in India the *dharma* is being proposed in the form of the Hindutva ideology as the only viable basis of the state, while some Muslims claim that only the implementation of the *Sharia* can establish a just polity. 'Political religion', then, is a term loaded with ambiguities: should religion be instrumentalised by politics, or should it be kept separate from the political sphere? Or alternatively, is it the case that religions of whatever type are constitutively political in their different ways, such that their political orientation will always come to light in the public sphere (May, 1999)? And if any of this is true, how can a social scientist study it?

We would therefore do well to be cautious about addressing the topic of 'political religion', whether in the context of Religious Studies, which some see as an illegitimate child of Christian theology, or International Relations, which might be characterised as extending the study of the political institutions of nation states to include the relations between states themselves. The inherited presupposition of both disciplines is that the secularisation and consequent privatisation of religion are fundamental to modernity, that any deviation from this canonical view represents a threat to the normative principles of liberal democracies, and that the politicisation of religion, its re-entry into civil society as a public actor, is some kind of distortion or anomaly whose study can safely be left to those whose interests run to social deviation and sectarianism.[1]

This is ironic, because the great political thinkers of the Enlightenment, such as Locke, Rousseau and de Tocqueville, although they approved of the separation of church and state, did so in the name of religious toleration, for they believed that religious liberty and political liberty were allies, not adversaries, and that underlying what Rousseau called 'civil religion' was not only a 'natural religion' but a properly theological issue of human wholeness and moral conscience (Reynolds and Durham, 1996; Fiala, 2005).

> Because of the Westphalian presumption, 'virtue-ethics' are contrary to the approach of Western governments and development agencies, which argue that 'religion' gets in the way of helping the poor or promoting development. What has to be remembered is that there is a close relationship between religious freedom and political freedom, and religious toleration often has been the beginning of political toleration, civil society, and democracy. (Thomas, 2003, pp 45-6)

It is this ambivalence of the linkage between politics and religion that leads me to address the problems raised for the study of religion in the highly politicised context of globalisation. To make secularity the presupposition of the 'scientific' study of religion is to overlook the fact that secularisation is itself a religious phenomenon, as the 'founding fathers' of the social sciences were well aware. The historical process of 'secularisation' in its literal sense – the forced reduction of sacred people and objects (monks and nuns, monasteries and convents, rulers and their bureaucracies) to the 'lay state' – at one and the same time posited and destroyed the dualism of sacred and secular. Fundamental to this process was the separation of church and state in Europe, which liberated not only the arts and sciences but also citizens and their consciences from ecclesiastical control. What was lost in this process was the complementarity of sacred and secular, the awareness that the one does not make sense without the other and that their duality does not make sense outside its Western European context of origin. Take away the secular, and the sacred uses its claim on absolute truth to monopolise power; but take away the sacred, and the secular withers because it is cut off from its sources of moral strength and imagination. The sacred means this world functioning as a mediator of transcendence; the secular implies that this same world is autonomous and sufficient unto itself (Loy, 2004, pp 27-8).

> What may be misleading about this discussion of an enervated sacral dimension is that it still seems to suggest *superimposing* something (for example, some particular religious understanding of the meaning of our lives) onto the secular world (that is, the world 'as it really is'). My point is the opposite: our usual understanding of the secular is a *deficient* worldview (in Buddhist terms, a delusion) distorted by the fact that one half of the original duality has gone missing, although

now it has been absent so long that we have largely forgotten about it. (Loy, 2004, p 28; emphasis in original)

The problems involved in taking for granted that secularity is an indispensable precondition for both the study of religion and the conduct of international affairs should by now be apparent. This chapter sets out to investigate in what sense religion can legitimately be political, to consider the implications of this for International Relations, and to ask whether the coming global civil society will in fact be secular in the same sense as its nation state predecessors, adverting throughout to the consequences of our reflections for Religious Studies.

The pitfalls of trying to yoke 'political' to 'religion'

In Indigenous societies such as those of Melanesia there is no real distinction between economic, political and 'religious' activity; it may also legitimately be asked what sense the concept of secularisation makes in civilisations such as the Chinese and Japanese, in which religion was always a this-worldly affair and continues to be so under conditions of rapid and thoroughgoing industrialisation and technological innovation. Where more other-worldly religions such as the great monotheisms have aspired to rise above politics and purify themselves of secular concerns, they have generally failed, even where they have striven to convince themselves otherwise. In its attempts not to be, religion usually finishes up being political; religions that have voluntarily withdrawn from the public arena, such as the Anabaptists of the left-wing Reformation and many varieties of contemporary fundamentalism, whether Christian or Islamic, as well as those which have tried to dominate it, such as the Roman Catholic church at certain stages in its history and Islam from the very beginning of its, have become political actors in so doing. Religions may choose to shun the public arena because they cannot dominate it or because it defines them in a way with which they disagree, but these are *public* acts by *social* actors in a *political* forum, in much the same way as the mere mutual awareness of two or more conscious subjects already constitutes communication; even if the people in question wish to avoid communicating explicitly, it is this that they are communicating! In Martin E. Marty's laconic formulation: 'Not to decide about religion in public life is to decide' (Marty, 2005, p 162).

There is considerable tension today between religious beliefs and practices forged in cultural settings such as ancient India and Palestine or medieval Europe and Arabia and their status in pluralist – which is taken to mean *ipso facto* secular – societies, not to mention the emerging global public sphere. One of the taken-for-granted orthodoxies of modernity is the 'privatisation' of religion once 'secularliberaldemocracy' has been established. The secularisation of society itself, we are told, inevitably decouples religion from politics and makes it a matter of personal preference and interior conviction. In this (now classical) 'liberal' view of society, religion has no business in the public sphere. Reason is public, but not religion; scientific theories and the evidence for them, like political decisions and the interests they represent, are properly matters of public debate, but not religious rituals and their mythological rationales, because there is no agreed medium in which they can be expressed apart from that imposed on them from without by secular reason. In the new public space created by globalisation and the 'real virtuality' (Castells, 1996, pp 410-18; May, 2003, 2005) of electronic communications media, it is not so much the *privatisation* (retreat into interiority) of religious convictions as the *individualisation* (isolation in autonomy) of the culturally uprooted and disorientated that is making possible the new universalisms of the 'next Christendom' (Jenkins, 2002) or the 'virtual *ummah*' (Roy, 2004): cut off from ties to community and place by social mobility or emigration, individuals absorb the shock of individualisation by identifying with idealised, ahistorical versions of all-encompassing religious world-views such as those of Buddhism, Christianity and Islam. The obverse of this globalisation of the religious is the consolidation of localised groups of true believers who demand space in the public sphere to be exclusively themselves.

It is at this point that the question of how to study religions in global public space becomes interesting. The founders of *Religionswissenschaft* took their scientific stand on comparativism and phenomenological method, a heritage which is indeed foundational for the discipline of Religious Studies, but in the context defined by orientalism and post-colonial theory this is increasingly regarded as a Western perspective which prematurely universalises 'religion' and approaches the religions as Christianity's 'religious others' (King, 1999; Masuzawa, 2005). The reluctance of the social sciences, including both International Relations and Religious Studies, to react to the global resurgence of religion exposes flaws in social science methodology that are becoming intellectually counterproductive and are stifling the contributions the study of religions could make to world peace. In such a context, 'political religion' becomes not only a proper but also an urgent topic for Religious Studies.

The more unambiguously 'religious' the religions are, the greater their potential to become political factors: this is my first proposition. If it can be substantiated, another follows: the complicity of Religious Studies in the ideology of neutrality towards its subject matter may have to be revised, for under these auspices there is a danger that students of religion will miss the very elements that make religions 'religious' and *consequently* 'political'. The stance of strict abstention from judgements of truth about religions is itself part of a practical-political programme stemming from the Enlightenment with its differentiation of science and art, politics and economics as autonomous spheres emancipated from religious control; in other words, 'secularised' (Casanova, 1994, p 214). This emancipation was the indispensable presupposition of modernity, and wherever it occurs there is tension with the religious traditions that previously presided over these spheres (although in East Asia, as we have seen, one may ask whether it ever made sense to speak of secularisation in this way). The proper place of religions in specifically 'modern' societies and their polities is to remain outside the public sphere in which rationality obtains, and hence beyond the possibility of political intervention.

The fascinating aspect of the new developments is that religions, in their fundamentalist and neofundamentalist forms, are eagerly placing *themselves* in this extra-social, a-political, de-culturated position. There is a sense in which anyone who expresses a firm conviction in public these days is liable to be labelled a fundamentalist; but it is also the case that there are fundamentalist movements that are well aware of their own political impact, thereby making calculated use of the secularisation of societies: the rise of *Hindutva* in secular India, the influence of the New Christian Right on neoconservative politics in the US and the tensions generated by radical Islamists in Europe are cases in point. The *study* of religions, at least as it is still institutionalised in most of our universities, continues to restrict itself to the intrinsic interest of the religions as historical and social phenomena, bracketing out any implications they might have for personal religious commitment or the public role of religion. Hence my question: is this a sufficient rationale for the study of religions in a world where the religions have once again become both political actors and personal identity markers on a global scale? Some scholars of religion are calling for the deployment of the resources of the religions themselves in the study of religion, in much the same way as heavily camouflaged Protestant Christian assumptions used to define the parameters of Religious Studies (Cabezón and Davaney, 2004; Cabezón, 2006).

The term 'political', too, deserves a moment's reflection. Politics is problem solving, not the application of ready-made theories to practice, which facilitates the creation of ideologies. This can become a significant temptation for religions, but ideology tends to politicise and instrumentalise and ultimately to falsify religions, even when they vehemently reject any such politicisation. The situation in Northern Ireland, of course, is a veritable laboratory for the study of such instrumentalisation (May, 1995). Hasenclever and Rittberger (2003, p 113) state that 'the causal pathway is unambiguous: The politicisation of religions leads to the escalation of given disputes and never to their de-escalation', and Lausten and Waever (2003, pp 165-6) are even more unequivocal: '*Religion plus securitization equals ideology*', but '*Ideology is quasi-religion, not religion per se*' (emphasis in original). In this framework, then, my reflections are not purely disinterested but try to envisage a future in which the study of religion will become more 'engaged' while preserving its 'scientific' integrity.

The 'Westphalian presumption' and the 'return of religion' in International Relations

It is said that within days of 11 September 2001 copies of the Qur'an were sold out across the US. The fact that 'they' attacked 'us' is not the purest of motives for a renewed interest in the world's religions, but there is no denying that the radicalisation of militant Islam has shaken many in the West out of their complacent assumption that the religions are the politically irrelevant expression of private convictions. Islam's emotional hold over its adherents and the sheer spiritual power it is capable of mobilising worldwide can be exaggerated (Roy, 1995, 2004), but the realisation that religion, *as* religion, can be a power factor has accelerated the revision already under way of the theories of 'secularisation' that dominated the social sciences for more than a generation (Wuthnow, 1992; Berger, 1999). It is becoming apparent that secularisation can affect different aspects of society and its political and administrative structures in different ways: it can mean the differentiation of autonomous spheres such as science and politics from religious tutelage, thus rendering them 'secular'; the decline of religious belief and practice, as can be observed particularly in Europe; and the marginalisation of religion by confining it to the private sphere (Casanova, 1994, p 211). These can occur either separately or together in various combinations. Secularisation is thus contextual, involving quite different dynamics in different historical and cultural situations. This discussion involves us immediately in a reassessment of certain aspects of the Enlightenment and their normative status for education and culture in the West.

Once the signatories of the Peace of Westphalia had conceded that the church was no longer coincident with society, as it had been in the form of 'Christendom' throughout the Middle Ages, and that the now divided Christian churches could enter into various political allegiances without thereby necessarily providing grounds for conflict (*cuius regio, eius religio*, loosely translated as 'the religion of the subject shall conform to the religion of the ruler'), the churches had unwittingly started down the road that was to see them become mere 'denominations' in secular pluralist states, and the states themselves had just as unwittingly set the stage for an international order of competing ideologies, in which at least some nation states are organised as societies that explicitly recognise ideological pluralism. The outcome of both processes was that 'the religious sphere became just another sphere' (Casanova, 1994, p 21) in the ideologically neutral public forum in which world-views interact and compete. Precisely this is now happening to Islam as it makes the painful passage from its cultural homelands to the multicultural societies of the West. The social sciences, whose foundational theorists such as Weber, Durkheim and Troeltsch wrestled with the relationship between religion and society, eventually took it as axiomatic that the privatisation of religion – in other words, secularisation – is the inevitable outcome of processes of modernisation and industrialisation and the indispensable presupposition of pluralist democracies and the rational conduct of public affairs; even Thomas Luckmann's 'invisible religion' and Niklas Luhmann's redefinition of it as a 'contingency formula' make this assumption (Casanova, 1994, p 35). As these processes proceed apace under the aegis of global economism, something like the universal 'end of religion' should be the result.

But it is now becoming apparent that in many contemporary situations – we may think of liberation theology in Latin America, Black consciousness in South Africa or engaged Buddhism in Southeast Asia – religion has made the transition from being a 'dependent' to an 'independent' variable (Gill, 1975, 1977). Large numbers of people can be simultaneously both secular and religious; in other words, *the privatisation of religion is not normative* as either the presupposition or the outcome of processes of industrialisation and democratisation (Casanova, 1994, pp 38-9), and religions, even those that repudiate culture and politics, are paradoxically becoming cultural and political factors in their own right. The salient point is that, in the case of religion, *both privatisation and deprivatisation can be voluntary.* There may then be 'legitimate forms of "public" religion in the modern world' which can *both* offer rationally grounded criticism of public policy while *also* allowing 'for the privatization of religion and for the pluralism of subjective religious beliefs':

> In order to be able to conceptualize such possibilities the theory of secularization will need to reconsider three of its particular historically based – that is, ethnocentric – prejudices: its bias for Protestant subjective forms of religion, its bias for "liberal" conceptions of politics and of the "public sphere", and its bias for the sovereign nation–state as the systematic unit of analysis. (Casanova, 1994, p 39)

Far from remaining corralled in the private sphere to which the theorists of modernity had confined it, religion has insisted on 'going public', making more and varied use of the space opened up by 'civil society' as an alternative either to co-opting the state or taking refuge in the privacy of face-to-face relationships. Hence,

> ... religion and politics keep forming all kinds of symbiotic relations, to such an extent that it is not easy to ascertain whether one is witnessing political movements which don religious garb or religious movements which assume political forms. (Casanova, 1994, p 41)

We are thus confronted with 'attempt[s] to indigenize modernity rather than to modernize traditional societies' (Thomas, 2003, p 22). The distinction between private and public spheres is being continually redefined by the religions themselves at all levels of society, from the family to the state, but most especially as actors in the 'open space' of civil society – even where they vehemently reject it. Religion may be 'political' even though it does not determine forms of government; the separation of church and state, or of the purely religious from the merely political, does not necessarily entail either the privatisation of religion or the secularisation of societies. All this holds good, however, under the one precondition, which is Enlightenment's greatest legacy to modernity and which religions from traditional Catholicism to contemporary Islam have found hardest to accept: the state's right and duty to protect the individual's freedom of conscience *from* religion, for

> ... from the normative perspective of modernity, religion may enter the public sphere and assume a public form only if it accepts the

> inviolable right to privacy and the sanctity of the principle of freedom
> of conscience. (Casanova, 1994, p 57)

In short, one could say that the publicness of religion sets up a dialectic of relationships between power, freedom and truth which generates tensions and sometimes open conflict between the religious community as such, its institutionalised form in the larger society and the beliefs and practices of its individual members.

In the light of this discussion, I suggest that neither Religious Studies nor International Relations is at present adequately equipped to disentangle the complex relationships between religion and politics. There has been much progress in creating an enhanced awareness of the interaction between researcher and subjects in anthropology and, since the work of the 'ethnomethodologists' in 'constructivist' sociology and political science (McSweeney, 1999, chs 6, 8), but each discipline has characteristic inhibitions when confronted with 'theology', or its equivalents in non-theistic religious traditions. By this I mean the intellectual labour of self-interpretation, the hermeneutic immanent within each identifiable tradition by which it continually explains itself to itself, thereby maintaining the continuity of its identity from generation to generation. Such activity, especially when it is the immediate inspiration of attempts to become active in the public sphere, is instinctively regarded by the liberal consensus as illegitimate because non-rational and therefore non-viable in the public forum. Whatever else it is, Religious Studies must be 'not-theology' and must never admit to any kind of normative presuppositions (Griffiths, 2006). The 'politics of religious studies' thus becomes a sub-species of 'political religion' (Wiebe, 1999, ch 10).

Towards an 'engaged' study of religions in global civil society

I suspect that the sense of 'political religion' I am striving to elucidate is just as intellectually unwelcome in Religious Studies as it is in International Relations, although attitudes are changing. On the side of Religious Studies, the sterile debate which pits 'theology' and other confessional commitments against the 'scientific' study of religions is gradually being overcome (see the many-sided debate in the *Journal of the American Academy of Religion*, vol 74, 2006 and also May 2004), and on the side of International Relations the 'return' of cultural identity and religious commitment to the purview of international politics is belatedly being proclaimed (Johnston and Sampson, 1994; Lapid and Kratochwil, 1996; Petito and Hatzopoulos, 2003). This welcome conjuncture urgently needs further intensive study from both sides, however. Religious Studies, as an aspiring social science, is most comfortable with the study of religions as phenomena, or, as we might say today, 'data' – institutions, symbolic structures, behaviour – as abstracted from the evidence of religious actors. In the eyes of some, this involves rigorous generalisation from a standpoint that is *not* that of those being studied ('the natives *don't* know best').[2] Even in cases of self-reflective participant observation and empathetic description researchers are faced with the problem of whether or not to accept as 'true' the meanings and intentions that religious actors themselves attribute to their actions. It is intentional actions that create the precondition for truth by their implicit requirement that such actions be meaningful and that their meanings be discernible and, if need be, defensible, so that actions can be approved of as 'right' because they conform to what is taken to be 'true'. If language is the continuation of action by other means (Hörmann, 1978), then it is meaningful actions themselves – that is, behaviours *and* the meanings attributed to them by actors – that are the basic units of the study of religions.

It is precisely these implicit meanings that are made explicit and 'objectified' when exposed to the pluralism of the – now global, but not necessarily secular – public sphere, thus initiating a crisis of meaning for many religious traditions. As Mary Douglas insisted, all meanings are social meanings, and 'the known cosmos is constructed for helping arguments of a practical kind' (Douglas, 1975, p xix; see pp 5, 8, 75, 122). But for many religious people it is an unfamiliar spectacle to see their cherished convictions become the premises of practical–political arguments with others whose interests and convictions differ radically from their own. Such conflicts are no longer restricted to the controlled environments of 'secular' democracies, but are global in scope, as recent attempts to enforce *laïcité* in France and Turkey and Pope Benedict XVI's unfortunate remarks on Islam in his Regensburg address illustrate. In such circumstances, it is undoubtedly advantageous for the social scientist to maintain an intellectual distance between their viewpoint as researcher and the truth claims being advanced by subjects. This need not entail that the student of religion must adopt an exclusively 'outsider' perspective, but one way or another they too have a viewpoint, one that can engage with that of the 'insiders' (McCutcheon, 1998). Perhaps it is the dawning realisation of this that is leading some scholars of religion with religious commitments to 'come out' and declare themselves 'religious' (see Cabezón and Davaney, 2004; Cabezón, 2006, pp 32-3). It could be argued that it is only by adopting the 'insider' perspective of those whose views of the world are at issue – by 'becoming' in some real sense what we study – that we are able fully to understand.

Conclusion

Materialist, positivist and otherwise reductionist rationales for the study of religions are not the antidote to ideology but are themselves ideological; this much is becoming clear. It is equally clear that religious faith itself, and not just its rationalisations in various 'theologies', can perform ideological functions. This is a challenge to both Religious Studies and International Relations. Neither discipline is comfortable when exposed to commitments, but it is commitments that make actions moral, and one step further back it is religious commitments that at the very least provide contexts of origin – and as a rule contexts of validity as well – for moral conviction. Ethics, although logically autonomous, is pragmatically in need of motivation and ideationally in need of 'plausibility structures', which the religions have historically provided – albeit sometimes by dubious means – and continue to provide. This is not to recommend a 'religious' study of religions, simply to note that students of religion are deceiving themselves if they think they can ignore 'theology', understood as the religions' own critical reflection on their practice and experience. In today's multireligious context, this involves entering into *inter*religious relationships as the religions experience them, thereby gaining access to their crises of self-understanding and their attempts to accommodate otherness within the constraints of their own ongoing efforts at self-definition. As Cabezón puts it, the Other may be problematic 'when he is TOO-MUCH-LIKE-US, or when he claims to BE-US', but 'it is equally true that the Other becomes problematic when *we* claim to BE-THEM' (Cabezón, 2006, p 33; capitals as in original). These are ethical questions, implicit in the very notion of dialogue, and they cannot be solved in the abstract, from outside, but only in a practical engagement with otherness as it touches truth – 'their' truth, but ours as well in as much as we allow our religiosity – and secularity – to engage with theirs. There is a problem-solving, conflict-resolving and peace-building potential implicit in the very fact of interreligious relations.

The alternatives are sobering. For the religions, if they fail to rise to the challenge of global pluralism and constructive interrelatedness, there is the bleak prospect of a plethora of rigid fundamentalisms, incapable of accommodating otherness and unable to enter the public sphere except to reinforce their obsessions and do battle with all who differ from them. For International Relations, the consequences would be even more disastrous than they are proving to be at present. For Religious Studies, the ultimate outcome of a sterile 'science envy' would be a steady loss of plausibility and legitimacy, ending in irrelevance and confirming Paul Griffiths' pessimistic forecast: 'This [assumption] makes the future of the nontheological academic study of religion just what it should be: bleak' (Griffiths, 2006, p 74). The admittedly large claim being made is that the empathetic study of religions in their interrelationships can make a political contribution to warding off the threat of fundamentalism while providing International Relations as a *praxis* with some purchase in its attempts to establish the bases of civilised behaviour in the global public forum. A negative outcome is not inevitable if Religious Studies, short of becoming somebody's particular 'theology' but also without succumbing to a dis- and uninterested scientism, can renew itself by coming to grips with the ethical and political challenges the religions must now meet in the emerging global civil society. As Richard Falk states:

> It is my contention that this effort to construct a democratic global civil society is informed by religious and spiritual inspiration, and if it is to move from the margins of political reality and challenge entrenched constellations of power in a more effective way, it will have to acquire some of the characteristics and concerns of a religious movement,

including building positive connections with the emancipatory aspects of the great world religions. (Falk, 2003, p 193)

The religions can confront politicians and the powerful, nationally but now also internationally in the inchoate global order, with serious questions about the normative presuppositions of their policies. Declarations of war, ecological destruction, economic imbalance, the wanton elimination of languages and cultures – all these and many other evils of globalisation may no longer be rationalised with spurious 'liberal' justifications (freedom of choice, economic growth, competition). When asserting the dignity of the human, the inviolability of nature and the common good, the religions – at their best – are bringing to bear on these problems historically rooted and communally tested value orientations. What might be termed their 'future nostalgia' – what Christian theology calls their eschatological vision – makes the religions factors to be reckoned with as the new global order of civil society takes shape. Both Religious Studies and International Relations – preferably in an explicit intellectual exchange – would be reinvigorated if this were recognised and integrated into their methodologies. Can social scientists rise to this challenge while preserving the integrity of our disciplines? This is not a soft option for idealists, but a hard intellectual and political task, and the way we go about it, I am convinced, will determine the future credibility – and fundability – of our disciplines.

Notes
[1] In International Relations, this is known as the 'Westphalian presumption'; see Petito and Hatzopoulos (2003).

[2] The most uncompromising proponent of this view is Segal (1992, 2006), and see the review of McCutcheon (2003) by Albinus (2006).

Acknowledgements
In its original form, this chapter was read as the annual Charles Strong Lecture at the 30th anniversary conference of the Australian Association for the Study of Religions, Adelaide, 7–9 July 2006. I would like to thank Professor Norman Habel and the Charles Strong trustees for the invitation to give the lecture and for their hospitality, and my colleagues Dr Bill McSweeney and Dr Geraldine Smyth OP, and my student Jude Lal Fernando, for helpful comments on earlier drafts.

Further reading
Appleby, R.S. (2000) *The ambivalence of the sacred: Religion, violence, and reconciliation*, Lanham, MD, Boulder, CO, New York, NY, Oxford: Rowman & Littlefield Inc.
Atack, I. (2005) *The ethics of peace and war: From state security to world community*, Edinburgh: Edinburgh University Press.

Beyer, P. (1994) *Religion and globalization*, London: Sage Publications.

Biggar, N. (2001) 'Forgiveness in the twentieth century: a review of the literature', in A. McFadyen and M. Sarot (eds) *Forgiveness and truth*, Edinburgh and New York, NY: T & T Clark, pp 181-217.

Cady, L. (2005) 'Secularism, secularizing, and secularization: reflections on Stout's *Democracy and tradition*, *Journal of the American Academy of Religion*, vol 73, pp 871-85.

Dower, N. (1998) *World ethics: The new agenda*, Edinburgh: Edinburgh University Press.

Ehteshami, A. (2005) 'Islam as a political force in international politics', in N. Lahoud and A.H. Johns (eds) *Islam in world politics*, London and New York, NY: Routledge, pp 29-53.

Falk, R. (1999) *Predatory globalization: A critique*, Cambridge: Cambridge University Press.

Falk, R. (2001) *Religion and humane global governance*, New York, NY: Palgrave.

Galtung, J. (1996) *Peace by peaceful means: Peace and conflict, development and civilization*, London: Sage Publications.

Gopin, M. (2000) *Between Eden and Armageddon: The future of world religions, violence, and peacemaking*, Oxford and New York, NY: Oxford University Press.

Gopin, M. (2002) *Holy war, holy peace: How religion can bring peace to the Middle East*, Oxford and New York, NY: Oxford University Press.

Herbert, D. (2003) *Religion and civil society: Rethinking public religion in the contemporary world*, Aldershot: Ashgate.

Loy, D.R. (2002) *A Buddhist history of the west: Studies in lack*, Albany, NY: SUNY Press.

Loy, D.R. (2003) *The great awakening: A Buddhist social theory*, Boston, MA: Wisdom Publications.

May, J. D'Arcy (2003a) *Transcendence and violence: The encounter of Buddhist, Christian and primal traditions*, New York, NY and London: Continuum.

Nagel, T. (1981) *Staat und Glaubensgemeinschaft im Islam. Geschichte der politischen Ordnungsvorstellungen der Muslime*, 2 vols, Zürich and München: Artemis.

Safi, O. (ed) (2003) *Progressive Muslims on justice, gender and pluralism*, Oxford: Oneworld.

Schweiker, W. (2004) *Theological ethics and global dynamics: In the time of many worlds*, Oxford: Blackwell.

Segal, R.A. (1989) *Religion and the social sciences: Essays on the confrontation*, Atlanta, GA: Scholars Press.

Shriver, D.W. (1995) *An ethic for enemies: Forgiveness in politics*, New York, NY: Oxford University Press.

Stout, J. (2004) *Democracy and tradition*, Princeton, NJ: Princeton University Press.

References

Albinus, L. (2006) 'Review of McCutcheon (2003)', *Journal of the American Academy of Religion*, vol 74, pp 524-8.

Berger, P. (1999) *The desecularization of the world: Resurgent religion and world politics*, Washington, DC and Grand Rapids, MI: Ethics and Public Policy Center and Eerdmans.

Cabezón, J.I. (2006) 'The discipline and its other: the dialectic of alterity in the study of religion', *Journal of the American Academy of Religion*, vol 74, pp 21-38.

Cabezón, J.I. and Davaney, S.G. (eds) (2004) *Identity and the politics of scholarship in the study of religion*, New York, NY and London: Routledge.

Casanova, J. (1994) *Public religions in the modern world*, Chicago, IL and London: University of Chicago Press.

Castells, M. (1996) *The rise of the network society. The information age: Economy, society and culture*, vol I, Oxford: Blackwell.

Douglas, M. (1975) *Implicit meanings: Essays in anthropology*, London: Routledge and Kegan Paul.

Falk, R. (2003) 'A worldwide religious resurgence in an era of globalization and apocalyptic terrorism', in F. Petito and P. Hatzopoulos (eds) *Religion in international relations*, New York, NY: Palgrave Macmillan, pp 181-208.

Fiala, A. (2005) *Tolerance and the ethical life*, London and New York, NY: Continuum.

Gill, R. (1975) *The social context of theology: A methodological enquiry*, London and Oxford: Mowbrays.

Gill, R. (1977) *Theology and social structure*, London and Oxford: Mowbrays.

Griffiths, P.J. (2006) 'On the future study of religion in the Academy', *Journal of the American Academy of Religion*, vol 74, pp 66-74.

Hasenclever, A. and Rittberger, V. (2003) 'Does religion make a difference? Theoretical approaches to the impact of faith on political conflict', in F. Petito and P. Hatzopoulos (eds) *Religion in international relations*, New York, NY: Palgrave Macmillan, pp 107-45.

Hörmann, H. (1978) *Meinen und Verstehen. Grundzüge einer psychologischen Semantik*, Frankfurt: Fischer.

Jenkins, P. (2002) *The next Christendom: The coming of global Christianity*, New York, NY: Oxford University Press.

Johnston, D. and Sampson, C. (eds) (1994) *Religion: The missing dimension of statecraft*, New York, NY and Oxford: Oxford University Press.

King, R. (1999) *Orientalism and religion: Postcolonial theory, India and the 'Mystic East'*, London and New York, NY: Routledge.

Lapid, Y. and Kratochwil, F. (eds) (1996) *The return of culture and identity in IR theory*, Boulder, CO and London: Lynne Rienner.

Lausten, K.B. and Waever, O. (2003) 'In defense of religion: sacred referent objects for securitization', in F. Petito and P. Hatzopoulos (eds) *Religion in international relations*, New York, NY: Palgrave Macmillan, pp 147-80.

Loy, D.R. (2004) 'Terror in the God-shaped hole: a Buddhist perspective on modernity's identity crisis', *The Journal of Transpersonal Psychology*, vol 36, no 2, pp 17-39.

McCutcheon, R.T. (ed) (1998) *The insider/outsider problem in the study of religion: A reader*, London: Cassell.

McCutcheon, R.T. (2003) *The discipline of religion: Structure, meaning, rhetoric*, New York, NY: Routledge.

McSweeney, B. (1999) *Security, identity and interests: A sociology of international relations*, Cambridge: Cambridge University Press.

Marty, M.E. (2005) *When faiths collide*, Oxford: Blackwell.

Masuzawa, T. (2005) *The invention of world religions: Or, how European universalism was preserved in the language of pluralism*, Chicago, IL and London: University of Chicago Press.

May, J. D'Arcy (1995) 'Instrumentalisierung des Christentums durch die Politik? Das Beispiel Nordirland', *Una Sancta*, vol 50, pp 141-50.

May, J. D'Arcy (1999) 'Contested space: alternative models of the public sphere in the Asia-Pacific', in N. Brown and R. Gascoigne (eds) *Faith in the public forum*, Adelaide: Australian Theological Forum, pp 78-108.

May, J. D'Arcy (2003b) 'God in public: the religions in pluralist societies', *Bijdragen. International Journal in Philosophy and Theology*, vol 64, pp 249-64.

May, J. D'Arcy (2004) 'The dialogue of religions: source of knowledge? Means of peace?', *Current Dialogue*, no 43, pp 11-18.

May, J. D'Arcy (2005) 'Alternative a Dio? Le religione nella sfera pubblica globale', in A. Autiero (ed) *Teologia nella Città, Teologia per la Città*, Bologna: Dehoniane, pp 95-109.

Petito, F. and Hatzopoulos, P. (eds) (2003) *Religion in international relations: The return from exile*, New York, NY: Palgrave Macmillan.

Reynolds, N.B. and Durham, W.C. (eds) (1996) *Religious liberty in western thought*, Atlanta, GA: Scholars Press.

Roy, O. (1995) *The failure of political Islam*, Cambridge, MA: Harvard University Press.

Roy, O. (2004) *Globalised Islam: The search for a new Ummah*, London: Hurst.

Segal, R.A. (1992) *Explaining and interpreting religion: Essays on the issue*, New York, NY: Peter Lang.

Segal, R.A. (2006) 'All generalizations are bad: postmodernism on theories', *Journal of the American Academy of Religion*, vol 74, pp 157-71.

Thomas, S.M. (2003) 'Taking religious and cultural pluralism seriously', in F. Petito and P. Hatzopoulos (eds) *Religion in international relations*, New York, NY: Palgrave Macmillan, pp 21-53.

Wiebe, D. (1999) *The politics of religious studies: The continuing conflict with theology in the Academy*, London: Macmillan.

Wuthnow, R. (1992) *Rediscovering the sacred*, Grand Rapids, MI: Eerdmans.

TWO

Australia's 'shy' de-secularisation process

Adam Possamai

Introduction

In many parts of the world religion has re-entered the public sphere to such an extent that it has undermined the 'hard line' secularisation thesis – that is, the assumption that religion would disappear in Western, modernised societies. Since this 'hard line' view should not be happening, views on secularisation have had to be revised. Some academics (for example, Bruce 2002, 2006; Norris and Inglehart, 2004) explain that secularisation is still happening but in a much less extreme process than first predicted, while others (for example, Richardson, 1985; Hadden, 1987; Brown, 1992; Warner, 1993; Kepel, 1994) propose that there is a reverse process and that secularisation is losing momentum. In accordance with this latter view, recent theories in the sociology of religion (see, for example, Martin, 2005; Casanova, 2006; Davie, 2006) have pushed the debate further by applying Eisenstadt's (2000) multiple modernities paradigm.

To illustrate this paradigm, I am using Martin's (2005) recent work on the matter in which he employs Casanova's definition of secularisation on social differentiation, 'meaning by that the increasing autonomy of the various spheres of human activity' (Martin, 2005, p 123). Religion is no longer an overarching system and is now seen as a sub-system of society alongside other sub-systems (for example, education, health, commercial, scientific institutions) such that all-encompassing claims of religion have much less relevance. Religion no longer has the place it had in societal structure and is no longer the dominant voice when it comes, for example, to politics, welfare and education. If religion is still strong in our culture, it is not the yesteryear pillar of Western social structure. Moving beyond this *fait accompli*, Martin's work pushes further our understanding of this process by underlining the different dynamics of secularisation, rather than simply assuming a single one as in many previous sociological studies. The fundamental argument of his latest work is that secularisation is not a clear-cut process that happens in all Western societies homogeneously or that will happen to all industrialising countries. Indeed, as the author argues in relation to Christianity:

> … instead of regarding secularization as a once-for-all unilateral process, one might rather think in terms of successive Christianizations followed or accompanied by recoils. Each Christianization is a salient of faith driven into the secular from a different angle, each pays a characteristic cost which affects the character of the recoil, and each undergoes a partial collapse…. (Martin, 2005, p 3)

Following this multilateral view of the process of secularisation, the reader is asked to observe that this process is not only different between North America and Europe, but is also distinctive within each region of these cultural areas. There is not one secular ending to Western history but rather various phases of secularisation and sanctification.

Martin's articulation of 'multiple secularisations' aligns itself with the very recent concept of 'multiple modernities' (Eisenstadt, 2000). For Eisenstadt (2000, p 2):

> The idea of multiple modernities presumes that the best way to understand the contemporary world – indeed to explain the history of modernity – is to see it as a story of continual constitution and reconstitution of a multiplicity of cultural programs. These ongoing reconstructions of multiple institutional and ideological patterns are carried forward by specific social actors in close connection with social, political, and intellectual activists, and also by social movements pursuing different programs of modernity, holding very different views of what makes societies modern.

The main point of the multiple modernities thesis is that the modernities outside of the Western world cannot fully be understood with the same categories and concepts used to understand Western modernities. Indeed, following this Western imposition on social transformations and ideals, Martin reminds us how the concept of 'secularisation' became an 'ideological and philosophical imposition on history rather than an inference from history' (2005, p 19). One can also remember Martin's (1995) earlier work considering the studies of Durkheim and Weber on the crisis of religious consciousness in modernity, which were so strong that secularisation became the undisputed paradigm among sociologists and thus was not regarded as deserving much study after the First World War. By understanding secularisation as a multilateral process, a type of 'multiple secularisations' thesis, Martin gives to researchers of religion a strong way out from this ideological imposition.

Even more recently, Casanova (2006) and Davie (2006) used this theory to differentiate the European case from that of the US. For many years, sociologists analysed the secularisation process in Europe believing that the rest of the world, when modernised, would follow this trend. The US, where religion is stronger in terms of church attendance and political activism, was seen as the exception to the secularisation rule. Now, with recent data, these authors have come to the conclusion that religion is thriving around the world (including countries that are modernised but not European or that are in the process of modernisation). This has led them to reverse the perspective and to view Europe as the exception. The contrast between the European and US case can provide an answer to this difference:

> Crucial is the question of why individuals in Europe, once they lose faith in their national churches, do not bother to look for alternative salvation religions. In a certain sense, the answer lies in the fact that Europeans continue to be implicit members of their national churches, even after explicitly abandoning them. The national churches remain there as a public good to which they have rightful access when it comes time to celebrate the transcendent rites of passages, birth, and death. It is this peculiar situation that explains the lack of demand and the absence of a truly competitive religious market in Europe. In contrast ... the United States never had a national church. Eventually, all religions in America, churches as well as sects, irrespective of their origins, doctrinal claims, and ecclesiastical identities, turned into "denominations", formally equal under the constitution and competing in a relatively free, pluralistic, and voluntaristic religious market. As the organizational form and principle of such a religious system, denominationalism constitutes the great American invention. (Casanova, 2006, p 16)

Needless to say, both Europe and the US have gone through a modernisation process that has differently affected their (de-)secularisation process. Earlier in her work, Davie (2002) put Europe and the US on the extreme of a continuum. At one point, she equated the European case with that of state or elite control of religion (in which there is a culture of obligation, for example going to church because one has to) and the US case with that of religious voluntarism (in which there is a culture of consumption or choice, for example I go to church because I want to as long as it provides what I need during a period of time I want to invest). In between she places Australia and Canada as hybrid cases.

Australia might have a specific modernity and a specific process of secularisation and de-secularisation. This chapter argues that there is an increased decentralisation, pluralism and voluntarism of religious life within Australia's specific modernity; and that these are not signs of religion's demise but of its vitality. It is the working assumption of this chapter that this phenomenon adds to Australia's diversity (Bouma, 2006) and the enrichment of its civil society (Ireland, 1999). After exploring Australian religious characteristics, I will then attempt to pinpoint Australia's specific de-secularisation process.

Australia's religious characteristics

Australia, this former English penal colony where the Anglican religion was first used as a tool for social control despite claims of a separation of church and state, saw its religious homogeneity changing after the Second World War as postwar migration and conversion to new religious movements transformed the cultural, religious and ethnic profile of Australian society. In 1947, Anglicans represented 39% of the population. In 2006, they dropped to 18.7% and are no longer the largest religious group in Australia. Catholics, on the other hand, thanks to migration movements, have become the largest group, with 25.8% of the population in the same year. What is also worth noting is that Australia is becoming less and less a Christian country, from 88% of the population in 1947 to 64% in 2006. It is also worth mentioning that attendance at mainstream churches is also in decline, from 20% of the population attending at least once a month in 1998 to 18.6% in 2002 (Bellamy and Castle, 2004). Without going into much detail, on the other hand, non-mainstream Christian groups such as the Pentecostals and non-Christian groups are growing in Australia. In the 'other' census category that includes groups such as Baha'i, Japanese religions, Scientology and Witchcraft, there was an increase of 33% between 1996 and 2001. In the same time frame, Buddhism increased by 79%, Hinduism by 42% and Islam by 40% (Bouma, 2006). These changes occurred behind the back of public and secular group notice from the mid-1970s to the early 1990s. The secular Australian government, while managing migrant intake,[1] always believed that when religious migrants came to Australia, they would simply see the 'light' of Australian secular society and slowly convert to the 'No religion' category. The secular government never thought that these migrant groups would add so much to the Australian religious landscape (Bouma, 2006).

To be fair with this debate, it is important to mention that the 'No religion' category, although it has decreased by 1.5% since 1996, has grown from 6.7% of the population in 1971 to 15.5% in 2001. We cannot thus conclude that people who leave churches necessarily remain religious and turn to other religions. For example, as found in other research in the UK, Heelas and Woodhead (2005) discovered that the relatively small growth of the holistic milieu does not compensate for the larger decline of the congregational domain. Indeed, the fall in numbers of Christian attendees is much higher than the growth of the spiritualities and other new religious movements. These non-Christian or non-mainstream Christian groups do not necessarily provide a spiritual refuge for all dissatisfied Christians: many of these church leavers can also become non-religious. However, there are nevertheless church leavers interested in other religious groups and this adds to Australia's religious diversity.

Faced with these changes, classical theories of secularisation are adequate to describe the current state of mainstream religious churches, but fail to address Australia's current religious diversification and religious revitalisation, especially among Pentecostals, Buddhists, Muslims and neo-pagan groups. With this increased vitality comes increased differentiation and thus increased competition between religious groups. Further, spirituality, as a more personal approach to the religious phenomenon, has grown over the past few years (see below). On top of this, although Australia's governmentality is still overtly secular, conservative Christians in national politics formed a coalition (the Lyons Forum) in 1992 to press for Christian values in government (Maddox, 2001). And a first in Australia, a political party, the Family First Party, representing a network of Pentecostal groups, won a critical seat in the Senate.

Davie (2002, pp 147-50) observes that on this continuum between religious obligation and religious voluntarism, Europe is slowly shifting towards the voluntarist end. As Australia is a hybrid case between these two models, one can wonder if Australia is shifting towards this voluntarist end as well? Bouma (2006) has recently claimed that for Australians, religion must be a low-temperature phenomenon. Religion is not something to get overtly enthusiastic about, and the cultural aspect of Australian identity will always prevent Australia moving towards the US model. As Bouma states, 'It is not characteristically Australian to trumpet encounters with the spiritual like some American televangelists' (Bouma, 2006, p 2). Following this observation, Bouma aptly describes the Australian soul in terms of religion and spirituality as 'a shy hope in the heart'. For this phrase, he was influenced by Manning Clarke's comment about the ANZAC spirit, 'A whisper in the mind and a shy hope in the heart'. As Bouma (2006, p 2) explains about religion and spirituality in Australia:

> A shy hope in the heart aptly expresses the nature of Australian religion and spirituality. There is a profound shyness – yet a deeply grounded hope – held tenderly in the heart, in the heart of Australia.[...] Australians hold the spiritual gently in their hearts, speaking tentatively about it. The spiritual is treated as sacred. What is held protectively in the heart is sacred; the sacred is handled with great care. Not all things that evoke awe and wonder are loud and noisy, brassy and for sale.

This shyness does not reflect a weak indication of the religious and spiritual vitality, and appears to stay and might even grow in modest size.

For this 'shy' approach to religion to reach the US voluntarist level in its full-blown proportion is, I believe, difficult in the Australian context. It is partly related to a strong Australian value, that of the tall poppy syndrome. This syndrome refers to the behavioural traits of Australians to cut down those who are 'superior' to them (Hughes et al, 2003). Respect for social position has long been the butt of Australian humour. People who expect that their claims to a higher class will give them a place in society soon find it more likely to exclude them from social life. Equally, those who put themselves on a pedestal are quickly brought down to earth. Australia has long been known for its dislike of 'tall poppies', and this applies to religious groups that are being 'too' successful and/or that move too close to the public sphere. For Australians, religion is not something to get overtly enthusiastic about. It is part of the ordinary Australian imaginary that is characterised by distaste for display – whether aesthetic or affective – and that includes religion and spiritualities that should not make any symbolic excess out of ordinary events (Sinclair, 2004). This value needs to be seen in contrast to another one, that of egalitarianism and of mateship with an inclination to support the underdog which is reflected in the entrenched Australian norm of a 'fair go'. In terms of religion, this 'fair go' attitude gives to every religious group a chance to establish itself (to a certain degree) in Australian society, thus adding to Australia's diversity, while not forgetting that these groups should take it easy about religion. Having described these two typical Australian values (Hughes et al, 2003), and taking into account that some groups are allowed to get taller than others (for example, the Roman Catholic church versus the Church of Scientology) and have a fairer go than others (for example, the Anglican church versus Islam) the de-secularisation process of Australia could thus be seen as stuck for a very long time between these two values which would make Australia always in a mid-point between the European exceptional case and the US voluntarist one.

A de-secularisation process in Australia?

Arguing with the multiple modernisation thesis that there are different types of de-secularisation processes in the world is only the beginning. What needs to be done now is to be able to characterise the specific de-secularisation process in Australia using an analytical method of analysis. For this, Dobbelaere (2002)'s theories of secularisation might be of help. He does not work on the different dynamics of secularisation (horizontal process) like Martin but on its different levels (vertical process). For Dobbelaere (2002), there are three levels. The first one is *societal secularisation* (also called, in his terms, '*laïcisation*' for the societal or macro level). It deals with the change of structure, which has occurred with the industrialisation of Western societies, and refers to a functional differentiation process. Through this process many sub-systems are developed and perform different functions that are structurally different. Religion, as an institution, is thus no longer an overarching institution but one of many. This is basically the definition of secularisation given by Casanova (2006) earlier in this chapter. The second dimension is *organisational secularisation* (also called, in his terms, 'religious change' for the organisation or meso level) and reflects changes at the level of religious organisations, such as churches, denominations, sects and new religious movements. At this level, the study of the decline and emergence of certain types of religious groups can be conducted. The last dimension, *individual secularisation* (also called 'religious involvement' for the individual or micro level), refers to the individual level and deals with the way an individual believes in a specific religion and how this person is integrated into a religious group.

As there are multiple processes of secularisation, there will thus be multiple processes of de-secularisation such as the political re-entering of the public sphere by certain religious groups (Kepel, 1994; Lawrence, 1998), the cultural transaction operated by religious and spiritual groups and individuals via consumer culture and popular culture (Bauman, 1998; Possamai, 2005a), and the growth of a type of religious social capital generated by the transnational networks of new immigrant and ethnic communities (Possamai and Possamai-Inesedy, 2008). However, this chapter now attempts to pinpoint the processes of de-secularisation in Australia.

Societal de-secularisation

> For the first time since the First World War ... when Irish Catholic Australians condemned Australian government involvement in Britain's war against the Prussian, Austro-Hungarian and Ottoman empires (but especially against the Irish rebels), every level of Australian politics had become saturated with debates over religion and its place in the secular body politic of the Commonwealth. Whereas a decade before, religion had hardly ruffled the surface of multi-cultural Australia.... (Jakubowicz, 2005, p 51)

Since the election of the conservative federal government in 1996 in Australia, preference for religious provision of services has become a policy priority. Senior church people have increasingly become influential with senior political operatives. The rise of the Pentecostal Hillsong church (Sydney) has drawn politicians to their gatherings and in 2004 a Pentecostal party won a Senate seat. Over the past 10 years, religion, it can be argued, has moved back into the mainstream of the political flow, but in a shy manner. While in the past politicians have kept their faith to the private sphere, public display of religiosity has become prominent over the Howard government's third term, but it is still far removed from US-type presidential races in which faith-based politics is of high importance (Maddox, 2005). The overt appeal to the Gospel and to Christian values are more common in the discourse of US presidents than Australian prime ministers.

We can thus argue that by having religion coming back to the public sphere of politics, we are faced with a process of de-secularisation at the societal level; however, comparatively speaking, this very 'shy' re-emergence of religion in political life is far from leading to an important impact.

Organisational de-secularisation

During the move to multiculturalism in the 1970s, non-mainstream religious groups developed in Australia. Increased diverse immigration corresponded to an increase in new religious movements around the same time (Bouma, 2005). It can be argued that increased congregationalism has had a resultant effect in the decrease in attendance of the mainstream churches in Australia. Such changes have meant that Australia has moved from a culture of 'obligation' towards a culture of 'consumption/choice'.

Australia is one of the most religiously diverse countries in the world (Bouma, 2006), and this has happened largely peacefully and without major clashes between religious groups. According to Bouma (1999) and Sheen (1996) there have, nevertheless, been incidents of discrimination, vilification, harassment and conflict in Australia. For Sheen (1996) new religious movements suffer at the hands of authority and the media. With regard to Islam, especially after 9/11, there were negative media portrayals, together with discriminatory rhetoric, policy and practices at the level of the state against Muslims (Poynting and Perry, 2007). However, according to Bouma (1999), and taking into consideration other countries, Australia appears to have an enviably low rate of the occurrence of religious intergroup hostility. Richardson (1999) believes that Australia has its share of controversy but not as much as in Western Europe. On the other hand, as Bouma has underlined from the Religious Freedom Act (HREOC, 1998), the current legal protections against discrimination on the grounds of religion or belief, at federal, state and territory levels, are inadequate, and existing blasphemy laws do not protect religions other than Christianity.

Nevertheless, there are now many more religious groups offering their 'product' in a religious market being tried out by many consumers. Indeed, Australia is home to many ideas and practices found in alternative spiritualities and new religious movements, and is currently hosting many New Age practices and ideas (Possamai, 2005b).

Another example is the religious groups that are part of new immigrant and ethnic communities and very often take on new forms to be capable of survival in the new land,[2] and are thus reaching beyond traditional ethnic and cultural boundaries. In Australia, these groups constitute the largest segment of the phenomenon of increasing religious diversity (Ireland, 1999). They celebrate and maintain a way of life and a religious culture from elsewhere, but they also are working in Australian society: not just resisting pressures for assimilation, but helping members translate the norms and values of their land of origin into the new Australian context.

At this level, it can be argued that Australia is going through a de-secularisation process because of the vitality of its religious diversity. A counter-argument could claim that the expansion of the number of religious groups does not mean that they attract more people than if there were fewer such groups (Bruce, 2002). However, this chapter follows the view of Yang and Ebaugh (2001, p 269), who refer to the 'new paradigm' in the sociology of religion 'that refutes secularisation theories: Internal and external religious pluralism, instead of leading to the decline of religion, encourages institutional and theological transformations that energize and revitalize religions [...] these changes have transnational implications for global religious systems – implications that are facilitated by the material and organizational resources that new [...] immigrants possess'.

However, stating the simple fact that Australia is welcoming a variety of new ethnic religious communities does not necessarily lead to a straightforward de-secularisation process. Immigrant new religions have different degrees of success in Australia with regard to acceptance and growth/continuation of practice by members. This has had a significant impact on the intensity of the de-secularisation process in Australia (for more information, see Possamai and Possamai-Inesedy, 2008).

Individual de-secularisation

As in many other Western countries, Australians appear to no longer need to belong to a specific religious group in order to 'believe'. The 'spiritual' revolution outside of an organised religion has been strong in Australia. Cases in point are the New Age and neo-pagan network (Possamai, 2005b), hyper-real religions (that is, religions such as Jediism and Matrixism created from popular culture by individuals) (Possamai, 2005a), Western appropriation of forms of Buddhism, or even traditional religions lived outside of their institutions, such as believing without belonging (Davie, 2002). Although churches are noting declines in attendance, it does not mean that people are less religious/spiritual.

Part of this phenomenon is the growth of spirituality in Australia (Tacey, 2000; Bouma, 2006) outside of religious groups and inside as well. As Wuthnow (2001, p 307) claims, 'many people who practice spirituality in their own ways still go to church or synagogue'. Indeed, social scientists find from various surveys (for example, Marler and Hadaway, 2002; Hughes et al, 2004) that the large majority of the people surveyed claim to be religious and spiritual at the same time. This claim might reflect a stronger engagement in religious practices and beliefs than, for example, a non-practising Catholic who still claims to be of that religion in the census.

At this individual level, it can be observed that Australia is being de-secularised through the growth of spirituality.

Australia's de-secularisation process

> The United States was born as a modern secular state, never knew the established church of the European caesaro-papist absolutist state, and did not need to go through a European process of secular differentiation in order to become a modern secular society. (Casanova, 2006, p 12)

The beginning of Australia saw religion being used as a tool of social control to help build a modern secular society. It was used by the state to 'civilise' the prisoner in penal colonies, the free settlers and the Indigenous inhabitants of the land. Although Australia was also born as a modern secular state, religion was used in conjunction with the state for this modernisation process. Overall, the colonisation process of Australia itself might explain its hybridity between the US (which started modernisation without any established church) and Europe (which had tensions with the established church during the modernisation process).

If religion and spiritualities are 'a shy hope in the heart', as Bouma (2006) details, the de-secularisation process could be characterised the same way. Religions and spiritualities are diversifying and are being revitalised in Australia, but this happens, as Bouma indicates, at a 'low temperature'. There are no overt claims from any religious group to take central stage at the societal level, but groups and individuals are discreetly active at the organisational and individual levels. As the definition of secularisation is always connected to how religion is defined (Casanova, 2006), one might thus think of the Australian secularisation process as 'a hopeless shy heartburn' at the organisational and individual level. Because religion has never been strong at the societal level in Australia, the Australian government saw religion as an issue of not much consequence that could be left forgotten like a social pain of *no* consequence that was supposed to heal itself. Now, the government can no longer ignore religions and spiritualities and this Australian religious diversity needs to be carefully managed (Bouma, 2005).

Conclusion

Concerns about the re-emergence of religion in Australia suggest that new forms of religious life may undermine powers of deliberation and voting among members, promote hate rather than negotiation and transform pluralism into parochialism. However, as analysed in this chapter, this re-emergence happens at the organisational and individual levels, and not strongly at the societal one. Against these fears are the hopes that civil society is enriched and revitalised as it diversifies, and that new forms of civic engagement, constituting a 'politics of pluralisation', are emerging (Ireland, 1999). Perhaps with this de-secularisation process, we can see new vitality in civil society, new forms of civic engagement and a new democratic politics in which democratic institutions are not corroded. However, this vitality is of a 'shy' type.

More research needs to be done on the various types of de-secularisation processes in the world. This chapter used Australia as a case study utilising as a method of analysis Dobbelaere's three levels of secularisation. A comparison between Australia and other countries will certainly provide an understanding of other types of de-secularisation processes around the world and fine-tune our understanding of the various types and sub-types of de-secularisation.

What is happening in Australia as a de-secularisation process might provide a source of knowledge and understanding that could become useful when dealing with religious and secular issues in the world. As Bouma (2005, p 49) explains:

> What has become clear to me is that religious diversity is not a disease to be overcome, but a cultural resource that can be used to enrich the capacity of a society to operate effectively in a global context.

Notes

[1] In 2001, 23% of the Australian population was born overseas.

[2] However, not all immigrants maintain a country-of-origin religious identity. Some turn away from the dominant tradition of their country of origin to join other religious affiliations (Warner and Wittner, 1998).

References

Bauman, Z. (1998) 'Postmodern religion?', in P. Heelas et al (eds) *Religion, modernity and postmodernity*, Oxford: Blackwell Publishing, pp 55-78.

Bellamy, J. and Castle, K. (2004) *2001 church attendance estimates*, NCLS Occasional Paper 3, Sydney, Australia: NCLS Research (www.ncls.org.au).

Bouma, G. (1999) 'Social justice issues in the management of religious diversity in Australia', *Social Justice Research*, vol 12, no 4, pp 283-95.

Bouma, G. (2005) 'Religious differentiation and religious revitalisation', *Canadian Diversity*, vol 4, no 3, pp 48-50.

Bouma, G. (2006) *Australian soul. Religion and spirituality in the twenty-first century*, Melbourne, Australia: Cambridge University Press.

Brown, C.G. (1992) 'A revisionist approach to religious change', in S. Bruce (ed) *Religion and modernization: Sociologists and historians debate the secularization thesis*, Oxford: Clarendon Press, pp 31-58.

Bruce, S. (2002) *God is Dead: Secularization in the West*, Oxford: Blackwell Publishing.

Bruce, S. (2006) 'Secularization and the impotence of individualized religion', *The Hedgehog Review*, vol 8, nos 1-2, pp 35-45.

Casanova, J. (2006) 'Rethinking secularization: a global comparative perspective', *The Hedgehog Review*, vol 8, nos 1-2, pp 7-22.

Davie, G. (2002) *Europe: The exceptional case. Parameters of faith in the modern world*, London: Darton, Longman & Todd.

Davie, G. (2006) 'Is Europe an exceptional case?', *The Hedgehog Review*, vol 8, nos 1-2, pp 23-34.

Dobbelaere, K. (2002) *Secularization: An analysis at three levels*, Bruxelles, Bern, Berlin, Frankfurt am Main, New York, Oxford, Wien: PIE-Peter Lang.

Eisenstadt, S.N. (2000) 'Multiple modernities', *Daedalus*, vol 129, no 1, pp 1-29.

Hadden, J.K. (1987) 'Toward desacralizing secularization theory', *Social Forces*, vol 65, p 608.

Heelas, P. and Woodhead, L. with Seel, B., Szerszynski, B. and Tusting, K. (2005) *The spiritual revolution: Why religion is giving way to spirituality*, Oxford: Blackwell Publishing.

HREOC (Human Rights and Equal Opportunity Commission) (1998) *Article 18: Freedom of religion and belief*, Sydney, Australia: HREOC.

Hughes, P. and Bond, S. with Bellamy, J. and Black, A. (2003) *Exploring what Australians value*, Adelaide, Australia: Openbook Publishers.

Hughes, P., Black, A., Bellamy, J. and Kaldor, P. (2004) 'Identity and religion in contemporary Australia', *Australian Religion Studies Review*, vol 17, no 1, pp 53-8.

Ireland, R. (1999) 'Religious diversity in a new Australian democracy', in G. Bouma (ed) *Managing religious diversity*, Melbourne, Australia: AARS Editions.

Jakubowicz, A. (2005) 'Religion and Australian cultural diversity', *Canadian Diversity*, vol 4, no 3, pp 51-5.

Kepel, G. (1994) *The revenge of God. The resurgence of Islam, Christianity and Judaism in the modern world*, Pennsylvania, PA: Penn State University Press.

Lawrence, B. (1998) 'From fundamentalism to fundamentalisms: a religious ideology in multiple forms', in P. Heelas (ed) *Religion, modernity and postmodernity*, Oxford: Blackwell Publishing, pp 88-101.

Maddox, M. (2001) *For God and country: Religious dynamics in Australian federal politics*, Canberra, Australia: Commonwealth of Australia.

Maddox, M. (2005) *God under Howard. The rise of the religious Right in Australian politics*, Sydney, Australia: Allen & Unwin.

Marler, P. and Hadaway, C. (2002) '"Being religious" or "being spiritual" in America: a zero-sum proposition?', *Journal for the Scientific Study of Religion*, vol 4, no 2, pp 289-300.

Martin, D. (1995) 'Sociology, religion and secularization: an orientation', *Religion*, no 25, pp 295-303.

Martin, D. (2005) *On secularization: Towards a revised general theory*, Aldershot: Ashgate.

Norris, P. and Inglehart, R. (2004) *Sacred and secular: Religion and politics worldwide*, Cambridge: Cambridge University Press.

Possamai, A. (2005a) *Religion and popular culture: a hyper-real testament*, Bruxelles, Bern, Berlin, Frankfurt am Main, New York, Oxford, Wien: P.I.E.-Peter Lang.

Possamai, A. (2005b) *In search of New Age spiritualities*, Aldershot: Ashgate.

Possamai, A. and Possamai-Inesedy, A. (2008) 'The Baha'i faith and Caodaism: migration, change and de-secularisation(s) in Australia', *Journal of Sociology*, vol 43, no 3, pp 301-17.

Poynting, S. and Perry, B. (2007) 'Climates of hate: media and state inspired victimization of Muslims in Canada and Australia since 9/11', *Current Issues in Criminal Justice*, vol 19, no 2.

Richardson, J.T. (1985) 'Studies of conversion: secularization or re-enchantment?', in P.E. Hammond (ed) *The sacred in a secular age. Toward revision in the scientific study of religion*, Berkeley and Los Angeles, CA: University of California Press, p 104.

Richardson, J. (1999) 'New religions in Australia: public menace or societal salvation?', *Nova Religio: The Journal of Alternative and Emergent Religions*, vol 4, no 2, pp 258-65.

Sheen, J. (1996) 'Living within the tensions of plurality: religious discrimination and human rights law and policy', in G. Bouma (ed) *Many religions, all Australians: Religious settlement, identity and cultural diversity*, Melbourne, Australia: Christian Research Association, pp 163-80.

Sinclair, J. (2004) 'Spirituality and the (secular) ordinary Australian imaginary continuum', *Journal of Media & Cultural Studies*, vol 18, no 2, pp 279-93.

Tacey, D. (2000) *Re-enchantment. The new Australian spirituality*, Sydney, Australia: HarperCollins.

Warner, S. (1993) 'Work in progress toward a new paradigm for the sociological study of religion in the United States', *American Journal of Sociology*, vol 98, no 5, pp 1044-93.

Warner, S. and Wittner, J. (eds) (1998) *Gatherings in diaspora: Religious communities and the new immigration*, Philadelphia, PA: Temple University Press.

Wuthnow, R. (2001) 'Spirituality and spiritual practice', in R. Fenn (ed) *The Blackwell companion to sociology of religion*, Oxford: Blackwell Publishing, pp 306-20.

Yang F. and Ebaugh, H. (2001) 'Transformations in new immigrant religions and their global implications', *American Sociological Review*, vol 66, no 2, pp 269-88.

THREE

Muslims, equality and secularism[1]

Tariq Modood

Introduction

Most European countries do not collect data on non-White citizens and residents, only on foreigners, but it seems that more than 5% and possibly up to 10% of citizens of EU15 are of non-European descent. Currently most of the largest, in particular the capital, cities of North West Europe, are about 15%–30% non-White (that is, people of non-European descent). Even without further large-scale immigration, being a young, fertile population, these proportions will grow for at least one generation more before they stabilise, reaching or exceeding 50% in some cities in the next few decades. The trend will include some of the larger urban centres of South Europe. A high degree of racial/ethnic/religious mix in its principal cities will be the norm in 21st-century Europe, and will characterise its national economic, cultural and political life, as it has done in 20th-century US (and will do so in the 21st). Of course there will also be important differences between Western Europe and the US. Among these is the fact that the majority of non-White citizens in European countries are Muslims (the UK, where Muslims form about a third of non-White citizens or minority ethnic groups is the exception). With an estimated 15 million plus Muslims in Western Europe today, about 4% of the population (Savage, 2004), they are larger than the combined populations of Finland, Denmark and Ireland. Many people in Europe fear this newly settled population. It is popularly associated with terrorism, and many centre-left intellectuals and social scientists see it as threatening the Enlightenment heritage of Europe. In virtually every country in Western Europe, there is a perception that Muslims are making politically exceptional, culturally unreasonable or theologically alien demands on European states. To counter this I shall show in this chapter that the claims Muslims are making in fact parallel comparable arguments about gender or ethnic equality. Seeing the issue in that context shows how European and contemporary the logic of mainstream Muslim identity politics is. In addition I argue that multicultural politics must embrace a moderate secularism and resist radical secularism. I shall focus on the case of Britain in particular.

British equality movements

Muslim assertiveness became a feature of majority–minority relations only from around the early 1990s; prior to this, racial equality discourse and politics were dominated by the idea that the dominant post-immigration issue was 'colour racism'. One consequence of this is that the legal and policy framework still reflects the conceptualisation and priorities of racial dualism.

Until 2004 it was lawful to discriminate against Muslims *qua* Muslims because the courts did not accept that Muslims were an ethnic group (although Jewish and Sikh people were recognised as ethnic groups within the meaning of the law). While initially unremarked on, this exclusive focus on race and ethnicity, and the exclusion of Muslims but not Jewish and Sikh people, came to be a source of resentment. A key indicator of racial discrimination and inequality has been numerical under-representation, for instance in prestigious jobs and public office. Hence, people have had to be (self-)classified and counted; thus group labels, and arguments about which labels are authentic, have become a common feature of certain political discourses. Over the years, it has also become apparent through these inequality measures that it is the Asian Muslim groups and not, as expected, the African-Caribbean groups, who have emerged as the most disadvantaged and poorest groups in the country (Modood, 1992; Modood et al, 1997). To many Muslim activists, the misplacing of Muslims into race categories and the belatedness with which the severe disadvantages of the Pakistani and Bangladeshi groups have come to be recognised mean that race relations are perceived at best as an inappropriate policy niche for Muslims, and at worst as a conspiracy to prevent the emergence of a specifically Muslim sociopolitical formation. One of the principal sources of these views was developments within anti-racism and the egalitarian political struggles more generally.

Just as in the US the colour-blind humanism of Martin Luther King Jr came to be mixed with an emphasis on Black pride, Black autonomy and Black nationalism as typified by Malcolm X, so too the same process occurred in the UK. Indeed, it is best to see this development of racial explicitness and positive blackness as part of a wider sociopolitical climate that is not confined to race and culture or non-White minority groups. Feminism, gay pride, Québecois nationalism and the revival of a Scottish identity are some prominent examples of these new identity movements that have become an important feature in many countries. In fact, it would be fair to say that what is often claimed today in the name of racial equality, again especially in the English-speaking world, goes beyond the claims that were made in the 1960s. Iris Young expresses well the new political climate when she describes the emergence of an ideal of equality based not just on allowing excluded groups to assimilate and live by the norms of dominant groups, but on the view that 'a positive self-definition of group difference is in fact more liberatory' (Young, 1992, p 157).

Equality and the erosion of the public–private distinction

This significant shift takes us from an understanding of 'equality' in terms of individualism and cultural assimilation to a politics of recognition, to 'equality' as encompassing public ethnicity. This perception of equality means not having to hide or apologise for one's origins, family or community, and requires others to show respect for them. Public attitudes and arrangements must adapt so that this heritage is encouraged, not contemptuously expected to wither away.

These two conceptions of equality may be stated as follows:

- the right to assimilate to the majority/dominant culture in the public sphere, with toleration of 'difference' in the private sphere;
- the right to have one's 'difference' (minority ethnicity, etc) recognised and supported in both the public and the private spheres.

While the former represents a classical liberal response to 'difference', the latter is the 'take' of the new identity politics. The two are not, however, alternative conceptions of equality in the sense that to hold one, the other must be rejected. Multiculturalism, properly construed, requires support for both conceptions. For the assumption behind the first is that participation in the public or national culture is necessary for the effective exercise of citizenship, the only obstacles to which are the exclusionary processes preventing gradual assimilation. The second conception, too, assumes that groups excluded from the national culture have their citizenship diminished as a result, and sees the remedy not in rejecting the right to assimilate, but in adding the right to widen and adapt the national culture, and the public and media symbols of national membership, to include the relevant minority ethnicities.

The public–private distinction is, then, crucial to the contemporary discussion of equal citizenship, and particularly to the challenge to an earlier liberal position. It is in this political and intellectual climate – namely, a climate in which what would earlier have been called 'private' matters had become sources of equality struggles – that Muslim assertiveness emerged as a domestic political phenomenon. In this respect, the advances achieved by anti-racism and feminism (with its slogan 'the personal is the political') acted as benchmarks for later political group entrants, such as Muslims. While Muslims raise distinctive concerns, the logic of their demands often mirrors those of other equality-seeking groups.

Religious equality

So, one of the current conceptions of equality is a difference-affirming equality, with related notions of respect, recognition and identity – in short, what I understand by political multiculturalism (Modood, 2007). What kinds of specific policy demands, then, are being made by or on behalf of religious groups and Muslim identity politics in particular, when these terms are deployed?

I suggest that these demands have three dimensions, which get progressively 'thicker', and are progressively less acceptable to radical secularists.

No religious discrimination

The very basic demand is that religious people, no less than people defined by race or gender, should not suffer discrimination in job and other opportunities. So, for example, a person who is trying to dress in accordance with their religion or who projects a religious identity (such as a Muslim woman wearing a headscarf, a *hijab*), should not be discriminated against in employment. Until the end of 2003 there was no legal ban on such discrimination in Britain. This is, however, only a partial 'catching-up' with the existing anti-discrimination provisions in relation to race and gender. It does not extend to discrimination in provision of goods and services, nor does it create a duty on employers to take steps to promote equality of opportunity.

Even-handedness in relation to native religions

Many minority faith advocates interpret equality to mean that minority religions should get at least some of the support from the state that longer-established religions do. Muslims have led the way on this argument, and have made two particular issues politically contentious: the state funding of schools and the law of blasphemy. The government has agreed in recent years to fund a few (so far, seven) Muslim schools, as well as a Sikh and a Seventh Day Adventist school, on the same basis enjoyed by thousands of Anglican and Catholic schools and some Methodist and Jewish schools. (In England and Wales, over a third of state-maintained primary and a sixth of secondary schools are in fact run by a religious group, but all have to deliver a centrally determined national curriculum.)

Some secularists are unhappy about this. They accept the argument for parity but believe this should be achieved by the state withdrawing its funding from all religious schools. Most Muslims reject this form of equality in which the privileged lose something but the under-privileged gain nothing. More specifically, the issue between 'equalising upwards' and 'equalising downwards' here is about the legitimacy of religion as a public institutional presence.

Muslims have failed to get the courts to interpret the existing statute on blasphemy to cover offences beyond what Christians hold sacred, but some political support has been built for an offence of incitement to religious hatred, as has existed in Northern Ireland for many years, mirroring the existing one of incitement to racial hatred. (The latter extends protection to cover certain forms of anti-Jewish literature, but not anti-Muslim literature.) Indeed, such a proposal was in the Queen's Speech in October 2004, but was part of the raft of legislation that was abandoned to make way for the General Election in May 2005, though was reintroduced in the Queen's Speech in May 2005 and placed before Parliament in June that year. Despite the controversy that this has created, few people seem to have noticed how the law on race is already being stretched to cover religion so that anti-Muslim literature is becoming covered in the way that anti-Jewish literature has been covered for decades.[2] Nevertheless, the government continued to have difficulties getting support for such legislation, not least from their own supporters, inside Parliament and outside it, where it especially provoked resistance from comedians, intellectuals and secularists, who feared that satire and criticism of religion was at risk. Finally, Parliament passed a bill in early 2006 to protect against incitement to religious hatred. Yet it was only passed after members of both houses of Parliament, supported by much of the liberal intelligentsia, forced the government to accept amendments that weakened its initial proposals. Unlike the incitement to religious hatred offence in Northern Ireland, and the incitement to racial hatred offence in the UK, mere offensiveness was not an offence, and moreover the incitement must require the *intention* to stir up hatred. Nevertheless, a controversy shortly after this bill was passed showed that the media was coming to voluntarily restrain itself. This was the case of the Danish Muhammad Cartoons Affair, the cartoons being reprinted in several leading European newspapers but not by any major organ in Britain, suggesting there was a greater understanding in Britain about anti-Muslim racism and about not giving gratuitous offence to Muslims than in some other European countries.

Positive inclusion of religious groups

The demand here is that religion in general, or at least the category of 'Muslim' in particular, should be a category by which the inclusiveness of social institutions may be judged, as they increasingly are in relation to race and gender. For example, employers should have to demonstrate that they do not discriminate against Muslims by explicit monitoring of Muslims' position within the workforce, backed up by appropriate policies, targets, managerial responsibilities, work environments, staff training, advertisements, outreach and so on (CBMI 2002; FAIR, 2002). Similarly, public bodies should provide appropriately sensitive policies and staff in relation to the services they provide, especially in relation to (non-Muslim) schools, social and health services; Muslim community centres or Muslim youth workers should be funded in addition to existing Asian and Caribbean community centres and Asian and Black youth workers.

To take another case: the BBC currently believes it is of political importance to review and improve its personnel practices and its output of programmes, including its on-screen 'representation' of the British population, by making provision for and winning the confidence of women, ethnic groups and young people. Why should it not also use religious groups as a criterion of inclusivity and have to demonstrate that it is doing the same for viewers and staff defined by religious community membership?

In short, Muslims should be treated as a legitimate group in their own right (not because they are, say, Asians), whose presence in British society has to be explicitly reflected in all walks of life and in all institutions; and whether they are so included should become one of the criteria for judging Britain as an egalitarian, inclusive, multicultural society. There is no prospect at present of religious equality catching up with the importance that employers and other organisations give to sex or race. A potentially significant victory, however, was made when the government agreed to include a religion question in the 2001 Census. The question was voluntary but only 7% did not answer it and so it has the potential to pave the way for widespread 'religious monitoring' in the way that the inclusion of an ethnic question in 1991 had led to the more routine use of 'ethnic monitoring'.

These policy demands no doubt seem odd within the terms of, say, the French or US 'wall of separation' between the state and religion, and may make secularists uncomfortable in Britain too. But it is clear that they virtually mirror existing anti-discrimination policy provisions in the UK. Moreover, Muslim assertiveness, although triggered and intensified by what are seen as attacks on Muslims, is primarily derived not from Islam or Islamism but from contemporary Western ideas about equality and multiculturalism. While simultaneously reacting to the latter in its failure to distinguish Muslims from the rest of the 'Black' population and its uncritical secular bias, Muslims positively use, adapt and extend these contemporary Western ideas in order to join other equality-seeking movements. Political Muslims do, therefore, have an ambivalence in relation to multicultural discourses. On the one hand, as a result of previous misrecognition of their identity, and existing biases, there is distrust of 'the "race" relations industry' and of 'liberals'; on the other hand, the assertiveness is clearly a product of the positive climate created by liberals and egalitarians (Modood, 2005). This ambivalence can tend towards antagonism as the assertiveness is increasingly being joined by Islamic discourses and Islamists. In particular, as has been said, there is a sense that Muslim populations across the world are repeatedly suffering at the hands of their neighbours, aided and abetted by the US and its allies, and that Muslims must come together to defend themselves. There is a useful analogy with the Black power movement here, not just in its internationalism but one could say that as Black nationalism and Afrocentrism developed as one ideological expression of Black power, so, similarly, we can see political Islamism as a search for Muslim dignity and power.

Those who see the current Muslim assertiveness as an unwanted and illegitimate child of multiculturalism have only two choices if they wish to be consistent. They can repudiate the idea of equality as identity recognition and return to the 1960s liberal idea of equality as colour/sex/religion etc blindness. Or they can argue that equality as recognition does not apply to oppressed religious communities, perhaps uniquely not to religious communities. To deny Muslims positive equality without one of these two arguments is to be open to the charge of double standards.

Hence a programme of racial and multicultural equality is not possible today without a discussion of the merits and limits of secularism. Secularism can no longer be treated as 'off-limits', or, as President Jacques Chirac said in a major speech in 2004, 'non-negotiable' (Cesari, 2004, p 166). Not that it is really a matter of being for or against secularism, but rather a careful, institution by institution analysis of how to draw the public–private boundary and further the cause of multicultural equality and inclusivity.

Secularism: different public–private boundaries in different countries[3]

At the heart of secularism is a distinction between the public realm of citizens and policies and the private realm of belief and worship. While all Western countries are clearly secular in many ways, interpretations and the institutional arrangements diverge according to the dominant national religious culture and the differing projects of nation state building; this makes secularism a 'particular' experience.

For example, the US has as its First Amendment to the Constitution that there shall be no established church; there is wide support for this and in the past few decades there has been a tendency among academics and jurists to interpret the church–state separation in continually more radical ways (Sandel, 1994; Hamburger, 2002). Yet, as is well known, not only is the US a deeply religious society, with much higher levels of church attendance than in Western Europe (Greely, 1995), but there is also a strong Protestant, evangelical fundamentalism that is rare in Europe. This fundamentalism disputes some of the new radical interpretations of the 'no establishment clause', although not necessarily the clause itself, and is one of the primary mobilising forces in US politics; it is widely claimed that it decided the presidential election of 2004. The churches in question – mainly White, mainly in the South and mid-West – campaign openly for candidates and parties, indeed raise large sums of money for politicians and introduce religion-based issues into politics, such as positions on abortion, HIV/AIDS, homosexuality, stem cell research, prayer at school and so on. It has been said that no openly avowed atheist has ever been a candidate for the White House and that it would be impossible for such a candidate to be elected. It is not at all unusual for politicians – in fact, for President George W. Bush, it is most usual – to publicly talk about their faith, to appeal to religion and to hold prayer meetings in government buildings. On the other hand, in establishment Britain, bishops sit in the upper chamber of the legislature by right and only the senior Archbishop can crown a new head of state, the monarch, but politicians rarely talk about their religion. It was noticeable, for example, that when Prime Minister Blair went to a summit meeting with President Bush to discuss aspects of the Iraq War in 2003, the US media widely reported that the two leaders had prayed together. Yet, Prime Minister Blair, one of the most openly professed and active Christians ever to hold that office, refused to answer questions on this issue from the British media on his return, saying it was a private matter. The British state may have an established church but the beliefs of the Queen's first minister are his own concern.

France draws the distinction between state and religion differently again. Like the US, there is no state church but, unlike the US, the state actively promotes the privatisation of religion. While in the US, organised religion in civil society is powerful and seeks to exert influence on the political process, French civil society does not carry signs or expressions of religion. Yet, the French state, contrary to the US, confers institutional legal status on the Catholic and Protestant churches and on the Jewish consistory, albeit carefully designating organised religions as '*cultes*' and not communities. We could express these three different national manifestations of secularism as in Table 3.1.

Table 3.1: Religion vis-à-vis state and civil society in three countries

	State	Religion in civil society
England/Britain	Weak establishment but churches have a political voice	Weak but churches can be a source of political criticism and action
US	No establishment	Strong and politically mobilised
France	Actively secular but offers top-down recognition	Weak; rare for churches to be political

Source: Adapted from Modood and Kastoryano (2006)

So, what are the appropriate limits of the state? Everyone will agree that there should be religious freedom and that this should include freedom of belief and worship in private associations. Family too falls on the private side of the line but the state regulates the limits of what is a lawful family (for example, polygamy is not permitted in many countries), not to mention the deployment of official definitions of family in the distribution of welfare entitlements. Religions typically put a premium on mutuality and on care of the sick, the homeless, older people and so on. They set up organisations to pursue these aims, but so do states. Should there be a competitive or a cooperative relationship between these religious and state organisations, or do they have to ignore each other? Can public money – raised out of taxes on religious as well as non-religious citizens – not be used to support the organisations favoured by some religious taxpayers? What of schools? Do parents not have the right to expect that schools will make an effort – while pursuing broader educational and civic aims – not to create a conflict between the work of the school and the upbringing of the children at home but, rather, show respect for their religious background? Can parents, as associations of religious citizens, not set up their own schools and should those schools not be supported out of the taxes of the same parents? Is the school where the private (the family) meets the public (the state); or is it, in some Platonic manner, where the state takes over the children from the family and pursues its own purposes? Even if there is to be no established church, the state may still wish to work with organised religion as a social partner, as is the case in Germany, or to have some forum in which it consults with organised religion, some kind of national council of religions, as in Belgium. Or even if it does not do that because it is regarded as compromising the principle of secularism, political parties, being agents in civil society rather than organs of the state, may wish to do this and institute special representation for religious groups, as many do for groups defined by age, gender, region, language, ethnicity and so on. It is clear then that the 'public' is a multifaceted concept and in relation to secularism may be defined differently in relation to different dimensions of religion and in different countries.

We can all be secularists, then, all approve of secularism in some respect, and yet have quite different ideas, influenced by historical legacies and varied pragmatic compromises, of where to draw the line between public and private. It would be quite mistaken to suppose that all religious spokespeople, or at least all political Muslims, are on one side of the line, and all others are on the other side. There are many different ways of drawing the various lines at issue. In the past, drawing them has reflected particular contexts shaped by differential customs, urgency of need and sensitivity to the sensibilities of the relevant religious groups (Modood, 1994, 1997). Exactly the same considerations are relevant in relation to the accommodation of Muslims in Europe today – not a battle of slogans and ideological over-simplifications.

Moderate secularism as an implication of multicultural equality

Multicultural equality, then, when applied to religious groups means that secularism *simpliciter* appears to be an obstacle to pluralistic integration and equality. But secularism pure and simple is not what exists in the world. The country-by-country situation is more complex, and indeed, far less inhospitable to the accommodation of Muslims than the ideology of secularism – or, for that matter, the ideology of anti-secularism – might suggest (Modood and Kastoryano, 2006). All actual practices of secularism consist of institutional compromises and these can be, should be and are being extended to accommodate Muslims. The institutional reconfiguration varies according to the historic place of religion in each country. Today the appropriate response to the new Muslim challenges is pluralistic institutional integration, rather than an appeal to a radical public–private separation in the name of secularism. The approach that is being argued for here, then, consists of:

1. A reconceptualisation of equality from sameness to an incorporation of a respect for difference.
2. A reconceptualisation of secularism from the concepts of neutrality and the strict public–private divide to a moderate and evolutionary secularism based on institutional adjustments.
3. A pragmatic, case-by-case, negotiated approach to dealing with controversy and conflict, not an ideological, drawing a 'line in the sand' mentality.

This institutional integration approach is based on including Islam into the institutional framework of the state, using the historical accommodation between state and church as a basis for negotiations in order to achieve consensual resolutions consistent with equality and justice. As these accommodations have varied from country to country, it means there is no exemplary solution, for contemporary solutions will also depend on the national context and will not have a once-and-for-all-time basis. It is clearly a dialogical perspective and assumes the possibility of mutual education and learning.

The recognition of Islam in Europe can in some countries, for example France, take a corporatist form, can be led or even imposed by the state in a 'top-down' way and can take a church or ecclesiastical model as its form. This may be appropriate for certain countries or at certain moments and could be (and usually is) consistent with the conception of multiculturalism outlined. However, it would not be my own preference for it would not represent the British multicultural experience and its potentialities at its best. A corporatist inclusion would require Muslims and their representatives to speak in one voice and to create a unified, hierarchical structure when this is out of character in Sunni Islam, especially the South Asian Sunni Islam espoused by the majority of Muslims in Britain, and of the contemporary British Muslim scene. Corporatism would very likely consist of state control of the French kind, with the state imposing its own template, plans, modes of partnership and chosen imams and leaders on Muslims. My own preference would be for an approach in which civil society played a greater role and would be more comfortable with a variety of Muslim voices, groups and representatives. Different institutions, organisations and associations would seek to accommodate Muslims in ways that worked best for them at a particular time, knowing that these ways may or ought to be modified over time, and Muslim and other pressure groups and civic actors may be continually evolving their claims and agendas. Within a general understanding that there had to be an explicit effort to include Muslims (and other marginal and underrepresented groups), different organisations – like my earlier example of the BBC – may not just seek this inclusion in different ways but would seek as representatives Muslims who seemed to them most appropriate associates and partners, people who would add something to the organisation and who were not merely delegated from a central, hierarchical Muslim body. The idea of numerical or 'mirror' representation of the population might be a guideline but it would not necessarily follow that some kind of quota allocation (a mild version of the corporatist tendency) would have to operate. Improvisation, flexibility, consultation, learning by 'suck it and see' and by the example of others, incrementalism and all the other virtues of a pragmatic politics in close touch with a dynamic civil society can as much and perhaps better bring about multicultural equality than a top-down corporatist inclusion. 'Representation' here would mean the inclusion of a diversity of backgrounds and sensibilities, not delegates or corporate structures. Recognition, then, must be pragmatically and experimentally handled, and civil society must share the burden of representation.

While the state may seek to ensure that spiritual leaders are not absent from public fora and consultative processes in relation to policies affecting their flocks, it may well be that a Board of Jewish Deputies model of community representation offers a better illustration of a community–state relationship. The Board of Deputies, a body independent of, but a communal partner, to the British state, is a federation of Jewish organisations, which includes synagogues but also other Jewish community organisations, and its leadership typically consists of lay people whose standing and skill in representing their community is not diminished by any absence of spiritual authority. It is most interesting that while at some local levels Muslim organisations have chosen to create political bodies primarily around mosques (for example, the Bradford Council of Mosques), at a national level, it is the Board of Deputies model that seems to be more apparent. This is certainly the case with the single most representative and successful national Muslim organisation, the Muslim Council of Britain (MCB), whose office holders and spokespeople are more likely to be chartered accountants and solicitors than imams. Most mosques in Britain are run by local lay committees and the *mullah* or imam is usually a minor functionary. Very few of those who aspire to be Muslim spokespeople and representatives have religious authority and they are not expected to have it by fellow Muslims. So the accommodation of religious groups is as much if not more about the recognition and support of communities than necessarily about ecclesiastical or spiritual representation in political institutions. The state has a role here that includes ensuring that Muslim civil society is drawn into the mainstream as much as it is to seek forms of representation within state structures.

Conclusion

The emergence of Muslim political agency has thrown British multiculturalism into theoretical and practical disarray. It has led to policy reversals in the Netherlands and elsewhere, and across Europe has strengthened intolerant, exclusive nationalism. We should in fact be moving the other way, and enacting the kinds of legal and policy measures that are necessary to accommodate Muslims as equal citizens in European polities. These would include anti-discrimination measures in areas such as employment, positive action to achieve a full and just political representation of Muslims in various areas of public life, the inclusion of Muslim history as European history, and so on. Critically, I have been arguing that the inclusion of Islam as an organised religion and of Muslim identity as a public identity is necessary to integrate Muslims and to pursue religious equality. While this inclusion runs against certain interpretations of secularism, it is not inconsistent with what secularism means in practice in Europe. We should let this evolving, moderate secularism and the spirit of compromise it represents be our guide. Unfortunately, an ideological secularism is currently being reasserted and generating European domestic versions of 'the clash of civilisations' thesis and the conflicts that entails for European societies. That some people are today developing secularism as an ideology to oppose Islam and its public recognition is a challenge both to pluralism and equality, and thus to some of the bases of contemporary democracy. It has to be resisted no less than the radical anti-secularism of some Islamists.

Notes

[1] The first half of this chapter borrows from and builds on my 'Muslims and the politics of difference' (2003a), with simultaneous publication in *Political Quarterly* (2003b). The second half borrows from and builds on parts of a joint chapter with Riva Kastoryano, 'Secularism and the accommodation of Muslims in Europe' (2006). For a fuller elaboration of the perspective on which this chapter is based, see my *Multiculturalism: A civic idea* (2007).

[2] The 1998 Crime and Disorder Act introduced the concept of a 'racially aggravated' offence that covers not just the intention of an act but also its consequences. It relates primarily to acts of violence but also in relation to amendments to the section of the 1986 Public Order Act that deals with threatening, abusive or insulting behaviour. So, the latter behaviour is not determined by intentions alone. Following '9/11' an Anti-Terrorism, Crime and Security Act was quickly passed and extended the phrase 'racially aggravated' to 'racially or religiously aggravated'. In 2003, the High Court upheld the conviction in the *Norwood* case, arguing that displaying a British National Party poster bearing the words 'Islam out of Britain' and 'Protect the British People' accompanied by a picture of the 9/11 attack on the Twin Towers amounted to an offence of causing alarm or distress. The High Court argued that evidence of actual alarm or distress was not necessary if it was determined that 'any right thinking member of society' is likely to be caused harassment, alarm or distress. It concluded, therefore, that the poster was racially insulting and, additionally, religiously aggravated. It seems, then – although this is only on the basis of one case – that Muslims in Britain may have stronger legal protection against a version of incitement to religious hatred than that provided in the 2006 Act (for further details see *Norwood v DPP* [2003] EWHC 1564 (Admin); CBMI, 2004).

[3] For the next two sections I am grateful to Riva Kastoryano both for some collaborative writing (Modood and Kastoryano, 2006) and for helping me to clarify our disagreements about the nature of institutional integration.

References

CBMI (Commission on British Muslims and Islamophobia) (2004) *Response to the Commission on Racial Equality's Code of Practice*, London.

Cesari, J. (2004) *When Islam and democracy meet*, New York, NY and Basingstoke: Palgrave.

FAIR (Forum Against Islamophobia and Racism) (2002) *A response to the government consultation paper, 'Towards equality and diversity: Implementing the Employment and Race Directives'*, London.

Greely, A. (1995) 'The persistence of religion', *Cross Currents*, vol 45, Spring, pp 24-41.

Hamburger, P. (2002) *Separation of church and state*, Cambridge, MA and London: Harvard University Press.

Modood, T. (1992) *Not easy being British: Colour, culture and citizenship*, London: Runnymede Trust/Trentham Books.

Modood, T. (1994) 'Establishment, multiculturalism and British citizenship', *Political Quarterly*, vol 65, no 1, pp 53-73.

Modood, T. (ed) (1997) *Church, state and religious minorities*, London: Policy Studies Institute.

Modood, T. (2003a) 'Muslims and the politics of difference', in S. Spencer (ed) *The politics of migration*, Oxford: Blackwell Publishing.

Modood, T. (2003b) 'Muslims and the politics of difference', *Political Quarterly*, vol 74, no 1, pp 100-115.

Modood, T. (2005) *Multicultural politics: Racism, ethnicity and Muslims in Britain*, Minneapolis, MN and Edinburgh: University of Minnesota Press and University of Edinburgh Press.

Modood, T. (2007) *Multiculturalism: A civic idea*, Cambridge: Polity.

Modood, T. and Kastoryano, R. (2006) 'Secularism and the accommodation of Muslims in Europe', in T. Modood, A. Triandafyllidou and R. Zapata-Barrero (eds) *Multiculturalism, Muslims and citizenship: A European approach*, London: Routledge.

Modood, T., Berthoud, R., Lakey, J., Nazroo, J., Smith, P., Virdee, S. and Beishon, S. (1997) *Ethnic minorities in Britain: Diversity and disadvantage*, London: Policy Studies Institute.

Sandel, M. (1994) 'Review of Rawls' political liberalism', *Harvard Law Review*, vol 107, pp 1765-94.

Savage, T. (2004) 'Europe and Islam: crescent waxing, cultures clashing', *The Washington Quarterly*, vol 27, no 3, pp 25-50.

Young, I.M. (1992) *Justice and the politics of difference*, Princeton, NJ: Princeton University Press.

FOUR

Section 116: the politics of secularism in Australian legal and political discourse

Holly Randell-Moon

Introduction

The theory referred to in sociology as the 'secularization thesis' (Nash, 2004, p 302) hypothesises that religion has gradually waned in cultural and social importance because Western modernity has secured a non-religious and secular foundation for liberal democracy. Secularism, however, does not necessarily imply secularisation as some religions, such as Christianity, can exercise a cultural power in 'Western' nations even as liberal secularism requires a separation of church and state. However, the idea of secularisation contributes to a framing of secularism as universal in its operation and diminishes the particularity of how secularisms and religions operate in specific cultural contexts.

The focus of this chapter is to interrogate the implications of liberal secular theories that conceptualise religion as outside of politics, and therefore institutional forms of power, by examining constitutional and legal understandings of secularism in Australia. Drawing on the critical insights on secularism in the work of anthropologist Talal Asad, it will be argued that secularism does more than represent politics as separate from religion; it functions to produce particular understandings of religion. The separation of religion from politics by secularism underpins the constitutional and legal frameworks that treat secularism as 'neutral' rather than implicated in the symbolic and political terms through which religion is understood in Australian culture.

The first section of the chapter gives a short overview of liberal secularism in order to contextualise representations of secularism in Australia's Constitution. From this vantage point I examine section 116 of the Australian Constitution, which outlines the relationship of religion to the state. Section 116 explains that:

> The Commonwealth shall not make any law for establishing any religion, or for imposing any religious observance, or for prohibiting the free exercise of any religion, and no religious test shall be

required as a qualification for any office or public trust under the Commonwealth.

Section 116 approximates a secular separation of church and state by protecting religious freedom from government intervention and prohibiting the official establishment of any one religion by the Commonwealth. The legal literature on section 116 and the cases concerning its applications qualify this separation by theorising a relationship between church and state in Australia as neutral rather than strictly demarcated. That is, the government neither prohibits nor establishes a specific religion. For example, Australian courts have upheld government assistance to church schools viewing it as 'indirect' through a framework of neutrality, whereas in the US such a practice has been prohibited constitutionally (Puls, 1998, p 148). The Australian legal literature surveyed in this chapter attempts to produce a consistent definition of secularism through the characterisation of the state's relationship to religious matters as neutral. Given the nature of Australia's constitutional arrangements, however, it will be shown how jurisprudence concerning religious matters necessitates that legal definitions must be established on a case-by-case basis. Thus any definition of religion is contingent and arbitrary according to different political circumstances.

The chapter concludes by arguing that theories of secularisation overlook ways in which the dominant religion in a culture can be integrated into government operations. This integration is often supported by ethnocentric assumptions of cultural compatibility between specific religions and a secular state. Particular attention is given to the comments of former Federal Treasurer Peter Costello, who attempts to frame aspects of Islam as 'illegitimate' because it seemingly combines both politics and religion. Such comments are demonstrative of an appeal to secularism as an unproblematic norm that also masks the symbolic status given to Christianity within Australian parliamentary and governmental arrangements. In this way, the representation of secularism within political spaces is not characterised by a 'distinct' separation of the secular from the non-secular, but is imbued with religiously informed cultural and social values.

Liberal secularism

Theories of liberal secularism attempt to both explain and justify a doctrine of separation between religion and politics in legal and governmental practice. From this paradigm, religious views comprise what political theorist John Rawls refers to as comprehensive doctrines that '[cover] all values and virtues within one rather precisely articulated system' (1993, p 152, n 17). Since a plural democracy contains individuals each with their own comprehensive doctrines,

> we must distinguish between a public basis of justification generally acceptable to citizens on fundamental political questions and the many

nonpublic bases of justification belonging to the many comprehensive doctrines and acceptable only to those who affirm them. (p xix)

In other words, since all citizens do not share the same religious beliefs, liberal secularism requires that these beliefs be privatised and that public decisions or justifications of government policy be political only. In this way it can be said by legal scholars that 'the idea of a secular liberal state, ie the state which neither gets involved with matters religious, nor inhibits in any way religious expression and activities, has been long understood as best encapsulated by the idea of the state's neutrality toward religion' (Sadurski, 1990, p 421). Within a model of liberal secularism, the practice by governments of separating church and state is viewed as protecting an individual's religious preference as well as maintaining equilibrium between individual religions by not according any one religion an official priority.

However, an understanding of secularism as self-evidently able to foster religious freedom and good (non-religious) governance relies on a series of particular assumptions concerning religion and the secularisation of 'Western' culture. The liberal model for separating church and state is reflected by a historical trajectory that sees secularisation involving the progressive diminution of (predominantly Christian) religions from democratic systems of government. David Nash defines the secularisation thesis as 'the argument that the importance of religious practice and belief is in inexorable (and inevitable) decline as a fundamental process introduced by the arrival of modern society and its consequences' (2004, p 303). While liberal democracies have claimed a secular foundation for political organisation, the presentation of secularisation as producing irreligiosity universalises secularism and undervalues the role of religion within contemporary political systems. Talal Asad argues that the 'separation of religion from power is a modern Western norm, the product of a unique post-Reformation history' (1993, p 28), which instantiates a conceptual separation of religion from power – as though religion retains a transhistorical essence (p 29). If secularism were constituted only by the absence of religion then secular countries such as the US, Britain, France (and Australia) would implement the separation of church and state in similar ways (Asad, 2003, p 5).

The 'separation of religion from power' has a number of effects, which include valorising liberal secularism as the best form of protection for religious freedom by appealing to its neutral or objective nature, and obscuring the specific religious frames that underpin secularism. David Theo Goldberg writes, 'the difference between the religious and the secular ... is in the conditions appealed to in justifying [particular political] claims as true' (1993, p 17), not necessarily between an irreligious secularity and religious power. Because secularism's emergence with modernity was based on 'the general standards for which the West took to be its own values universalized' (p 4), the predominantly Christian frames of reference that make up secular ideals of political comportment are rendered invisible in contemporary political discourses (Imtoual, 2004, p 83). Importantly, and for the purposes of this chapter, secularism has a discursive power that can appeal to a separation of the secular from the non-secular without specifying how this separation produces a particular understanding of religion (Asad, 1993, p 28) and how religion in turn informs the use of secularism in various cultural contexts. It is to the implications of these ideas and the specific ways liberal secularism is seen to have its practical application in section 116 of the Australian Constitution that the chapter now turns.

Secularism and Australia's Constitution

Section 116 of Australia's Constitution contains provisions for the protection of religious freedom and the preservation of religious diversity through the prohibition of a state-established religion. The section can be broken into four clauses:

1) The Commonwealth shall not make any law for establishing any religion, or
2) for imposing any religious observance, or
3) for prohibiting the free exercise of any religion, and
4) no religious test shall be required as a qualification for any office or public trust under the Commonwealth.

In the Australian political system the Constitution grants the Commonwealth of Australia (hereafter referred to as either 'the Commonwealth' or 'Australia') the power to create laws, and the Federal Parliament decides on what laws need to be made (Eburn, 1995, p 78). Section 116 works as a restriction to the Commonwealth's powers to create laws with respect to religion. The section is modelled on and has counterparts in US constitutional provisions for religious freedom. But unlike the US provisions, section 116 is not binding on State and Territory governments despite being located in the Chapter of the Constitution dealing with matters relating to the States (Hogan, 1981, p 219; McLeish, 1992, p 209; Puls, 1998, p 141). Theoretically this means that State and Territory governments are not obliged to provide religious protection, although all but South Australia prohibit religious discrimination (Maddox, 2001, p 106; Imtoual, 2006). The following section considers the cases brought before the High Court that involve section 116 and the legal literature concerning its application in order to draw out some insights about interpretations of secularism and religion in Australian legal discourse.

Judicial applications and interpretations of section 116

The High Court of Australia has addressed some cases with respect to the free exercise and establishment clauses of section 116 (so far the clauses dealing with religious observance and religious tests for public office have not been examined by the court). Regarding the free exercise provision, in the case of *Krygger v Williams*

(1912) 15 CLR 366, the court found that compulsory military training did not constitute a prohibition of religious freedom (Hogan, 1981, pp 219–20). Later the court ruled in favour of the Commonwealth's proscription of organisations considered detrimental to the war effort in the case of *Adelaide Company of Jehovah's Witnesses Inc v Commonwealth* (1943) 67 CLR 116. This was on the basis of giving priority to the protection of the community (which was seen to benefit from the Second World War) over individual freedom to exercise religion (Hogan, 1981, p 220). In the most recent case, *Kruger v Commonwealth* (1997) 190 CLR 1, Indigenous plaintiffs contended that the Aboriginals Ordinance (NT) of 1918–57, which removed Indigenous children from their families, breached a number of constitutional rights, including the right to the free exercise of religion (Eastman and Ronalds, 1998, pp 337–8). The court, whilst recognising the rights existed, rejected the application because the legislation authorised forms of welfare and was not concerned with religious practices (Gageler and Glass, 1998, p 58).

Because the High Court is concerned with examining the scope of government power (which is the structure of the Constitution), the legislation involved in the above cases was viewed as not directly concerning the limitation of the free exercise of religion and therefore was upheld. This potentially produces a narrow framework for what comprises religious freedom. By contrast, when deciding whether Scientology constituted a religion for the purposes of tax exemption in *Church of The New Faith v Commissioner of Pay-Roll Tax* (Vic) (1983) 154 CLR 120, the High Court argued for a wide definition of religion in section 116 as its purpose was to protect those 'minority religions out of the main streams of religious thought' (as cited in COA, 2000, para 4.22). *Krygger v Williams* (1912), the Jehovah's Witnesses case (1943) and *Kruger v Commonwealth* (1997) limit the freedom of 'minority' beliefs based on the scope of Commonwealth power (notwithstanding section 116's free exercise clause), whereas the court widens the definition of religion in the Scientology case to uphold 'minority' beliefs. Although the different applications of section 116 in these cases may appear somewhat contradictory, they do make sense in the context of a liberal concept of neutrality that neither favours specific religious beliefs, by guaranteeing the freedom to exercise those beliefs above secular laws or policies, nor prohibits their establishment.

In 1981 the Attorney-General of Victoria challenged Commonwealth legislation that provided aid to denominational schools in the States and Territories in *Attorney-General (Vict); Ex Rel Black v The Commonwealth* (1981) 146 CLR 559. This funding went predominantly to Roman Catholic schools (Puls, 1998, p 143). The court found that the money disbursed to the States for educational purposes did not specifically 'establish any religion' and consequently the section did not apply to State aid (Eburn, 1995, p 83; Hogan, 1981, pp 222–3). Importantly, in this case Justice Wilson determined that the section of the Constitution dealing with religious matters 'cannot answer the description of a law which guarantees within Australia the separation of church and state' (as cited in Wallace, 2005). Representations of Australia as a secular nation, discussed below in more detail, are problematic if the separation of church and state is only partially legitimated in the High Court's interpretations and applications of section 116.

Australian constitutional interpretations revolve around the scope of Commonwealth powers. Australia has no legal document of civil liberties, such as a Bill of Rights, so most political rights and freedoms are inferred from the Commonwealth's powers not to make laws in specific areas of civil life. This means that religious freedoms found by the High Court are not positive freedoms in the sense that they guarantee a right to religious freedom. Rather, religious freedoms are negative in that they derive from the actions (or inaction) of the state. By adopting a neutral attitude towards religious matters, degrees of religious freedom are enabled when the Commonwealth neither favours nor prohibits particular religions.

However, for some legal scholars, the characterisation of the state's relations to religion as neutral implies an equation between neutral and non-political. Legal scholar Joshua Puls argues:

> the extent to which religious guarantees of the First Amendment [in the United States] have been litigated, and the extent to which religious loyalties permeate American public life, are indications of the politicisation of religion and the evangelisation of politics in the United States. (1998, p 163)

The implication is that a formal and legally binding right to freedom of belief unduly politicises religion. This would serve no purpose in Australian culture, which is 'neither sectarian nor dogmatically suspicious of relations between government and religion', and thus 'the section has been faithful to its purpose and has served Australia well' (p 164). Puls' argument that the litigation of religious matters in Australia is marginal and therefore demonstrative of a dispassionately religious climate confuses the judicial structures for judging religious matters as neutral with their consequences of marginalising religious matters as non-political. That is, the characterisation of the law as neutral makes invisible the selective and contextual interpretations of the High Court regarding section 116 that necessitate the judgement of religious matters on a case-by-case basis. As such, religion is politicised in and through the legal system and constitutional interpretations of section 116. The framing of the judiciary as neutral towards religion is political.

Defining religion as non-political in legal discourse

The assumption behind interpretations of the implementation and scope of section 116 is the adoption of neutrality towards religion by the government. The central aim of this implementation is the desire not to politicise religion by either directly preferencing or explicitly avoiding it. As a result, a great deal of time is spent by legal scholars trying to accommodate an apolitical view of religion with respect to its legal definitions and applications. Wojchiech Sadurski, for example, argues that the maintenance of state neutrality towards religion is enabled by two principles of secularity, 'the separation of the state and religion, and the freedom of religion' (1990, p 422). These are covered by the free exercise and non-establishment clauses in section 116, where 'the separation of state and religion is often seen as the best guarantee of religious freedom' since 'citizens can freely pursue their religious lives according to their own wishes, and obviously a state-established religion tends to interfere with the free exercise of non-established religions' (p 422). There is, however, a tension between the two clauses as one, the free exercise clause, calls for government accommodation of religion and the other does not. This is because the free exercise clause has what Sadurski refers to as 'an expanding dynamic built into it' that attempts to protect not only dominant but marginalised religions as well (p 423). This has the effect of necessitating an expansive definition of religion for cases dealing specifically with religious recognition, as in the Scientology case, in order to accommodate religious freedom as broadly as possible. In cases relating to the non-establishment clause, the court already knows what the religion is since the concern is whether or not that religion is officially tied to and established by the state (Sadurski, 1989, p 842). Sadurski argues that the burden on the court in non-establishment cases is:

> making sure that the government-regulated sphere of public life is uncontaminated by religious (or anti-religious) considerations. The principal insight here is that religion must remain a private matter for every individual, and that social life ... must remain unaffected by religious or anti-religious motivations of the policy-makers and legislators. Consequently, the public decision-makers must know clearly and precisely what is to count as 'religion', and how to demarcate the non-religious concerns, in order to screen off the religion-conscious considerations from their decisions. (1989, p 841)

It is difficult to envisage how the public spheres of law and government can remain 'uncontaminated' by religion when interpretations of section 116 produce a jurisprudence where religion can only be ruled upon on a case-by-case basis. This produces a tension between determining what is religious and what is political precisely at the same time as they are inextricably linked. Because the judiciary determines religious freedom in a case-by-case way, secularism's viability is connected to the politics of the state even as the state's relation to religion is cast as 'neutral'. The judicial realm is 'contaminated' by the state's ability to govern, which has effects for how religion is accommodated. What comprises 'religious freedom' in the above cases is subject to the interests of the state's engagement in foreign and military policy as well as the implementation of domestic policies predicated on the racialised marginalisation of Indigenous peoples and their religious freedoms in *Kruger v Commonwealth* (1997). The point is that religion cannot be de-politicised if it can only be decided by politics within and through government legislation and the legal system. Michael Eburn observes 'the freedom of religion [in Australia] is protected by the political process and the "goodwill" of government, rather than by being enshrined in the foundation documents of the nation' (1995, p 77). Claims to the neutral nature of secularism mask the ways in which it enables the politicisation of religion, and so the 'problem' of determining what is religious or political only occurs if the 'objective' understanding of secularity and neutrality is upheld.

Puls writes that if a solution to determining what is or is not a state-established religion suggested that 'Australia and the United States are both multicultural, pluralistic societies' but 'they are societies founded on, and still principally directed by Judeo-Christian values', it would be 'controversial' (1998, pp 157–8). While it may be true according to the logic of secularism that Australia has no state-established religion (and by this inaction of establishment a right to religious freedom is enabled), this does not mean that the terms through which a secular state operates are free from religion or the privileging of particular religious values. Alia Imtoual notes that secularism's development from the European Enlightenment meant that religious plurality was an approach to different Christian denominations as opposed to what would contemporaneously be referred to as religious plurality between different religions (Imtoual, 2004, p 83; see also Asad, 2003, pp 181–201; Mahmood, 2006; Pecora, 2006, pp 25–66). This 'historical relationship between Western "secularism" and Christian modes of thought' (Imtoual, 2004, p 83) is implicated in the governmental structures that privilege Christianity (such as the inclusion of the Lord's Prayer and swearing on the Bible in parliamentary arrangements) even as secularism is upheld by not 'officially' establishing Christianity as a state-religion. Approaching secularism as neutral makes invisible the politicisation of religion through legal and governmental mechanisms and positions secularity as a universal rather than historically and culturally contingent.

The politics of secularism and religion

Talal Asad writes in *Genealogies of religion* that 'there cannot be a universal definition of religion, not only because its constituent elements and relationships are historically specific, but because that definition is itself the historical product of discursive processes' (1993, p 29). Secularism does not simply separate religion from the state but constitutes the forms religion can take. The implied religious plurality in the implementations of secular neutrality in section 116 draw on a notion of liberal pluralism that sees a tension between unity and individual beliefs as producing a state of equanimity through freedom of choice. Returning to Rawls' theory of political liberalism, he argues that the interaction of subjects within political operations occurs in this way:

> Political liberalism assumes that, for political purposes, a plurality of reasonable yet incompatible comprehensive doctrines is the normal result of the exercise of human reason within the framework of the free

> institutions of a constitutional democratic regime. Political liberalism
> also supposes that a reasonable comprehensive doctrine does not reject
> the essentials of a democratic regime. (1993, p xvi)

This theory understands religion as separate from political processes because it is
not strictly political (it is comprehensive) but is nevertheless compatible because
it is 'reasonable' and therefore democratic. Religious freedom is dependent upon
a necessary association between cultural plurality and tolerance because this
ensures freedom of choice to express difference. Democratic political systems
are productive in ensuring this freedom. This model of secularity presumes, as
Rawls suggests, that any given religion within a liberal pluralist society will be
'compatible' with democratic principles. That is, these religions or (comprehensive
doctrines) can be integrated in various ways into a political system because they
have democratic principles. Given that, as Goldberg notes, modernity framed
specific 'Western' cultural and religious values as universal, secularism can
reproduce itself as a neutral arbiter of religions even as it formed within specific
Protestant–Christian values. This in turn means that equations between cultural
compatibility and democracy are not directed towards the already dominant
religion in a culture but can be projected onto cultures and religions considered
'other' (see Randell-Moon, 2006).

This is evidenced in mainstream political discourses about the supposed
'compatibility' of Islam with secular states such as Australia. In a speech to the
Sydney Institute (a conservative organisation that hosts weekly speakers on political
issues) in February 2006, former Federal Treasurer Peter Costello argued that
Sharia law, a form of Islamic law, is intrinsically irreconcilable with the democratic
practices of government in Australia, principally the separation of church and
state. In contrast to Sharia law, Costello argued 'there is not a separate stream of
law derived from religious sources that competes with or supplants Australian law
in governing our civil society' (Costello, 2006). This positions Australian law as
neutral towards and unconnected with religious matters in opposition to Sharia
law. However, the federal government already has a series of discursive strategies
which place Christianity at the centre of Australian political life, such as the
opening of parliament with (Christian) prayer and the swearing in of government
senators and members on the Bible (Maddox, 2001, pp 109, 114).

If religious values, such as Christian values, can operate within and through state
mechanisms, the question of Sharia law's location outside them is supported by
understandings of cultural compatibility that relate specific religions to national
identity. The main subject of Costello's speech was a critique of what he referred
to as 'mushy multiculturalism' that promotes a cultural diversity detrimental to
core Australian values: 'there is a predominant culture just as there is predominant
language. And the political and cultural institutions that govern Australia are
absolutely critical to that attitude of harmony and tolerance' (Costello, 2006).
This 'harmony and tolerance' is predicated on an alignment of Australian values
with a specifically Anglo-Celtic language and culture that is universalised as

'predominant'. This 'predominant language' deploys secularism to reproduce an implicit cultural binary that scripts some 'comprehensive' religions in opposition to a 'reasonable' and ostensibly 'apolitical' (Protestant) Christianity.

The conflation of law and religion in representations of Islam attempts to displace ethnocentric ideals of Australian culture with questions of 'cultural difference'. Asad argues that 'the attempt to understand Muslim traditions by insisting that in them religion and politics (two essences modern society tries to keep conceptually and practically apart) are coupled must ... lead to failure' (1993, p 28). The universalisation of secularism by Costello works to construct particular religions along ethnocentric lines as compatible with secular law, because they can seemingly exist outside of the political process, and others as incompatible because they are 'excessively' political. Secularism is implicated in the terms that produce Australianness and reproduce hegemonic forms of power that marginalise non-Christian religions. Far from weakening the cultural importance of religion, secularisation contributes to political and cultural contexts that legitimate some expressions of religions over others.

Conclusion

The relationship of religion to politics in Australia is much more complex than 'secular neutrality' implies. Assumptions of government neutrality, through an ideal of secularism, mask the ways in which the government can favour mainstream religions in Australian culture such as Christianity. The implementation and interpretations of section 116 demonstrates how religion is integrated into the legal system according to political contingencies. That is, the public sphere of law and government cannot remain neutral or unconnected from religion if interpretations of section 116 produce a jurisprudence where religion can only be ruled upon on a case-by-case basis. There are power relations that disperse the political representations of religions unequally and that are tied to discourses of cultural compatibility with secularism. Appeals to secularism as an unproblematic norm attempt to mask the specific frames through which particular religions are viewed. Federal Treasurer Costello utilises ethnocentric discourses of secularism to frame Islam as conflating religion and politics, thereby suggesting Islam is inherently incompatible with Australia's secular government. This overlooks the discursive strategies that centre Christianity in government operations, such as the opening of parliament services with prayer, precisely because secularity assumes religion is essentially exclusive to politics. This enables secularity to be understood as objective and universal and obfuscates the particular cultural and political investments in representations of secularism in mainstream legal and political discourse.

References

Asad, T. (1993) *Genealogies of religion: Discipline and reasons of power in Christianity and Islam*, Baltimore, MD/London: Johns Hopkins University Press.

Asad, T. (2003) *Formations of the secular: Christianity, Islam, modernity*, Stanford, CA: Stanford University Press.

Commonwealth of Australia Constitution Act (1900) (2003) Chapter V, The States, s 16.

COA (Commonwealth of Australia) Joint Standing Committee on Foreign Affairs, Defence and Trade (2000) *Conviction with compassion: A report into freedom of religion and belief*, Report No 97, November.

Costello, P. (2006) 'Worth promoting, worth defending: Australian citizenship, what it means and how to nurture it', Address to the Sydney Institute, 23 February (www.treasurer.gov.au/tsr/content/speeches/2006/004.asp?p?=1).

Eastman, K. and Ronalds, C. (1998) 'Using human rights' law in litigation: The practitioner's perspective', in D. Kinley (ed) *Human rights in Australian law*, Sydney: The Federation Press, pp 319–42.

Eburn, M. (1995) 'Religion and the Constitution – an illusory freedom', *Australian Religion Studies Review*, vol 8, no 2, Spring, pp 77–85.

Gageler, S. and Glass, A. (1998) 'Constitutional law and human rights in D. Kinley (ed) *Human rights in Australian law*, Sydney: The Federation Press, pp 47–62.

Goldberg, D. T. (1993) *Racist culture: Philosophy and the politics of meaning*. Oxford/Cambridge: Blackwell.

Hogan, M. (1981) 'Separation of church and State: Section 116 of the Australian Constitution', *The Australian Quarterly*, vol 53, no 2, Winter, 214–28.

Imtoual, A. (2004) '"Whiteness" studies, Christianity and religious racism in "secular" Australia,' in S. Schech and B. Wadham (eds), *Placing race and localising whiteness*, Conference Proceedings for the 'Placing Race and Localising Whiteness' Conference, Flinders University, South Australia, 1–3 October 2003, Adelaide: Flinders Press, pp 82–8.

Imtoual, A. (2006) '"I didn't know if it was illegal for her to talk about my religion in a job interview": young Muslim women's experiences of religious racism in Australia', *Australian Religion Studies Review*, vol 19, no 2, pp 189–206.

Maddox, M. (2001) *For God and country: Religious dynamics in Australian federal politics*, Canberra: Department of the Parliamentary Library.

Mahmood, S. (2006) 'Secularism, hermeneutics, and Empire: the politics of Islamic reformation', *Public Culture*, vol 18, no 2, pp 323–47.

McLeish, S. (1992) 'Making sense of religion and the Constitution: A fresh start for section 116', *Monash University Law Review*, vol 18, no 2, pp 207–36.

Nash, D. (2004) 'Reconnecting religion with social and cultural history: secularization's failure as a master narrative', *Cultural and Social History*, vol 1, pp 302–25.

Pecora, V. P. (2006) *Secularization and cultural criticism: Religion, nation and modernity*, Chicago, IL/London: University of Chicago Press.

Puls, J. (1998) 'The wall of separation: section 116, the First Amendment and constitutional religious guarantees', *Federal Law Review*, vol 26, no 1, pp 139–64.

Randell-Moon, H. (2006) '"Common values": Whiteness, Christianity, asylum seekers and the Howard Government', *Australian Critical Race and Whiteness Studies Journal*, vol 2, no 1, pp 1–14.

Rawls, J. (1993) *Political liberalism*. New York: Columbia University Press.

Sadurski, W. (1989) 'On legal definitions of "Religion"', *The Australian Law Journal*, vol 63, no 12, December, pp 834–43.

Sadurski, W. (1990) 'Neutrality of law towards religion', *Sydney Law Review*, vol 12, March, 420–54.

Wallace, M. (2005) 'The 1981 Australian High Court Constitutional Coup and its consequences', *New Matilda*, July 27.

FIVE

Dreams of the autonomous and reflexive self: the religious significance of contemporary lifestyle media

Gordon Lynch

Introduction

Lifestyle media, with its early origins in popular manuals of etiquette and household management, seeks to explore options and to offer advice in such areas of everyday life as personal relationships, finance, health, fashion and choices over career and real estate. There are a number of interesting ways in which contemporary lifestyle media intersect with religious tradition. Best-selling religious writers such as T.D. Jakes and Rick Warren have produced lifestyle literature from a particular Christian perspective (for example, Jakes, 2002; Warren, 2003), and lifestyle media often carries implicit or explicit reference to alternative spiritualities, ranging from explicit discussions of meditation, energy and spiritual well-being, to more implicit visual images conveying serenity in the context of calm, simple and natural surroundings. Traditional religious literature has even been refracted through the genre of lifestyle media, such as in the case of *Revolve*, a best-selling version of the New Testament presented in the format of a lifestyle magazine for teenage girls. Whilst the re-branding of religion and spirituality through various lifestyle media is an important area for study (Schofield Clark, 2007), my attention in this chapter will be focused on mainstream commercial lifestyle media in the UK that explores issues of lifestyle concern without any explicitly religious or spiritual frame of reference. A central concern in this chapter will be to examine how such 'secular' contemporary lifestyle media can be seen as an example of what Thomas Luckmann has referred to as the 'invisible religion' of late modern Western society, and to think about the implications of this for the study of religion and the sacred in contemporary culture.

The approach I will adopt here is to offer a theoretical reading of the content and significance of lifestyle media, with particular reference to lifestyle television shows in the UK. This initial theoretical discussion is, of course, meant to be a provocation for further research, and a fuller understanding of the phenomenon of lifestyle media would inevitably require a much more detailed analysis of the whole 'circuit of culture' in which this media functions, including empirical work with both producers and users of this media (see, for example, Jackson et al, 2001). Nevertheless, through this discussion I hope to be able to demonstrate how contemporary lifestyle media might be analysed in the light of wider debates about religion, media and contemporary culture.

A key theoretical framework that I will use as a starting point for this chapter is taken from Thomas Luckmann's (1967) seminal book, *The invisible religion*. Luckmann's central hypothesis was that late modernity is witnessing the eclipse of specialised, institutional forms of religion and the emergence of a new social form of religion characterised by an emphasis on the self-realisation and self-expression of the autonomous self. In keeping with other secularisation theorists, Luckmann argued that the modernisation of society leads to the growing influence of secular institutions (for example, in education, health and welfare) that in turn limit the epistemological authority and social function of specialised religious institutions (Luckmann, 1967, p 85). This social process is mirrored by a similar process within the consciousness of the individual as religious belief becomes increasingly confined to a specialised and privatised 'religious sphere' and becomes less significant as a basis for making decisions about the conduct of everyday life (1967, p 86). These processes do not tend to make one kind of institutional religion more successful than another. Nor, given Luckmann's definition of religion as a world-view, does it make sense to suggest that the decline of institutional forms of religion means the end of religion in Western society – for the decline of specialised, institutional religion does not mean that people without formal religious commitments lack any kind of meaningful world-view. Rather, Luckmann argued that modernisation has led to a fundamental shift in the nature of religion in Western society away from specialised, institutional religion towards a new social form of religion that lies beyond the boundaries of what sociologists have traditionally treated as 'religion'.

In Luckmann's (1996) view, this new social form of religion is characterised by 'low levels of transcendence': an emphasis on the experience and development of the autonomous self within the horizons of this life rather than on the significance of supernatural orders above or beyond this life. This focus on the significance of the self reflects the priorities of late modern liberal democratic society in which the autonomous individual plays a central role as voter and consumer (Taylor, 2004). The new social form of religion does not therefore seek to induct individuals into a formal code or set of doctrines that provide a single, clear, authoritative structure for life, but rather offers a range of resources that individuals may seek to take up and use in different ways in the particular biographical context of their lives. Supporting this process are a range of 'secondary institutions' that compete in an increasingly open marketplace of symbols and frameworks for making sense of life (Luckmann, 1967, p 104). Luckmann's thesis thus proposes a fundamental shift in the way in which religion is practised and thought about in late modern society, away from the influence of specialised, institutional forms of religion towards the emergence of a new, more diffuse, form of religion that meets the concerns of autonomous, expressive individuals seeking to find a meaningful way through their lives without any strong reference to a supernatural order above and beyond them.

Luckmann's thesis has found support in the subsequent empirical work of sociologists of religion such as Robert Wuthnow (1998), Wade Clark Roof (1999), and Paul Heelas and Linda Woodhead (Heelas et al, 2005) that demonstrates the growing importance of concerns of self-realisation and self-expression in the contemporary religious marketplace. There are also clearly certain points on which Luckmann's thesis requires qualification. Confident predictions of the decline of institutional religion made by sociologists of religion in the 1960s have been borne out to a reasonable degree in Western Europe (particularly in relation to the Christian church), but have proven so far to be less true in North America or indeed other parts of the world. Debates about 'European exceptionalism' in relation to the secularisation thesis suggest that Luckmann's thesis needs to be more nuanced depending on the particular social and cultural context to which it is applied (see Davie, 2002). Furthermore, Luckmann's thesis does not take sufficient account of factors that may support the continued significance of some forms of institutional religion (for example, the importance of specialised forms of religion for maintaining a sense of identity and community in minority ethnic or immigrant communities; see Bruce, 1995). Nevertheless, Luckmann's thesis poses important questions currently facing Western sociology of religion, namely 'What are the dominant values overarching contemporary culture?' and 'What it is that secularization has brought about in the way of a socially objectivated cosmos of meaning?' (Luckmann, 1967, p 40).

In this chapter, I suggest that contemporary secular lifestyle media can usefully be interpreted through Luckmann's thesis about the emerging new social form of religion. In particular, I argue that such lifestyle media can be seen as one particular example of a 'secondary institution' that supports the individual's project of trying to live a meaningful and fulfilled existence within the horizons of this life. In doing so, I first offer an explanation of how 'lifestyle' has become a significant area of concern within late modernity and suggest that the notion of 'lifestyle' is a helpful concept for further clarifying Luckmann's notion of the individual pursuit of meaning, identity and value. I then go on to examine how the content of British lifestyle television programmes offers guidance on matters of lifestyle choice from the perspective of particular ideological positions and discursive formations, and therefore attempts to serve as a particular kind of moral and existential resource within the horizon of lifestyle concern. Finally, I turn to broader questions about what this might suggest for the study of religion and the sacred more broadly in contemporary culture.

The significance of lifestyle in late modernity

In recent literature on the social and cultural significance of 'lifestyle', two contrasting definitions of lifestyle can be identified. The first of these definitions understands lifestyle in terms of a distinctive and recognisable style of living associated with particular social and cultural groups (see, for example, Sobel, 1981; Chaney, 1996). Within this approach it makes sense, for example, to speak of 'yuppie' or 'hippie' lifestyles as ways of living that demonstrate particular attitudes and practices in relation to work, relationships, finance, interior design, social activism and life goals and which are practised by identifiable groups within wider society. The second definition associates the concept of lifestyle with 'individuality, self-expression and a stylistic self-consciousness' (Featherstone, 1991, p 83), and views a lifestyle as something constructed by autonomous, reflexive, rational and expressive individuals. The first of these definitions thus tends to understand lifestyle in terms of shared patterns of attitudes and behaviour in particular social groups, whereas the second defines lifestyle in terms of the idiosyncratic choices of autonomous individuals.

Neither of these definitions can be accepted without some qualification. The notion of collective lifestyles associated with particular social groups may have an obvious appeal among those wishing to classify society for marketing purposes (a point I have discussed elsewhere in relation to the literature on 'Generation X'; see Lynch, 2002). But such an emphasis on collective styles of living has been criticised for failing to give sufficient weight to the choices of autonomous individuals who may mix and match across different 'styles' of living, a point made both by those who have argued that contemporary culture has taken a 'postmodern' turn and by those who have sought to critique the notion of collective lifestyle associated with the sub-cultural theory of the Birmingham Centre for Contemporary Cultural Studies (see, for example, Muggleton, 2000; Bennett and Kahn-Harris, 2004). At the same time, the notion that a lifestyle is simply the bricolage of choices made by autonomous individuals fails to acknowledge the significance of variables such as age, gender, ethnicity and socioeconomic status in shaping and limiting the choices that individuals make within particular social contexts (Furlong and Cartmel, 1997).[1] Furthermore, individual lifestyle choices (for example, choices about fashion) are intelligible only within shared social and cultural frameworks of interpretation. Satisfactory accounts of lifestyle therefore need to take account of both structure and agency when thinking about the ways in which lifestyles are constructed.

Despite the complexities of defining lifestyle, this concept is still arguably helpful in giving greater focus to Luckmann's notion of the invisible religion focused on self-realisation and self-expression. The idea of lifestyle helps to clarify the terrain in which the concerns of contemporary individuals are lived out and in which specific challenges of self-realisation and self-expression are grounded. The different dimensions of lifestyle concern – relationships, health, style, career choice, housing, finance and use of leisure time – represent the existential horizon within which the new social form of religion is practised. Understanding more clearly the beliefs and values that shape people's choices in these different aspects of their everyday lives, as well as the cultural resources that offer guidance in relation to these decisions, will help us to develop more satisfactory answers to Luckmann's question of what constitutes the operational values of a secular world-view.

Before moving on to analyse the kind of discourses, beliefs and values associated with contemporary 'secular' lifestyle media, it is important briefly to note why 'lifestyle' has become such an important field of concern in late modern society. Four interrelated factors have played an important role in this.

Firstly, the notion that individuals could be concerned with questions of lifestyle has become possible because of particular changes in Western concepts of selfhood. Writers such as Colin Campbell (1987) and Charles Taylor (1989) have noted how Western culture since the Reformation has placed a greater emphasis on the importance of the cognitive and affective life of the individual self. The Reformation itself led to greater attention being paid to the spiritual significance of the inner life of the individual (for example, among Calvinists anxiously scrutinising their thoughts and feelings for evidence of whether or not they were numbered among the elect). By the 18th century, such self-awareness was becoming increasingly detached from this particular form of Protestant theology and came to be seen more and more as a pleasure and a virtue in its own right. This positive view of the individual's moods and feelings went on to find expression in the 'cult of sensibility', supported by the burgeoning interest in reading and emoting to works of fiction (Mullan, 1997), and by the late 18th century had found more complex expression in the emerging Romantic movement. Alongside this emphasis on the importance of self-awareness and self-expression, the Enlightenment had placed a strong emphasis on the significance of the observations and reflections of the autonomous self. The Cartesian 'cogito ergo sum' placed the rational, thinking individual at the heart of the universe, and the rational individual played a central role in idealist and empiricist philosophies that underpinned revolutions in scientific, economic and political thought. By the end of the 18th century the title of Jane Austen's novel *Sense and sensibility* gave a neat summary to the different aspects of rational and expressive selfhood that were playing an increasingly important role in Western society. While the notion of the rational and expressive self has faced subsequent challenges in Western culture, for example from psychoanalytic and post-structuralist theory, it retains considerable influence in contemporary understandings of selfhood and, as we shall note shortly, forms the epistemic ground from which lifestyle decisions are made (see Luckmann, 1996; Wuthnow, 1998, pp 157f).[2]

A second key factor for the emergence of lifestyle concern has been the process of the aestheticisation of everyday life. Part of this process has involved the weakening influence of traditional notions of transcendence in Western culture, both in terms of belief in the influence of an external God in the day-to-day affairs and in the significance of the notions of heaven and hell as a basis for making decisions about one's belief and conduct in this life. Bauman (1998a) traces the initial weakening of these traditional notions of transcendence back to the cultural movement of Renaissance humanism and its desire to 'make man the measure of man'. From the late 17th century, the growth of Deism also placed divine influence outside the sphere of everyday life while also promoting the idea of nature as a source of truth that underpinned later Romantic concepts of the importance of the creative and expressive self in tune with nature (Taylor, 1989). Such developments weakened the existential horizon in which the will and acts of God and the fate of the eternal soul were significant areas of concern, and made possible an existential horizon in which well-being in this world and this lifetime became more important. An emphasis on the importance of the choices and resources of everyday life was further encouraged by the growth of consumer culture from the 19th century onwards which emphasised the symbolic significance and pleasure of commodities, and of cultural and artistic movements which collapsed the boundaries between art and everyday life and claimed that the practice of everyday life should itself now be considered an art form (Vaneigem, 1983; Featherstone, 1991, pp 65–82). By the start of the 20th century, Georg Simmel (1997) was referring to such attentiveness to the quality of everyday life as a central feature of the new mysticism that he discerned in the cultural spaces created by the receding influence of Christianity. Such cultural movements reinforced the assumption that meaning, purpose, pleasure and well-being were to be found primarily in relation to the sphere of everyday life and thus support the notion that choices about styles of living should be of central concern for contemporary existence.

A third significant factor for the emergence of lifestyle concern has been the growing awareness of choice as a defining characteristic of modernity. The contemporary West has been described by Giddens as a 'post-traditional' society in the sense that there is no longer any single overarching symbolic framework by which its members interpret their lives, order their relationships and measure their behaviour. The collapse of such a traditional Western framework could be located initially in the increasing differentiation of various forms of Christian denominations and sects since the Reformation, which opened up the possibility of increasing choice in one's religious affiliations and commitments (Bruce, 2002). Certainly the pluralism of multicultural, late modern, liberal democratic societies makes it hard to escape an awareness of alternative beliefs, values and ways of living. As Giddens (1994, p 75) puts it, 'in post-traditional contexts, we have no choice but to choose how to be', a state Peter Berger (1979) referred to as the 'heretical imperative'. Such an awareness of having to make choices is not only a product of cultural pluralism, but also of technological changes that have made it possible to greatly increase variation in the design and production of commodities. Henry Ford's quip that you could have his cars 'in any colour you want as long as it's black' has become redundant in a late capitalist consumer culture focused on high levels of product differentiation through design, manufacture and marketing (Featherstone, 1991; Lash and Urry, 1994). The use of branding further associates this growing range of commodities with different forms of imagined lifestyle (Pavitt, 2000). While this sense of the need to choose does not necessarily induce widespread existential angst in contemporary Western society – 'most people manage somehow', observes Peter Berger (1979, p 24) – the pluralism of post-traditional consumer culture nevertheless heightens the sense that how one chooses to live is a matter of choice rather than tradition or fate.

Finally, a fourth, and more recent, factor to be noted in the emergence of lifestyle concern has been the growth of what Pierre Bourdieu has referred to as the 'new petite bourgeoisie'. While the changing notions of selfhood, the aestheticisation of everyday life and the increasing awareness of choice have made lifestyle concern an unsurprising consequence of the unfolding of modernity, it is among the burgeoning middle classes of the mid- to late 20th century that questions of lifestyle have become most acute. The exponential increase in household expenditure on consumption in the postwar period (funded in more recent decades by house price inflation and easier access to consumer credit) has led to a growing section of society that has increasing levels of disposable income and more leisure time to think about how to spend it. The rise of lifestyle concern and lifestyle media should therefore be understood in relation to particular economic changes in society that have led to a growing middle class. While the lifestyle concerns and interests of the new middle classes do not impinge solely on this class – see, for example, Bauman's (1998b) discussion of the significance of the symbols and values of consumer culture for the 'new poor' – it is also not unreasonable to see contemporary lifestyle concern (and the assumption that lifestyle should be a matter of concern) as a particularly middle-class phenomenon.

These factors indicate that far from being a neutral or timeless phenomenon, the preoccupation with issues of lifestyle in contemporary Western culture is the product of a particular process of cultural evolution involving changing notions of selfhood and transcendence, the shift from a feudal to a late capitalist, liberal democratic society, and changing patterns of social class. A more detailed historical account of this process would be valuable, but this broad outline suggests that contemporary lifestyle concern is an expression both of longer cultural trends as well as more recent social, technological and economic changes. In the next part of this chapter, we examine how a particular form of 'secular' lifestyle media – British lifestyle television programmes – are constructed as media texts that address the existential horizon of lifestyle concern.

Analysing lifestyle television programmes in Britain

Before offering this analysis, it is important to make some brief comments by way of defining the genre of lifestyle television programmes. In using the term 'lifestyle' television programme, I am referring specifically to programmes that seek to explore, or offer guidance on, different areas of lifestyle ranging from personal relationships, health, finance, parenting, household management, career choice, choices about the area/country in which one lives and more specific decisions about real estate. Lifestyle television programmes form part of the wider genre of reality television shows, and one which explicitly acts as a resource for making decisions in these different realms of lifestyle choice. In quantitative terms, lifestyle television programmes do not form a major element of normal weekly television scheduling in the UK. But despite the greater volume of drama and light entertainment on these channels, however, lifestyle television programmes often achieve a high level of public attention, with presenters on some programmes becoming celebrities in their own right and advice books based around the programme content becoming bestsellers. Lifestyle television programmes often occupy key slots in midweek early evening primetime viewing – particularly on the terrestrial channels BBC2 and Channel 4, which tend to aim at more middle-class audiences – and achieve viewing figures comparable to other successful drama and entertainment shows, and certainly normally higher than those achieved by religious programmes. In the case of Channel 4, for example, lifestyle television programmes such as 'Grand Designs', 'Relocation, Relocation', 'Super Nanny', 'You Are What You Eat', 'Wife Swap' and 'Property Ladder' regularly feature in the channel's top 30 shows according to weekly ratings compiled by the Broadcasters' Audience Research Board (www.barb.co.uk). Despite Channel 4's relative success in developing award-winning current affairs programmes on religion, these rarely achieve comparable ratings.

In the recent evolution of British lifestyle television shows, two more specific sub-genres have emerged. The first has a standard format of 'ordinary' people facing some kind of lifestyle decision or crisis who are then helped through this by an expert or experts who (normally) guide them to a successful resolution of it. This sub-genre can be described as a *narrative of lifestyle redemption facilitated by experts*. Examples of this type of programme include 'What Not to Wear', 'Life Laundry', 'How Clean is Your House?', 'Honey I Ruined the House', 'Super Nanny' and 'Location, Location, Location'. The second genre adopts a 'fly-on-the-wall' perspective on individuals, couples or families who make radical lifestyle changes and explores the challenges, pleasures and difficulties associated with these changes. External 'experts' do not play a role in such programmes and the lifestyle experiments explored in these programmes are as likely to be unsuccessful as they are successful. This second sub-genre could then be described as *vicarious narratives of lifestyle experimentation*, in which the audience is offered a chance to explore the idea of lifestyle change without actually taking any risks themselves. Examples of such programmes include 'Get a New Life', 'Wife Swap', 'Grand Designs' and 'No Turning Back'.

The recent genre of secular British lifestyle television programmes offers particular symbolic resources for contemporary lifestyle concern in three important ways. Firstly, these programmes tend to maintain an ideological perspective on lifestyle choice as purely the activity of autonomous and reflexive individuals. From this perspective, it is entirely up to individuals to make their own choices about their lives, and the notion that wider social factors may shape or influence those choices tends to be obscured. A couple of examples may help to illustrate this point. On the programme 'You Are What You Eat', the dietician Gillian McKeith challenges individuals to review their eating and exercise habits and to make changes towards a healthier lifestyle. Within the programme, good and bad dietary habits are presented as a matter of individual choice. A successful shift towards healthier habits is therefore possible if the programme's participants, aided by the expert dietician, decide to make the necessary changes. This focus on diet as a matter of individual choice may be useful in prompting individuals to think about their dietary habits, but also neglects evidence that poor diet is often correlated with low income and living in inadequately resourced communities (see, for example, Eaton, 2002). Similarly in an episode of 'Wife Swap' broadcast originally in July 2004, a White housewife married to a millionaire swapped places with a Black, working single mother living in North London. One of the central plot lines of the programme focused on the attempt by this White woman from an affluent background to persuade the eldest son of the other woman to go out and find work. Again the fact that this young man had left school with no qualifications and with little apparent interest in finding work was represented by the programme in terms of lack of motivation on his part. There was no discussion of why such a high proportion of young Black men in Britain leave school with very poor qualifications or none, or what social and cultural factors make it difficult for young Black men to enter the workforce. Examples such as these illustrate an underlying ideological position within these programmes that constructs lifestyle as a matter of individual choice and which neglects social and cultural factors that influence and limit lifestyle choice. As noted, when discussing definitions of lifestyle earlier, seeing lifestyle simply in terms of the choices of autonomous and reflexive individuals represents an inadequate understanding of how lifestyle choices function in real-world settings. Nevertheless it is significant that as symbolic resources for addressing lifestyle concern these programmes tend to offer an essentially neoliberal ideology of self and society which obscures the ways in which equality and opportunity are not available to people in contemporary society (Chaney, 1996, p 19).

A second way in which these programmes offer resources for issues of lifestyle concern relates to the particular discourses that they draw on as a basis for making particular lifestyle choices. Although these television programmes do not normally prescribe a particular set of wider lifestyle tastes and practices as being right or wrong (with the exception of moralising discourses concerning health and hygiene), they do more often represent lifestyle choice as needing to reflect a balance between utility and fantasy, and between the thoughts and desires of the rational and expressive self. This balance, effectively between Enlightenment and Romantic discourses of selfhood, has been described by Mike Featherstone (1991, p 86) in terms of a 'calculating hedonism' in which the dreams of the autonomous self are kept in balance with what can be reasonably achieved within the various limitations of everyday life. This tension between utility and fantasy recurs throughout these television programmes. For example, in 'How Clean is Your House?', the two cleaning experts seek to encourage changes in participants' approach to housework by using both rational and expressive discourses. 'How long would it take you each day to keep this kitchen clean?', one of the experts asks a participant, inviting a rational calculation of the benefits of a cleaner and healthier kitchen compared to the limited cost in time and effort of doing the cleaning work. At the end of the programme, with the participant's home transformed into a cleaner, healthier and tidier environment, the experts also encourage the participant to say how they feel about the new state of their home – an invitation which often elicits gasps, shrieks or tears. The transformation of the household in this programme is therefore encouraged on the basis of both rational and expressive discourses. Similarly in 'Location, Location, Location', one of the expert presenters keeps advising participants on their second visit to a prospective property to 'use their heads rather than their hearts' in judging its strengths and weaknesses. Alongside this, however, participants are also encouraged to say how they feel about a property and whether they can imagine themselves in it, while the presenters' voiceovers make frequent reference to participants' search for their 'dream home'. While keeping the question of particular lifestyle tastes and values relatively open, these programmes nevertheless tend to offer a particular framework for thinking about how to make lifestyle choices that reflect Enlightenment and Romantic discourses that have been central moral sources in the formation of notions of the self in Western modernity (Taylor, 1989).

A third way in which these programmes seek to address issues of lifestyle concern is, as we have noted in relation to a particular sub-genre of lifestyle television, through the use of experts. These experts fulfil the role of what Lash and Urry (1994, p 108) refer to as 'reflexivity enhancers', increasing others' ability to be thoughtful, skilled and creative consumers in the marketplace of lifestyle choice. The role of these experts in relation to participants and viewers is somewhat ambivalent, however. This ambivalence is reflected in the ambiguous status of 'secondary institutions' that seek to offer informative resources for understanding and living one's life while not crossing over into authoritative statements about how one 'should' live one's life associated with more traditional 'primary' institutions. Thus, on the one hand, individuals in post-traditional, late modern society wish to find refuge from the anomie of uncertainty about how to live one's life to the fullest. Yet at the same time, they do not want to feel coerced or told how to live. As a consequence, the role of the television lifestyle expert is both powerful and fragile. As Zygmunt Bauman (2000, p 64) puts it, in the marketplace of lifestyle choice 'it is by courtesy of the chooser that a would-be authority becomes an authority'. Furthermore, while the experts may be informative guides there is also a sense in which they are not fundamentally different to participants and viewers. The expert is regarded as an expert because they have put time and effort into acquiring skills and knowledge that anyone, in principle, could achieve. The television expert is therefore different to the priest or shaman in traditional societies. The wisdom of such traditional guardians of truth was not gained through means generally available to everyone and their right to give guidance was a function of their social status rather than their competence in a specific area (Giddens, 1994, p 65). The authority of the television expert is generally treated with deference in lifestyle television shows: participants often have to surrender power to these experts by behaving in ways instructed by the expert or by symbolic acts such as temporarily giving over the keys to one's house. The format of some programmes may even involve the expert acting in ways that humiliate participants – both providing viewers with the opportunity for the vicarious enjoyment of others' incompetence in their lifestyle choices and reinforcing the technical competence of the expert. Yet at the same time, the expert's authority is only temporary and specific to a particular area of lifestyle concern. The fundamentally non-hierarchical assumptions of liberal democratic society are therefore not threatened by this temporary deference to the expert.

Conclusion

From this brief analysis of these mainstream lifestyle television shows, it is possible to develop a prima facie argument for how such media might function as a secondary institution supporting the new social form of religion – the pursuit of the free, meaningful, authentic and aspirational life. The programmes typically offer a neoliberal view of the world, in which the autonomous individual is free to pursue their lifestyle choices, provide moral discourses of reason, emotion, health and hygiene to guide these choices, and reinforce these ideas through the mediating role of the lifestyle expert. Attention to such programmes can therefore arguably sketch out more of the contours of the new social form of religion identified by Luckmann.

But to what extent is an analysis like this really concerned with religion at all? Luckmann's thesis may be an interesting and informative one, but if he is essentially interested in analysing the secular moral sources of the post-Christian West, then would this not be better described in terms of the analysis of cultural values? In short, does Luckmann's use of the term 'religion' – in his formulation of the new social form of religion – really add anything to his argument, or help us to understand more clearly what it means to study 'religion' in our rapidly changing cultural landscape?

There are clearly parts of Luckmann's conceptual framework that are problematic. His functionalist definition of religion – as any symbolic framework that enables one to give meaning to the raw biological data of human life – has been criticised as virtually indistinguishable from the concept of 'culture'. To talk about moral discourses of the free and expressive self as the new social form of religion may therefore have a certain rhetorical flourish in terms of pointing to the significance of these discourses in de-Christianised societies, but tells us little about religion as a specific cultural form in the contemporary world. So is this chapter really misplaced in this particular book? Has attention to Luckmann led us too far from the study of contemporary religion and spirituality into a more generic study of contemporary cultural values?

I would suggest that this is not necessarily the case, for two reasons. Firstly, understanding the cultural significance of lifestyle media can make us more sensitive to the importance of the existential horizon of lifestyle concern in contemporary cultural life. Such sensitivity is important for making sense of trends in contemporary religion, such as the rise of specialist religious lifestyle media, niche consumer goods to support particular religious lifestyles, and the reframing of religious tradition as a resource for negotiating lifestyle concerns. This does not necessarily entail the abandonment of broader religious metaphysics – Christian lifestyle media may still, for example, place lifestyle choice in the context of God's will and one's eternal destiny – but the gravitational pull for middle-class religion to focus on issues of lifestyle concern is increasingly strong. Analysing mainstream secular lifestyle media can also help us to identify ideologies – such as neoliberal notions of self and society – that can also be found in religious lifestyle media.

Secondly, however, I would argue that analysing contemporary lifestyle media in the light of Luckmann's thesis raises important questions as to whether the self has become sacred in late modernity. I have recently suggested elsewhere (Lynch, 2007) that the study of religion can be constructively focused around the study of sacred objects (objects, here, meant in the sense of object relations theory rather than simply material objects), with religions understood as social-cultural systems oriented in relation to sacred objects. Revising Luckmann's questions about the changing moral sources of post-Christian society in the light of this, it might be possible to ask whether the self has acquired the status of a sacred object in contemporary cultural life. Such a suggestion may appear counter-intuitive – sacred objects are typically seen as supra-human forces beyond the self. But is it possible for the self itself to act as a sacred force in contemporary cultural life, binding people into particular identities, perceptions and experiences of embodiment? Rather than the sacred voice from heaven or from the pages of a holy text, are people in contemporary culture hailed by the sacred call of their deepest feelings and aspirations, filtered through their capacity for rational, technical competence? There is a prima facie case for arguing that this is so. Over the past 10 years and more, Paul Heelas has done important work in arguing for the increasing influence of the cult of the individual in contemporary social life (see, for example, Heelas, 1996, 2000, 2002), arguing that Western cultural discourses of the self represent the primary gravitational force over contemporary religion and spirituality. But this question can benefit from further attention. To what extent are the apparently sacred qualities of the self analogous to the qualities of sacred objects perceived beyond the self? And to what extent do people in the contemporary world really live out their lives in the existential horizon of lifestyle concern, guided by the sacred call of the dreams of the autonomous and reflexive self? It is easy to make broad generalisations on these questions, when yet more careful empirical work is needed. But attention to the question of the sacredness of the self, and sensitivity to the cultural importance of lifestyle concern, represent important issues for the ongoing challenge of making sense of religion and spirituality in the contemporary world.

Notes

[1] In this sense, Giddens (1994, pp 75f) suggests that it may be more satisfactory to see the individual in late modern society as faced by 'decisions' rather than 'choices', as the word 'choice' may imply a greater range or equality of options than may exist in practice for a particular individual.

[2] On the basis of his empirical research, Wuthnow suggests that in the late 20th century the idea of the 'soul' in the US was increasingly being taken to refer to an aspect of depth in the self that should shape the conduct of everyday life.

References

Bauman, Z. (1998a) 'Postmodern religion?', in P. Heelas (ed) *Religion, modernity and postmodernity*, Oxford: Blackwell Publishing, pp 55-78.

Bauman, Z. (1998b) *Work, consumerism and the new poor*, Milton Keynes: Open University Press.

Bauman, Z. (2000) *Liquid modernity*, Cambridge: Polity Press.

Bennett, A. and Kahn-Harris, K. (2004) *After subculture: Critical studies in contemporary youth culture*, Basingstoke: Palgrave.

Berger, P. (1979) *The heretical imperative: Contemporary possibilities of religious affirmation*, New York, NY: Doubleday.

Bruce, S. (1995) *Religion in modern Britain*, Oxford: Oxford University Press.

Bruce, S. (2002) *God is Dead: Secularization in the West*, Oxford: Blackwell Publishing.

Campbell, C. (1987) *The romantic ethic and the spirit of modern consumerism*, Oxford: Blackwell Publishing.

Chaney, D. (1996) *Lifestyles*, London: Routledge.

Davie, G. (2002) *Europe: The exceptional case: Parameters of faith in the modern world*, London: DLT.

Eaton, L. (2002) 'UK food poverty could contravene UN human rights', *British Medical Journal*, 21 September, vol 327, no 7365, p 618.

Featherstone, M. (1991) *Consumer culture and postmodernism*, London: Sage Publications.

Furlong, A. and Cartmel, F. (1997) *Young people and social change: Individualization and risk in late modernity*, Buckingham: Open University Press.

Giddens, A. (1994) 'Living in a post-traditional society', in U. Beck, A. Giddens and S. Lash *Reflexive modernization: Politics, tradition and aesthetics in the modern social order*, Cambridge: Polity Press, pp 55–109.

Heelas, P. (1996) 'On things not being worse, and the ethic of humanity', in P. Heelas (ed) *Detraditionalization*, Oxford: Blackwell Publishing, pp 200-18.

Heelas, P. (2000) 'Expressive spirituality and humanistic expressivism: sources of significance beyond church and chapel', in S. Sutcliffe and M. Bowman (eds) *Beyond New Age: Exploring alternative spirituality*, Edinburgh: Edinburgh University Press, pp 237-54.

Heelas, P. and Woodhead, L. (2002) 'Homeless minds today?', in L. Woodhead (ed) with P. Heelas and D. Martin, *Peter Berger and the study of religion*, London: Routledge, pp 43-72.

Heelas, P., Woodhead, L., Seel, B., Szernszynski, B. and Tusting, K. (2005) *The spiritual revolution: Why religion is giving way to spirituality*, Oxford: Blackwell Publishing.

Jackson, P., Stevenson, N. and Brooks, K. (2001) *Making sense of men's magazines*, Cambridge: Polity Press.

Jakes, T.D. (2002) *The great investment: Balancing faith, family and finance to build a rich spiritual life*, Dallas, TX: G.P. Putnam.

Lash, S. and Urry, J. (1994) *Economies of sign and space*, London: Sage Publications.

Luckmann, T. (1967) *The invisible religion*, New York, NY: Macmillan.

Luckmann, T. (1996) 'The privatization of religion and morality', in P. Heelas, S. Lash and P. Morris (eds) *Detraditionalization: Critical reflections on authority and identity*, Oxford: Blackwell Publishing, pp 72–86.

Lynch, G. (2002) *After religion: 'Generation X' and the search for meaning*, London: DLT.

Lynch, G. (2007) 'What is this "religion" in the study of religion and popular culture?', in G. Lynch (ed) *Between sacred and profane: Researching religion and popular culture*, London: IB Tauris, pp 125–42.

Muggleton, D. (2000) *Inside subculture: The postmodern meaning of style*, Oxford: Berg.

Mullan, J. (1997) 'Feelings and novels', in R. Porter (ed) *Rewriting the self: Stories from the Renaissance to the present*, London: Routledge, pp 119–34.

Pavitt, J. (2000) *Brand new*, London: V&A Publications.

Roof, W.C. (1999) *Spiritual market-place: Baby-boomers and the re-making of American religion*, Princeton, NJ: Princeton University Press.

Schofield Clark, L. (ed) (2007) *Religion, media and the market-place*, Piscataway, NJ: Rutgers University Press.

Simmel, G. (1997) *Essays on religion*: New Haven, CT: Yale University Press.

Sobel, M. (1981) *Lifestyle and social structure: Concepts, definitions and analyses*, New York, NY: Academic Press.

Taylor, C. (1989) *Sources of the self: The making of modern identity*, Cambridge: Cambridge University Press.

Taylor, C. (2004) *Modern social imaginaries*, Durham, NC: Duke University Press.

Vaneigem, R. (1983) *The revolution of everyday life*, London: Rebel Press.

Warren, R. (2003) *The purpose driven life: What on earth am I here for?*, Grand Rapids, MI: Zondervan.

Wuthnow, R. (1998) *After heaven: Spirituality in America since the 1950s*, Berkeley, CA: University of California Press.

Part 2
Marginalisation of religious and spiritual issues

This Part considers the emergence of social scientific disciplines within the context of modernity, and the ways in which values underpinning these disciplines might serve to marginalise issues in relation to religion and spirituality. Given discussions among researchers in a number of fields about the importance of religion and spirituality in the lives of individuals and for communities, it is pertinent to ask questions about the theoretical underpinnings of social science disciplines and the challenges that are posed by religious and spiritual questions.

This Part begins with a contribution from Maria Frahm-Arp, who argues that religion is a crucial but often ignored aspect of social research in African contexts (Chapter Six). She argues that social research usually focuses on the impact of race and gender without taking into consideration the effect of religion and religious discourses. Lareen Newman has a similar focus in Chapter Seven insofar as she argues that social demographic research around fertility in Australia has largely ignored the role and influence of religion. Her chapter critiques this omission. Caroline Humphrey's chapter (Chapter Eight) considers how the secular and scientific underpinnings to the social sciences can play a limiting role, in that religious or spiritual experiences and world-views are overlooked. Humphrey argues that secular, scientific and spiritual and religious world-views can co-exist, particularly in the context of globalisation and multicultural societies. According to Ursula King, women's studies and gender studies in the West have largely operated within a dominant secular framework. Nonetheless this blindness to religion is being increasingly recognised and critiqued. Furthermore, not only has religion been a contributing factor in the rise of the women's movement, for King, but also she argues that a wide range of religious ideas has impacted on gender and feminist thinking and practice. King highlights that a large body of literature on women's spirituality, feminist spirituality, and spirituality and gender has emerged. Natassja Smiljanic explores legal study and theorisation, highlighting that often these have been devoid of human emotion. For Smiljanic, engaging spiritually with law means engaging emotionally, so that academic work might be informed by personal experiences and feelings, part of a personal and political spiritual journey, where reading 'shamanically' means accessing other states of consciousness, to see the worlds in different ways.

SIX

Studying religion in Sub-Saharan Africa

Maria Frahm-Arp

Introduction

In Sub-Saharan Africa the high rate of HIV/AIDS infection, unemployment, economic instability and dynamic religious changes from the rise of African independent churches to the current popularity of Pentecostal and Charismatic Christianity and Catholicism[1] are startling, concerning and intriguing. In order to understand these, little consideration is normally given to the religious world-view of the people in this area and the place of religion within the sociopolitical shifts that have taken place. In this chapter I would like to explore the idea of taking religion seriously as a social variable,[2] as something to help us understand why and how people collectively act. To unpack this idea more fully I will pick up on some salient issues featured in the early sociological study of religion and show how these have impacted on the way that religion has been studied in Africa. With this as the base of my argument I will examine some examples of the way in which contemporary Christianity and African religions[3] have been studied and finally propose the first steps of an inclusion of religious variables into the broader study of societies in postcolonial Africa.

Religion, culture and systems of knowledge

Durkheim was fascinated by the power and energy of what he called the sacred and the profane. For him the function of religion within society was of key importance and he proposed that religious systems offer people conceptual frameworks – the categories of which are used to organise human experiences. He proposed that religions could give the individual person a sense of empowerment and that rites and rituals gave one a sense of belonging (Durkheim, 1947, p 416). Societies 'owe to it [religion] not only a good part of the substance of their knowledge, but also the form in which this knowledge has been elaborated' (Durkheim, 1947, p 9). His theory did not negate religious systems but suggested that they were society worshipping/representing itself; in doing so he recognised the inherently symbolic nature of religion (Lambek, 2002, p 35).

Working with and expanding Durkheim's ideas, studies of African religions and African independent churches were largely carried out within a structural–functionalist paradigm (Evan-Pritchard, 1956; Wilson, 1961; Sundkler, 1961 [1936]; Peel, 1968; Fabian, 1971). Influenced by Durkheim and early 20th-century ideas about race, no religion was regarded as false but there was an undeniable hierarchy of religions from the most primitive to the most sophisticated/civilised. In this respect studies like these contributed to the 'scientific proof' within earlier sociology and anthropology that African traditional religions were 'primitive' and 'uncivilised'. These studies also failed to 'address "social change" in a theoretically adequate way' (Meyer, 2004, p 447). Much of this stems from Durkheim's general weakness to address historical change, thereby viewing societies, religions and traditions as static (Lambek, 2002, p 36). While intriguing, African religions and culture were seen as the 'other' and could therefore be the noble-savage, the erotic and the dangerous. I have highlighted these theoretical positions because they have shaped an often unhelpful canvas on which general notions of African society and religion have been built. In order for us to work with religion meaningfully we need to recognise that we are not dealing with an inferior 'other' but with divergent expressions of the sacred in a global world.

Durkheim (1947), Evans-Pritchard (1956) and Wilson (1961 [1936], 1971) opened up an important awareness that concepts of time, space, body, gender relations, personhood, family, the divine, the spiritual and the community are not understood in a universal way. There are, however, some issues common across many Sub-Saharan African religions such as the concepts of personhood, community, dis-ease, spirits and healing. The community, for example, is made up of the living and the living dead or ancestors. A person is a person because they are in relationship with other people. When good people die they remain part of the community in the form of the living dead. They need to be honoured and their opinions need to be consulted by the community. Spirits are regarded as part of the 'other world' and are otherworldly beings that can bring about good and bad fortunes/events. Above all is *Nkosi*,[4] or the divine being who remains aloof and removed. Dis-ease includes anything that affects the material, spiritual, emotional or physical well-being of one or more members of the community. Therefore if one person is ill or has had their car stolen, it is a matter that affects the whole community and must be collectively rectified – this includes consulting the ancestors who often have more insight and power into the causes of dis-ease than living people. Misfortune can be healed through an *nganga* 'herbalist' who has knowledge of *muti*[5] but not access to the spirits and ancestors, or a *sangoma* – a healer who uses their access to the spirits, ancestors and knowledge of *muti* to heal people or cast harmful curses (Mbiti, 1975; Morris, 2006, pp 148-59).

Perplexed by the ever-rising HIV/AIDS rates, a team of researchers have been doing ground-breaking research in southern Africa showing how an awareness of religion can impact social research. Interviewing rural and urban people, they found that patients with illnesses made decisions about their health and treatment not only based on bio-medical models of healthcare intervention but on their understanding of dis-ease, personhood and community drawn from one or more religious frameworks. A startling finding was that many HIV/AIDS sufferers were not disclosing their status or accepting bio-medical forms of treatment because HIV/AIDS was not seen as an individual problem, but affected the whole community. Disclosing a positive status would negatively impact the larger social body, which was regarded as more important than the individual (ARHAP, 2006).

Yamba's research (1997, p 222) showed that in Zambia many rural people were turning to African discourses of witchcraft to explain the HIV/AIDS pandemic which in their experience the bio-medical model was unable to explain or cure. This has led to explosive witchfinding and killing as it was believed that the cause of AIDS could be traced back to people placing curses on one another out of envy and fear. In many other parts of Sub-Saharan Africa witchfinding and witchcraft have also increased, stemming from issues of social inequality, envy, deprivation and the struggle to cope with the ambiguities of modernity (Geschiere, 1997; Niehaus et al, 2001; Jensen and Buur, 2004, p 208). For example, neighbours become jealous of one man's financial success and so they place a curse on him and he becomes ill. The neighbours then offer to help the man out with his business and soon they have taken it over from the ailing entrepreneur who continues to suffer from a mysterious illness.

Healing from witchcraft and dis-ease has been at the centre of the creation and continuation of African independent churches such as the ZCC, Aladura and Shembe churches. Most of these churches were begun by prophets or prophetesses who experienced some form of spiritual healing after suffering from physical and/or emotional distress. During their recovery they gained the ability to heal people and using these powers they established a following. This understanding of the role of illness is drawn from traditional African religions, such as those practised by the Zulus in South Africa. Here the ability to heal is regarded as a sign of divine or spiritual gifting. These churches are distinctive in that they use Christian concepts, particularly the power of the Holy Spirit, to solve their daily problems that they generally understand within an African religious paradigm. Their clothes, songs, dances, sticks and sashes are all symbols of healing and spiritual victory over dis-eases (Kiernan, 1990).

Throughout Sub-Saharan Africa Pentecostal and Charismatic churches have grown at a rapid rate during the past 25 years (Meyer, 2004, pp 447-8) and many of their converts are drawn to these churches because they offer healing from the distresses of life in modernising Africa (Maxwell, 2006, p 96). Unlike the earlier African independent churches these churches do not condone *muti*, *ngangas* or ancestors but regard them as evil. Members are continually told not to be involved with these demonic practices and to free themselves from such influences through the power of the Holy Spirit and blood of Christ, which saves all believers from the curses of the *sangmas* or angry ancestors. Meyer shows how these churches do not negate these powers but keep them alive in the consciousness of the people by damning them as evil (Meyer, 1998). In South Africa many of the younger Black members of Pentecostal and Charismatic churches are drawn to these churches because a demonisation of ancestor veneration frees them from the *angst* of not venerating the spirits of their departed grandparents or great-grandparents of whom they have no knowledge. Largely due to the apartheid project, which broke down the family unit, many young Black people growing up in rural and urban areas have little or no knowledge of their fathers; this means that they also do not know who the ancestors of their fathers are and are therefore unable to venerate them (Frahm-Arp, 2006, pp 160-5). Within African religion dis-eases are often believed to be the result of angry ancestors and by venerating the living dead people can improve their misfortune, but as these young people do not know who their ancestors are they are unable to honour them. The Pentecostal and Charismatic Christian theology, which demonises these practices and maintains that any ill fortune can be overcome by the power of the Holy Spirit, is therefore a reassuring gospel which frees these young people from the anxiety of the power of unknown forebears (Frahm-Arp, 2006, pp 150-70).

Politics and religion in Sub-Saharan Africa

Widespread dis-ease among many communities in Africa is largely accounted for by the situations of political unrest and oppression. Marx argued that social inequality was due to the class system, which he defined as 'persons who have the same position and perform the same role in the production of food, machines, and goods. The upper classes derive their privilege from ownership of the means of production, and the lower classes own nothing but their own labor power' (Pampel, 2000, p 35). Coupled with this he maintained that the economic organisation, the manner in which the material resources of society were ordered – the base structure – affected how the ideological powers within a society – the realm of ideas, beliefs, laws, and politics; in other words, the superstructure – were shaped and understood (Engels and Marx, 1992 [1848]). Therefore, in practice, ideological power was shaped by the class struggle in which the bourgeois attempted to maintain their control over the material resources. The function of religion was therefore to help people, especially the poor, cope with the pain of life and to direct their focus onto rewards in the afterlife. He criticised religion for not being a catalyst of social change and regarded it as a 'false consciousness that distorted the social and material reality to keep people in their place within the capitalist system' (Deal and Beal, 2004, p 12).

During the 1970s and 1980s African scholars began to use aspects of Marxist theory to critique religious, political and economic institutions on the continent. This contributed to some provocative shifts in understanding religion in Africa, namely the importance of religion as an ideological power which could be used as a hegemonic tool to keep people suppressed, the sense of alienation experienced by people in a modernising world, the relationship between the superstructure and the base or infrastructure in the shaping of religious practices and the idea that religious belief or belonging may help people to cope with their material reality (Ranger, 1986; Cone, 1997).

Religion began to be seen in terms of a politics of resistance. The Marxist approach was part of a larger move away from explaining religion to interpreting it (Fabian, 1979; Geetz, 1984). In Sub-Saharan Africa the focus of attention was drawn to the African independent churches like the Zionist churches in South Africa and the Aladura/Spirit churches north of the Limpopo, which had been mushrooming since the 1910s but flourished during the 1960s and 1970s. These were first understood as apolitical movements of safety and later as material or symbolic forms of resistance (Ranger, 1986; Comaroff and Comaroff, 1991). At the same time within mainline Christianity some priests and lay people began to embrace Marxist ideals of proletariat revolt, giving birth to Black and African theology (Bujo, 1992; Cone, 1997).[6]

The importance of religion in the political imagining is also central in understanding postcolonial Africa. In more traditional African religious philosophy the political body is made up of all those who participate in the rituals, and membership is validated through participation (Mbiti, 1975, p 126). In Protestant and Pentecostal and Charismatic forms of Christianity, belief, not ritual, is of central importance. By understanding the different forms of religious affiliation and their implications we may be better able to understand the political tenure and the sense of belonging exercised by particular groups of people (Ellis and Ter Haar, 2004); but Gifford cautions that religions alone are not the sole powers at play in the political arena, nor do they seem able to bring about substantial political change (Gifford, 1998).

Mbembe adds further provocative insights when he argues that politics in postcolonial Africa is a potent weave between 'the production of violence, and the arrangements for allocating privileges and means of livelihood' (2001, p 43). The authoritarian regimes are a 'trinity of violence, transfers and allocation' (2001, p 45). And the concept of transfer and allocation begins with the African religious philosophy of individual indebtedness to a collective heritage that provided 'the material and identitary infrastructure without which the individual could undertake nothing' (2001, p 47). Christianity proclaims salvation for all people and is therefore underpinned by a powerful universalising project that justified the colonisation and conversion of Africa. Mbembe (2001, pp 228-9) argues that the shape of postcolonial politics has been deeply influenced by the political structures put in place by the colonisers and these structures were based on Christian ideologies of morality, authority and personhood. This has influenced politics in two ways: firstly, the structure of the political systems are authoritarian and conquering, the legacy of Christian invasion and conversion, and, secondly, the vast majority of the people have relatively recently converted to Christianity, a process which involves the destruction of worlds, misunderstandings, and hybridisation as ancient references are lost, fragmentary new memories rewritten and customs redistributed (Mbembe, 2001, p 229). This collectively amounts to an unstable human imaging because '(b)eliefs are fundamental to the structure of a human universe as a realm of significations. Collective beliefs support collective representations' and are thus central in uniting people into one moral community (Steedman Jones, 2001, p 203). These appreciations of religion go some way to explaining why, on a deep level, so many African communities struggle to find a collective and unified voice to oppose current oppression.

Modernising Africa

As economic rather than political survival has become the more pressing problem for Sub-Saharan Africa and countries try to participate in the global neoliberal capitalist market, there has been a shift in religious expression such that global religious movements have found resonance in the African imagining. In his study Weber (1958) showed sensitivity to the differences within religions, particularly Christianity, and how these could affect socioeconomic conditions (Ling, 1980, p 15). Yet, his theory was limited in that he understood modernisation as being a process by which societies became more rational and bureaucratically structured such that charismas waned and religions were ultimately abandoned, although this has not happened in many modernising non-European countries. Weber focused his attention on the Orient and the Occident, allowing Africa and Latin America to be ignored and thus slip into 'insignificance'. Despite these shortcomings, Weber's ideas about religion and economics continue to hold merit and some scholars have used them in analysing why upwardly mobile people are drawn to Pentecostal and Charismatic Christianity in Sub-Saharan Africa. The possibility of Pentecostal and Charismatic Christianity leading to concrete political and economic reform in Africa has been argued for by Ellis and Ter Haar (2004), but their research lacks specific quantitative evidence. Martin (2002, pp 1-27) more cautiously suggests that this form of Christianity can be a vehicle for cultural change. Gifford (1998, 2004) and Maxwell (2006) both show that in Central and Southern Africa these churches are bringing about reform in the behaviour and social imagining of individuals such that people are leading sober, hardworking lives in which they aim to be good citizens, but this had not led to any long-term or direct political or economic change within a country as a whole.

Through their teaching, networks and focus on a lifestyle free from drinking, gambling, womanising and ancestor veneration these churches help their members to change the way they live, husband their resources and give them a sense of spiritual empowerment to conquer ill fortune by the power of the Holy Spirit (van Dijk, 1992). In Ghana the establishment of churches based on prosperity theology has become one of the fastest ways for individuals, working as pastors, to rise out of poverty (Gifford, 2004, p 192). While these churches are enormously popular, Ghanaians have begun to express deep unease about preachers as numerous stories of fraud, sexual lapses, theft and corruption emerge on an almost daily basis (Gifford, 2004, p 191). Some of these churches in South Africa have effective business networks that offer mentoring and training to members who are striving towards career success. Research found that the support people received from these churches positively affected their advancement in the corporate world (Frahm-Arp, 2006, pp 173-210). Multiple social and emotional factors contribute to the rapid rise of Pentecostal Charismatic churches in Sub-Saharan Africa but at root most seem popular because they profess to have the answers to Africa's material problems, and express these in terms and idioms which people naturally respond to (Gifford, 2004, p 196).

Gender and the roles of men and women

One of the many confusing issues in the modernising Africa is gender and changing concepts of the body. Bryan Turner showed how the body functions on different levels and is continually being shaped, controlled and coded in different ways – much of this stemming from religious beliefs and practices (1992, pp 115-38). Within Africa Islam, Christianity and African religions have different ideas of gender roles and understandings of the body. Under Islamic law and African religions men may have multiple wives, yet how women are allowed to present themselves publicly varies markedly. Islamic law requires women to cover themselves either with a full veil or modest clothes and a headscarf, yet traditional cultural practices in Sub-Saharan Africa require women to remain bare-chested. With the exception of some African independent churches, Christianity only allows monogamous forms of marriage where both men and women should wear modest clothes. What is strictly controlled are the things that enter the body rather than the adornment of the body. This brief overview suggests that the religious perceptions of gender and sexuality can impact how a society is ordered and controlled (Gerami, 1996, p 17).

Understandings of male and female power are also affected by religious teachings. Paula Girshick Ben-Amos' study of the Olokun cult among Edo women in Nigeria is part of a growing body of research suggesting that through participation in spirit cults not just the priestesses but women generally are able to redefine themselves and realise real social status, power and independence from men, both within and outside the cult meetings (1994, p 119). Religious participation may therefore change how a woman sees herself or is seen by her community, giving her status and roles different from what she would have had if she had not been part of the cult. In Pentecostal Charismatic churches the roles of men and women in African societies are being reshaped around the ideal of the nuclear family. Within these family structures women are expected to be under the headship of their husbands but the husbands are called on to provide both materially and emotionally for their families, thus giving women leverage to demand faithfulness to them and their children (Frahm-Arp, 2006, pp 246-76; Maxwell, 2006, pp 92-3). An analysis of Christian pamphlets in Ghana and Nigeria revealed the contradictions and paradoxes within contemporary West African gender ideologies. Female writers tried to establish romantic and utopian ideals in their tracks while the male authors held to conservative biblical principles of masculine headship (Newell, 2005, p 296).

Shaping new identities in a global world

Contradictions, ambiguity and change between colonial and postcolonial bureaucratic systems, rural and urban advances in technology and modern or traditional identities are recurring themes in Sub-Saharan Africa and the plethora of religious expressions reflect this. Maxwell (1995, p 334) argues that cycles of religious change have been common in 20th-century southern Africa as the various forms of Charismatic Christianity have tended to become bureaucratised, leading younger generations to generate fresh sources of renewal, and in situations of extreme tension, like liberation wars, resacralised ancestors cults. Morris (2006) identified four types of religious movements that have emerged in response to the impact of capitalism: cults of affliction, prophetic cults, witch-cleansing movements and independent churches. Since the late 19th century these have developed in various forms and at different times in response to social distress and change (Morris, 2006, pp 168-77). These variations all offer alternative ways for people to see themselves and make meaning of their worlds as modernisation, globalisation, consumerism and technology all profoundly affect identity and identity formation.

Within Africa and its diaspora there is a body of scholarship arguing for the existence of an essential African culture, personhood and identity which can be found in African art, music, religion and culture – the origins of this Afrocentric culture are both in geographical Africa and in the struggle for Africa (Sfola, 1978, p ix; Asante and Asante, 1985, p 4; Sanders, 1996, pp 3-6). Yet an exploration of the different shapes of identity formation being proposed by the various religious bodies suggests that the question of African identity and personhood is deeply contested. This chapter has shown that in the sea of change and choice people are shaping new concepts of themselves in line with their altering social situations and aspirations – in this process global religions are playing a dominant role in helping some people reshape their identities. Two examples are most striking – the immigration of people from, for example, Nigeria and Ghana to Britain and the Netherlands,[7] and upwardly mobile people who move out of rural villages and townships into the metropolitan suburbs in Sub-Saharan African countries.[8] In both cases people's social and economic realities have changed as they have moved away from their childhood homes to other locations; in the process their sense of self and identity is deeply affected and for many people joining Pentecostal and Charismatic churches becomes a way to maintain links with home and/or to validate a break away from old familial ties to create new family units that reflect their new identities as upwardly mobile people (van Dijk, 1997; Engelke, 2004).

Working with religion as a social variable

In this chapter I have shown how religion plays a role in the social, political and economic life of communities in Sub-Saharan Africa. To work with religion as a variable we need to have an appreciation for the multiple forms of religion, the fact that people can hold one or more religious positions, simultaneously acting from a different religious paradigm in accordance with the situations in which they find themselves. Religions are not static and provide networks – systems of structure, meaning, belonging and knowledge transfer. They help people to cope with oppression or to exercise agency using religious ideological or structural power to alter the situations people find themselves in. Various religions can therefore be catalysts for change and revolution, politically, as Black and African theologies tried to do, or culturally, as Pentecostal Charismatic churches do when they inspire people to change their lifestyles, spending habits and sense of self. Religions often aim to provide the answers or give the reasons for crisis; paradoxically this may include laying blame on the members themselves for situations of national, political or economic despair. For many people religious teachings and infrastructure offer them a means by which to negotiate the multiple networks of power both in the public and private sphere, thus empowering them to affect change within their lives.

Class, race and gender are variables that affect how people see themselves and are seen, what power they exercise or lack and what voice they may or may not have. Similarly, in terms of religion an individual's positionality may influence the social voice they have, how they are viewed and view themselves, and the degree of agency they exercise in negotiating the structural forces around them. In studying Sub-Saharan Africa we need to take religion seriously, understanding that it plays a part in how people make healthcare decisions, determine their political affiliation, shape their familial structures, foster a sense of responsibility, understand their gender roles, and spend their money. Raising the question of religion in Africa means more than asking if people are religious or not. For the variable of religion to have significance we need to view it in relation to other social variables such as class, race and gender. Political and economic developments also need to take religion seriously as a factor which may influence the daily expression of these factors in individuals' lives, for example how people vote, spend their money and where they choose to live.

Conclusion

Society, politics and religion have all been shifting in Africa over the past century, and in ways such that they influence each other, and any detailed study of societies in Africa needs to take these shifts in politics, economics, gender and religion into account.

In this chapter I have looked at the influence of Weber, Marx and Durkheim because these early sociologists regarded religion as an important social factor. I have shown how, influenced by their thinking, the study of religion in Africa took on a particular form which was not always helpful or valid. Picking up on current research the importance of religion as a means to negotiate changing social realities and thereby exercise agency has opened up a space to include religion within the numerous social variables used to understand society. Therefore Gifford (1998, 2004), Meyer (2004) and Maxwell (2006) all argue that to understand Kenya, Ghana and Zimbabwe scholars need to look at the role that religion is playing in how people think about themselves, which political parties they support and how they spend their money. In this chapter I have also suggested that religion influences the variables of gender, class and race and can therefore aid us in understanding more fully family dynamics, political affiliation and various forms of political structures, how people deal with poverty and illness, work and upward mobility, and the rapidly shifting social, economic and political landscape – all of which affect identity.

Notes
[1] Here I will concentrate on Christianity and African religions, but note that Islam is also growing at a rapid rate, particularly in North Africa.

[2] By social variable I mean a concept that in its empirical measure can take on multiple values, such that religion is a variable in which Christianity, Islam, African religions and so on are the values/attributes. In a more refined study of Christianity, Christianity would be the variable and the different denominations/ movement/traditions would be the values.

[3] Following Blakely et al (1994, pp 15-17) I refer to African religions as the religions practised in the geographical location of Africa but do not exclude religions from this region that have travelled through the African diaspora. These religions are not static but variable and flexible and therefore I do not refer to them as 'African traditional religions'.

[4] In this chapter I am using isiZulu words to denote the concepts of medication, witchcraft, healers and diviners.

[5] *Muti* is the collective term used for the specific plants, herbs, body parts and inanimate objects which are understood to contain power that can be used for healing or to curse enemies.

[6] The leaders of these positions argued that religions should be at the forefront fighting for the liberation of the poor and oppressed. Black theology added that people should be proud to be Black Africans and that they were not inferior to any other race group. African theology maintained that the Christianity brought to Africa by the Europeans skewed the gospel because it was presented in a culturally

specific light that undermined African cultures and believed that African cultural practices should be included into Christianity.

[7] In 2003 4,060 Ghanaians migrated to Britain and 529 migrated to the Netherlands, and in the following year 2,385 Ghanaians migrated to Britain and 533 to the Netherlands. In 2003 7,690 Nigerians migrated to Britain and 463 to the Netherlands, and in the following year 4,845 Nigerians migrated to Britain and 498 to the Netherlands (Migration Policy Institute statistics). For qualitative studies on their religious involvement see Ter Haar's (1998) study.

[8] Migration from the rural to the urban metropolis in Sub-Saharan Africa is not a straightforward phenomenon as people tend to keep their ties to the rural villages and towns, returning for family occasions and continually sending financial support to extended families in these areas. For more details of migration in South Africa see Lehohla (2006); for migration and religion in Zimbabwe see Maxwell (2006); and for migration and religion in Ghana see Meyer (1998).

References

ARHAP (African Religious Health Assets Programme) (2006) *Report*, Cape Town: ARHAP (www.arhap.ucf.ac.za).

Asante, M. and Asante, K. (eds) (1985) *African culture: The rhythms of unity*, London: Greenwood Press.

Ben-Amos, P.G. (1994) 'The promise of greatness: women and power in an Edo possession cult', in T.D. Blakely, W.E.A. van Beek and D.L. Thomson (eds) *Religion in Africa*, London: James Currey, pp 119-34.

Blakely, T.D, van Beek, W.E.A. and Thomson, D.L. (eds) (1994), *Religion in Africa*, London: James Currey.

Bujo, B. (1992) *African theology in its social context*, Maryknoll, NY: Orbis Press.

Comaroff, J. and Comaroff, J. (1991) *Of revelation and revolution: Christianity, colonialism, and consciousness in South Africa*, vol 1, Chicago, IL: Chicago University Press.

Cone, J. (1997) *Black theology and Black power*, Maryknoll, NY: Orbis Press.

Deal, W. and Beal, T. (2004) *Theory for religious studies*, London: Routledge.

Durkheim, E. (1947) *Elementary forms of religious life*, London: George Allen & Unwin.

Ellis, S. and Ter Haar, G. (2004) *Worlds of power: Religious thought and political practice in Africa*, Johannesburg: Wits University Press.

Engelke, M. (2004) 'Discontinuity and the discourse of conversion', *Journal of Religion in Africa*, vol 34, no 12, pp 82-109.

Engels, F. and Marx, K. (1992 [1848]), *The Communist manifesto*, London and New York, NY: Bantam Classics.

Evan-Pritchard, E. (1956) *Nuer religion*, London: Oxford University Press.

Fabian, J. (1971) *Jamaa: A religious movement in Katanga*, Evanton, IL: Northwestern University Press.

Fabian, J. (1979) 'The anthropology of religious movements: from explanation to interpretation', *Social Research*, vol 46, no 1, pp 4-35.

Frahm-Arp, M. (2006) 'Women of valour: professional women in South African Pentecostal churches', Unpublished PhD, Warwick: University of Warwick.

Geetz, C. (1984) *Local Knowledge*, New York: Basic Books.

Gerami, S. (1996) *Women and fundamentalism: Islam and Christianity*, London: Garland Publishing.

Geschiere, P. (1997) *The modernity of witchcraft, politics and the occult in postcolonial Africa*, Charlottesville, VA: University Press Virginia.

Gifford, P. (1998) *African Christianity: Its public role*, Bloomington, IN: Indiana University Press.

Gifford, P. (2004) *Ghana's new Christianity: Pentecostalism in a globalising African economy*, London: Hurst and Company.

Jensen, S. and Buur, L. (2004) 'Everyday policing and the occult: notions of witchcraft, crime and "the people"', *African Studies*, vol 63, no 2, pp 193-212.

Kiernan, J. (1990) *The production and management of therapeutic power in Zionism within a Zulu city*, Lewiston, NY: Edwin Mellen Press.

Lambek, M. (ed) (2002) *A reader in the anthropology of religion*, Oxford: Blackwell.

Lehohla, P. (2006) *Studies reveal the circular nature of urban migration* (www.statssa. gov.za/news_archive/04May2006_1.asp).

Ling, T. (1980) *Karl Marx and religion in Europe and India*, London: Macmillan Press.

Martin, D. (2002) *Pentecostalism: The world their parish*, Oxford: Blackwell.

Maxwell, D. (1995) 'Witches, prophets and avenging spirits: the Second Christian Movement in North-East Zimbabwe', *Journal of Religion in Africa*, vol XXV, no 3, pp 309-39.

Maxwell, D. (2006) *African gifts of the spirit: Pentecostalism and the rise of a Zimbabwean transnational religious movement*, Oxford: James Currey.

Mbembe, A. (2001) *On the postcolony*, Berkeley, CA: California University Press.

Mbiti, J. (1975) *An Introduction to African religions*, London: Heinemann.

Meyer, B. (1998) '"Make a complete break with the past": memory and post-colonial modernity in Ghanaian Pentecostalist discourse', *Journal of Religion in Africa*, vol 27, no 3, pp 316-49.

Meyer, B. (2004) 'Christianity in Africa: from African independent to Pentecostal-Charismatic churches', *Annual Review of Anthropology*, vol 33, pp 447-74.

Morris, B. (2006) *Religion and anthropology: A critical introduction*, Cambridge: Cambridge University Press.

Newell, S. (2005) 'Devotion and domesticity: The reconfiguration of gender in popular Christian pamphlets from Ghana and Nigeria', *Journal of Religion in Africa*, vol 35, no 3, pp 296-323.

Niehaus, I., Mohlala, E. and Shokane, K. (2001) *Witchcraft, power and politics: Exploring the occult in the South African Lowveld*, Cape Town and London: David Philip and Pluto Press.

Pampel, F. (2000) *Sociological lives and ideas: An introduction to the classical theorists*, Boulder, CO: Worth Press.

Peel, J. (1968) *Aladura: A religious movement among the Yoruba*, London: Oxford University Press.

Ranger, T. (1986) 'Religious movement and politics in Sub-Saharan Africa', *African Studies Review*, vol 29, no 2, pp 1-69.

Sanders, C. (1996) *Saints in exile: The holiness-Pentecostal experience in African American religion and culture*, Oxford: Oxford University Press.

Sfola, J. (1978) *African culture and the African personality: What makes an African person African*, Ibadan: African Resources Publishers.

Steedman Jones, S. (2001) *Durkheim reconsidered*, Cambridge: Polity Press.

Sundkler, B. (1961) *Bantu prophets in South Africa*, London: Oxford University Press.

Ter Haar, G. (1998) *Halfway to paradise: African Christians in Europe*, Cardiff: Cardiff Academic Press.

Turner, B. (1992) *Max Weber: From history to modernity*, London: Routledge.

van Dijk, R. (1992) 'Young puritan preachers in post-independence Malawi', *Africa*, vol 62, no 2, pp 159-81.

van Dijk, R. (1997) 'From camp to encompassment: discourse of transsubjectivity in the Ghanaian Pentecostal diaspora', *Journal of Religion in Africa*, vol 27, no 2, pp 135-60.

Weber, M. (1958) *The Protestant ethic and the spirit of capitalism*, New York, NY: Charles Scribner's Sons.

Wilson, M. (1961 [1936]) *Reaction to conquest: Effects of contact with Europeans on the Pondo of South Africa* (2nd edn), London: Oxford University Press.

Wilson, M. (1971) *Religion and the transformation of society: A study in social change in Africa*, Cambridge: Cambridge University Press.

Yamba, C. (1997) 'Witchfinding and AIDS in Zambia', *Africa*, vol 67, no 2, pp 200-23.

SEVEN

Demographic fertility research: a question of disciplinary beliefs and methods

Lareen Newman

Introduction

This chapter explores the changing place of religion as a variable of interest within demographic research on fertility and family size in Australia. Fertility rates are of social, political and academic interest because of the implications for future social and economic trends. Currently each woman in Australia is having, on average, fewer than two children, and each nominal couple is not replacing itself. At this rate, and without considerably higher immigration, the Australian population is likely to decrease in size over the next 50 years, leading to an undesirably high ratio of non-working to working population (McDonald and Kippen, 1999; UN Secretariat, 2000). Since about 2000, researchers and politicians have therefore increased their interest in better understanding influences on fertility behaviour, in particular to avoid 'fertility gaps' where people would have additional children under different circumstances. A particular focus has been on economic and work-based constraints, perhaps as these are deemed most amenable to government policy. Less attention has been paid to social factors, including those that could be influenced through religious affiliation or contact with faith communities, such as attitudes towards different family sizes or social support for parenting.

Religion in demography

In investigating factors associated with population-level fertility change, and differences among areas and groups, religion was once 'at the forefront' of demographic research (McQuillan, 2004, p 25). Denomination is the variable traditionally included on demographic surveys, although religiosity may also be measured (as frequency of attendance at services or activities). Average family size has fluctuated over time in Australia, but a general decline commenced around the 1870s, mirroring trends in Northern and Western Europe (Day, 1965). There have also been obvious denominational differences, with Australian Census data from 1911 and 1921 suggesting that the first to begin limiting family size were women born in England and Wales, who were mostly of the Church of England,

Methodist or Presbyterian churches (Ruzicka and Caldwell, 1982, p 214). In contrast, Roman Catholic women who had come mainly from Ireland, and Lutherans from Germany, limited their family size later (Ruzicka and Caldwell, 1982, p 214). The most rapid fertility decline in Australia, from 1911 to 1966, occurred among non-Catholics (Borrie, 1975, p 53). Historical variation in family size was long dominated by the difference between Catholics and non-Catholic Christians (Borrie, 1975). Catholics not only had larger average family sizes but also higher proportions of families with five or more children (Day, 1965, p 158). However, from the mid-1970s these differences began to disappear as Catholic fertility declined towards the level of non-Catholics. The difference has continued to decline to be insignificant at the aggregate level (Hugo, 2004, p 24), and by the 1996 Census there was little obvious difference to research. The fertility of major non-Christian groups (for example, Muslim or Buddhist groups) has not become a major research focus, perhaps because these groups each represent only a few per cent of the population, although they do have interesting fertility behaviour. Data standardised by age and marital status, for example, show that Islamic women recorded the highest fertility in Australia in 1996, 37% above that for all women (Carmichael and McDonald, 2003, p 62).

The influence of the secularisation paradigm

The 'loss of the difference' in the fertility of mainstream Christian groups appears to have coincided with a trend in Australian demography, from the 1980s on, towards a greater research focus not on the **issue** of fertility (which could have maintained interest in group *differences*) but on the **problem** of fertility *decline* and increasing *childlessness*. Considering that the secularisation paradigm was also rising in popularity over this period, I suggest that this further discouraged demographic interest in the supposed 'disappearing issue' of religion, although some general quantitative analysis that touched on religion did occur (for example, Meyer, 1999). While economic theories explain fertility change and decline through the impact of having children on current expenditure and capital investment, other theories give more weight to cultural change (Lesthaeghe and Willems, 1999). The latter is particularly associated with increasing secularisation and postmodernisation, which are in turn (and most importantly for this discussion) associated with the increased questioning of meta-narratives and traditional authority, growing distrust and rejection of organised religious influences, and the rejection of social control on individual lifestyle (Inglehart, 1977; Lesthaeghe, 1998). Lesthaeghe (1977) explains the cultural changes associated with declining fertility as changes in thinking and lifestyle, from 'traditional' to 'postmodern' orientations. Most importantly, his analysis of one hundred years of Belgian data, from 1870 to 1970, showed secularisation (measured as lack of church attendance) to be the strongest predictor of fertility decline through its negative influence on traditional moral and religious barriers, which reduced the proportion of the population marrying and increased age at marriage (Lesthaeghe, 1977, pp 230-1).

The declining demographic interest in religion may have been further encouraged by observation of increasing individualism and rationalism, which in turn may account for an increasing research focus on 'rational decision making' about family formation. This has been associated with the more conscious planning of education and career, and consideration of the financial costs of childrearing. This increasing focus on the 'rational' possibly led to assumptions that the 'irrational' (including aspects of religion) was no longer influential on fertility behaviour. Bouma (2006, p xiii) points out that, after all, the dominant sociological view of the latter half of the 20th century was that religion and the state were supposed to wither away as modern, secular rationalism rendered the religious, the mystical and the spiritual unnecessary. Drawing on Broom (1995), the argument could be made that demographers either individually or collectively operated on assumptions and methods that became more 'masculine' (increasingly focusing on the rational, the economic, the quantifiable, the public and the work-based), while underplaying the significance of the 'feminine' (the irrational, the spiritual and emotional, the social, the qualitative, the private and the family-based). This can be supported by the fact that, until very recently, feminism had also more or less passed demography by (Presser and Sen, 2000).

Religion and secularisation in Census data

Increasing secularisation in Australia appears to be supported by Census data, as shown in Table 7.1. The proportion recording a denomination decreased from just under 90% up to 1971, to 73% by 2001, while the proportion reporting 'No religion' rose. Bouma (2006) explains, however, that a decrease in the proportion reporting a denomination and the assumed causal influence from secularisation should not be taken to mean that religion is becoming less influential in Australian life or that Australians are now irreligious, antireligious or lacking in spirituality. Rather, he sees such changes as a reflection that, in secular societies, religion and spirituality are becoming more detached from the monopolistic control of formal organisations, so that people may still 'believe but not belong'. He also sees such change reflected in the declining popularity of traditional religious groups and the rising popularity of newer groups (Bouma, 2002). In light of this it is interesting to note that the proportion of Australians reporting 'No religion' fell slightly between 1996 and 2001 (see Table 7.1), while 71% of Australians in the prime childbearing age groups (20–39) in 2001 still recorded a religious affiliation (Weston et al, 2004).

'Rediscovering' religious influence through qualitative research

This section explains how qualitative research found that, despite the assumed loss of religious influence on fertility and family size in Australia, aspects of religion are still influential. The research is from the author's PhD that had the driving question

Table 7.1: Religious response in the Australian Census (1947–2001) (%)

	1947	1961	1971	1976	1986	1996	2001
A denomination	88.6	88.9	87.0	80.0	na	na	73.0
'No religion'	0.3	0.4	6.7	na	12.7	16.5	15.5
Inadequately described	0.2	0.2	0.2	na	0.4	0.3	1.9
Not stated	10.9	10.5	6.1	na	11.9	8.7	9.8

Note: Changes since 1961 in the proportion 'Not stated' and 'Inadequately described' do not fully account for changes in 'No religion', suggesting that most of the increase in 'No religion' between 1971 and 1996 came at the expense of stated groups. The main transfer was out of Anglican and MPCRU groups (Methodist, Presbyterian, Congregational, Reformed and Uniting), while the increase in 'No religion' between 1947 and 1971 was mainly due to a wording change which allowed 'No religion' to be recorded for the first time (Bouma, 2006, p 54).

Sources: Inglis (1965); Bouma (1997, 2002); ABS (2004, and unpublished)

of 'What influences family size in Australia today?' (Newman, 2006). It used census analysis to show socioeconomic patterns of average family size in metropolitan Adelaide, and in-depth interviews to provide a deeper understanding of these patterns. In 2003-04 the author conducted semi-structured interviews with 38 mothers and 24 fathers who had between one and seven children, including at least one child aged between one to six years. Parents were recruited mainly through publicly run kindergartens. Questions related to individuals' perceptions of influences on family size, while a self-completed questionnaire provided demographic details for each family (for further detail about the methodology see Newman and Hugo, 2006).

Based on expectations from the theoretical literature it was surprising during the early stages of interviewing to find parents frequently saying that the size of family they had grown up in had influenced their feelings about the family size they were likely to have themselves. Two thirds of mothers and almost half the fathers said this. For a considerable proportion it also seemed linked with the presence or absence of a religious upbringing:

> 'I suppose being one of three [children] I just assumed [I'd have about that number].... Also, I've grown up in a Christian family and so we'd always had the church family, and there were always a lot of people in our home.... You see a lot of large families in churches. I'm sure it's not the same ratio as in society in general, and part of that might be the teaching in the Bible about the value of human life and that a child is a gift from the Lord ... things like "God said to Adam and Eve be fruitful and multiply".... But we can't separate it because both of us were brought up in a Christian family.... It's certainly not because we're Christians we'll have more children, and I know lots of people in the church who don't [have children]. But there must be something there because I think there seem to be more bigger families

within the church.' (Mother, aged 34, upper-middle status area, four children, aged 1, 4, 7 and 9, always Uniting church, attendance weekly in childhood and now)

Current or intended family size also appeared larger for those raised in Catholic families or identifying with newer religious groups. For some, the number of aunts, uncles and cousins that they had had also influenced the range of family size they would consider. Sometimes religiously influenced social factors played a part in this:

'I thought I would never have children because I didn't expect to get married ... at school I was very tall and not overly popular ... until 18 when I met my husband.... He always wanted to get married and have children. That's important to him and his family.... We used to go round there for Sunday lunches and it was always really alive, full of energy, and it made me realise that having a big family would be really nice. Every weekend there was some kind of family show with big groups of people.... [My family] didn't really do Sunday lunches, we weren't religious. [So] we always wanted to have a big family, four children, influenced by his family.' (Mother, aged 31, highest status area, one child, aged 1, no religion in childhood, now Lutheran with high attendance/importance)

As the size of family and the denomination developed into a theme of influence, and this was contrasted with interviews that did not mention them, the issues were explored further in subsequent interviews. The apparent relationship was also tested using quantitative data from the questionnaire. Based on a vague curiosity to explore the 'old' religious influence on family size I had included some closed questions on religion on a previous survey of Adelaide couples thinking of starting a family. Therefore on the parent questionnaire I had repeated 'current religious denomination', 'frequency of attendance' and 'degree of importance of religion/spirituality in influencing your life'. And following findings from the small survey, and a hunch that childhood religion might also be influential, I asked the parents for their childhood denomination and attendance. The analysis of responses highlighted some interesting links between religion and family size. For example, mothers who had been 'raised in a particular religion' and had attended religious services weekly in childhood were more likely to already have three or more children (or to have one or two but believe they would have three or more) compared with mothers who believed they were unlikely to have more than one or two children; they were also more likely to currently see religion or faith as important in guiding their lives. Tests showed that the difference in childhood religious attendance for those with larger and smaller families was statistically significant.

Cross-checking with Census data

Based on these findings, I decided to see if any relationships existed between family size and religion for the whole state of South Australia. The qualitative data had suggested exploring average family size for *all* Christian denominations, not just traditional mainstream groups. Another interview theme had been that some mothers with a university degree (and often also a professional occupation) had gone against the generally accepted demographic trend that 'family size declines as education level rises', as they already had four or five children. I hypothesised that their religious background somehow negated this traditional relationship. I ordered customised 1996 Census data to analyse family size and mother's religious denomination and level of education, choosing data for women aged 40-44 who could be considered to have almost finished childbearing. (The latest data available was for 1996, as the 'number of children ever born' question is asked only every 10 years.)

Detailed analysis of the qualitative and quantitative data on religion, education and fertility from the project can be found in Newman and Hugo (2006). For this chapter it suffices to say that the Census data showed particular denominations *within* the Christian grouping to have average family sizes well above the norm of 2.01 children (metropolitan Adelaide) and 2.33 (country South Australia), as shown in Table 7.2. Women in New Protestant/New Christian groups had the largest families (2.47 children in the city and 2.78 in the country), while city women with 'No religion' had the smallest, with 1.85 children.

When education level was added, a substantially higher proportion of university-educated women had no children when compared with women of all education levels (24% and 14% respectively). University-educated women were also *less* likely to have three or more children (23% and 32%). The proportion with no children was even higher for university-educated women with 'No religion' (29% with none, and only 17% with three or more). Table 7.3 shows that, among the university-educated, average family size ranged from as low as 1.33 children for postgraduates with 'No religion', up to 1.95 for Lutheran postgraduates. Excepting the very small group of Other Protestant/Other Christians, the largest family size for university-educated women was for New Protestant/New Christian women with a bachelor's degree (2.12).

Considering that postgraduates with 'No religion' had the smallest family size, and that the university-educated are also those most likely to have 'No religion' (Newman and Hugo, 2006), the focus away from religion in fertility research may reflect the background of, and accordingly the issues important to, those doing demographic research. Perhaps researchers have ignored religious influences either because they were not personally important or, at least according to the secularisation paradigm, were not *supposed* to be important, even if they were still important to, and influencing the behaviour of, those Australians who recorded a religious denomination and/or had lower levels of education (in fact, at least 70% of the population). Perhaps religious influences also remained hidden due

Table 7.2: Average family size and religion,[a] women aged 40–44 years, South Australia (1996)

Religion	Adelaide Statistical Division			Rest of state		
	Mean number of children	Number of women	% of women	Mean number of children	Number of women	% of women
New Protestant/New Christian[b]	2.43	1,023	2.6	2.78	345	2.5
Other Protestant/ Other Christian[c]	2.33	191	0.5	2.35	37	0.3
Buddhist/Hindu/ Muslim/Jewish	2.21	802	2.1	2.46	57	0.4
Other Old Protestant[d]	2.11	2,480	6.4	2.40	1,022	7.5
Orthodox	2.10	1,115	2.9	2.33	98	0.7
Catholic	2.08	8,925	23.1	2.42	2,130	15.7
Lutheran	2.05	1,367	3.5	2.49	1,379	10.1
Uniting church	2.01	4,781	12.4	2.33	2,775	20.4
Anglican	2.00	6,753	17.5	2.32	2,210	16.3
Other religions[e]	1.97	189	0.5	1.93	56	0.4
Not stated/ inadequately described	1.93	3,317	8.6	2.19	1,133	8.3
'No religion'[f]	1.85	7,719	20.0	2.16	2,346	17.3
Total	2.01	38,662	100.0	2.33	13,588	100.0

Notes: [a] According to ABS (1996) Australian Standard Classification of Religious Groups.
[b] Includes Brethren, Jehovah's Witnesses, Latter Day Saints, Pentecostal.
[c] 'Other Protestant' includes Aboriginal Evangelical Missions, Born Again Christian, Congregational and Wesleyan Methodist; 'Other Christian' includes Religious Society of Friends and Christian Science.
[d] Includes Baptist, Methodist, Reformed, Presbyterian, Salvation Army.
[e] 'Other religions' include for example Australian Aboriginal Traditional Religions, Baha'i, Chinese and Japanese Religions, Nature Religions, Sikhism and Church of Scientology.
[f] Represents No religion, Agnosticism, Atheism, Humanism and Rationalism.

Source: Compiled from unpublished data, ABS 1996 Census of Population and Housing

to the continuing domination of quantitative research methods which supported traditional lines of inquiry and were hard to overthrow in the face of some researchers' beliefs that 'demography without numbers is social waffle' (Coleman, 2000, p 357). In thinking about where and when religion and spirituality are researched, it is important to remember Greenhalgh's (1996) view that all disciplines are socially constructed and historically situated bodies of knowledge and networks of individuals that affect which aspects are given prominence. Indeed, researchers can play a major role in preventing change if they frame their

Table 7.3: Average family size, religion and education level, women aged 40–44 years, Adelaide (1996)

Religion	Total	Post-graduate	Bachelor	Under-graduate and assoc diploma	Skilled/basic vocational	No post-school
New Protestant/New Christian	2.43	**1.94	2.12	2.42	2.34	2.51
Other Protestant/Other Christian	2.33	*0.60	**2.20	**2.00	**2.52	2.56
Buddhist/Hindu/Muslim/Jewish	2.21	1.50	1.72	1.96	1.61	2.48
Other Old Protestant	2.11	1.55	1.97	2.28	2.23	2.11
Orthodox	2.10	1.36	1.58	1.78	2.07	2.22
Catholic	2.08	1.59	1.81	2.03	2.06	2.16
Lutheran	2.05	1.95	1.82	1.96	2.14	2.08
Uniting church	2.01	1.80	1.83	2.01	2.06	2.04
Anglican	2.00	1.69	1.92	2.00	1.98	2.03
Other religions	1.97	1.58	**1.83	**1.45	**1.91	2.13
Not stated/inadequately described	1.93	1.44	1.71	1.79	1.88	2.05
'No religion'	1.85	1.33	1.50	1.69	1.80	2.05
Total	2.01	1.53	1.74	1.95	2.01	2.11

Notes: * = <10 women in cell; ** = <25 women in cell.

Source: Compiled from unpublished data, ABS 1996 Census of Population and Housing

research questions to reflect their cultural myths (Thurer, 1994, p 291). One leading demographer notes that knowledge building should be seen as:

> ... a series of "sub-narratives" from different disciplinary perspectives and orientations ... [of which] different parts ... have been highlighted at different times depending on policy interests, improvements in technical skills, availability of data, changes in societal settings, and the degree of satisfaction with the dominant sub-narratives of the day. (van de Kaa, 1996, p 389)

Qualitative insights on religion's influence

The in-depth parent interviews give some insight into the pathways of religious influence lying behind the quantitative patterns. They partly reflect traditional demographic explanations identified by McQuillan (2004), including religious doctrine (for example, attitudes to abortion, contraception and non-marital childbearing) and broader sociocultural messages supportive of parenthood (for example, praise of large families, the importance of family, gender role pressure supporting motherhood). However, the interviews also support Westoff and Potvin's findings (1967) that the social systems of religions provide a primary source of informal social relations that affect family size preferences. The interviews also suggest that religious families and communities may be valuing, and therefore providing practical support for, parenting, which is not offered where such religious influence is absent. In the Adelaide interviews some parents, for example, talked of religious–family influences on their confidence and support networks for parenting:

> 'When I got married I thought we'll have children, but as for how many, I don't know that I ever really contemplated it ... I was one of two but I think two might have been a bit boring! [laughs] [Husband's family of five] was so nice, big house, everybody always went there for parties ... my immediate family wasn't like that.... And [husband]'s family has a lot to do with their Christian beliefs – family is the core and God's in the middle of that.... [Fifth child just happened but] no question of me terminating the pregnancy. My Christian belief is that God never pushes you over the edge.' (Mother, aged 41, highest status area, five children aged 4 to 11, Anglican weekly in childhood, Lutheran now, religion very important in life)

One father (a Church of Christ associate pastor) felt that his faith encouraged anti-materialistic views that countered the fertility-lowering influences of materialism, consumerism and individualism that have accompanied secularisation:

> 'Our Western world is very materialistic, very self-centred [so] having children is just a nuisance factor and ... a lot of people are choosing not to have any [children] or to have them very late.... People are very much finance-driven that they *have* to have the best car, the holiday every year ... they put those things and finance before children.... We chose to have a large family rather than have expensive holidays.... I've never been one for desiring a lot of wealth [and] our children enjoy the simple things.... Part of our belief too, in our Christian [*sic*] ... we actually believe that there are models of servanthood, caring for others, putting others before yourself.' (Father, aged 42, lower-middle status area, seven children aged 2 to 20, no religion in childhood, Church of Christ very important from age 14, now associate pastor)

Religiously influenced environments could also play a key role in validating larger families:

'In the Catholic education system four [children] was of no consequence, but we've since put [daughter] in public education and you're introduced as "a mother of four", like it's something different! I do remember when I was pregnant with my fourth … this woman came up to me and said "Ooh you're *brave!*" … and I said what does *that* mean? [and she said] "Well four – it's a lot having four".' (Mother, aged 44, highest status area, four children aged 2 to 11, Catholic weekly in childhood, Catholic religion now very important)

However, two mothers explained that family size could be limited by religiously buttressed views about 'proper' mothers and 'proper' childcare held by the grandparent generation (in these cases all Italian-born Catholics who had migrated to Australian in the 1950s):

'The only negative influence in our family has been from my husband's parents who didn't want us to have the third child…. [They] looked after the children [while I was at work] and they didn't want us to put them into childcare…. Childcare would have been easier…. It's more his mother's influence and she's just someone who's fairly set in her opinions…. They kept saying "Don't have a third child" and we kept saying, "Well we intend to"….' (Mother, aged 34, highest status area, two children aged 2, 3½, pregnant with third, Anglican rarely in childhood, no religion now but somewhat important in life)

Some parents whose religious family background had positively influenced them to have children appeared to have been more openly encouraged, or to have been exposed to role models which perhaps subconsciously encouraged them more, to set partnership and parenthood as goals in life, *alongside* education and career. Parents in three larger families also mentioned church-based pre-marriage counselling that encouraged them to consider partners' family size preferences, which according to Cannold (2005) is particularly important in avoiding circumstantial childlessness:

'We never seriously considered only two [children]…. [It was] three even before we were married. People who marry you often say it's good to think about these things, and we did then, and three was … sort of the aim.' (Father, aged 36, upper-middle status area, three children aged 2, 4 and 6, Uniting Church weekly in childhood and now, very important now)

In summary, all of the interview themes discussed suggest that religious upbringing and religious communities are acting as cultural resources which can influence the number of children people have, and that they can support people to have larger families through providing social support and validation for parenting.

These aspects could be more widely considered by demographers in developed countries and those interested in exploring religion's influence in society. The findings also support Southworth's (2005, p 77) observation that faith communities and religious organisations continue to influence contemporary social life and behaviour despite the secularisation paradigm.

Religion in demography: future directions

The research discussed in this chapter occurred at an opportune time, with Bouma (2002) believing that globalisation and the events of September 11 have focused attention on religion per se, and McQuillan (2004, p 25) seeing recent developments in demography, including research on fertility change in Muslim populations, as generating renewed interest in the 'old question' of religious influence on fertility. This is also reflected in new research proposals stimulated by the re-introduction of a religion question in the UK's 2001 Census (Howard and Hopkins, 2005) as well as several papers related to fertility in the US (Lehrer, 2004) and Spain (Adsera, 2006). A variety of issues around family size and fertility could be further explored in social science, including pathways of influence associated with religious upbringing (including religious socialisation or lack thereof in childhood); links with current beliefs about religion versus spirituality; differences between those affiliated with traditional and newer denominations, or between those attending growing and youthful congregations compared with declining and ageing ones; influences related to attitudes towards marriage and partnership; the influence on family size of religious family and community support for parenting (or lack thereof); and pathways by which university-educated women with 'No religion' have smaller families or no children. However, in researching religious influence it should be remembered that behaviour is not purely a reaction to the contemporary environment but also reflects a lifetime of accumulated experiences. People of childbearing age today (20-40, born roughly mid-1960s to mid-1980s) were not only socialised in these eras but are also likely to have been influenced by the attitudes, views and values of their parents who grew up probably between the 1930s and 1950s. Hence, a variety of religious influences from any time over the previous three quarters of a century could have influenced today's parenting generation, so that research on contemporary issues should benefit from including the lifecourse perspective which has become more popular in social science over the past few years, along with a family history perspective which is often ignored.

Conclusion

This chapter provides research insights for those interested in religion in particular and those interested in social science in general. It has argued that lack of attention to religious influences on contemporary Australian fertility resulted partly from researchers adhering to an unquestioning belief in the hegemony of secularisation, along with a continued preference for aggregate-level quantitative analysis at the expense of qualitative methods, which effectively contributed towards a 'closed shop' on research topics. The empirical project highlighted how, through mixed method research, qualitative methods can provide room for new themes to emerge or old themes to be rediscovered, while quantitative data can test emerging hypotheses. The chapter also showed benefits in disaggregating data rather than aggregating to traditional groupings that may hide important trends and differences. In particular, the chapter has shown how qualitative research methods which talk to 'the actors' allow the voices of those in faith communities to be heard and explored, rather than the research being limited by traditional theory, disciplinary interest or popular debate. The former quite clearly leads to a broader and deeper understanding of influences on social behaviour, and in relation to fertility encouraged (re)exploration of *social and family* influences on fertility which have been overshadowed by the contemporary research focus on *economics* (work and finances). This chapter will hopefully leave readers encouraged to be more reflexive about the beliefs, assumptions, theories, methods and politics that colour their research so that the knowledge they help build comes closer to the truth about how the world really is for those who are the focus of their research.

References

ABS (Australian Bureau of Statistics) (2004) *Australian social trends 2004*, catalogue no 4102.0 (www.abs.gov.au/ausstats, 5/03/05).

Adsera, A. (2006) 'Marital fertility and religion in Spain 1985 and 1999', *Population Studies*, vol 60, no 2, pp 205-21.

Borrie, W.D. (1975) *Population and Australia: A Demographic analysis and projection*, First Report of the National Population Inquiry, Canberra: AGPS.

Bouma, G. (1997) 'Increasing diversity in religious identification in Australia: comparing 1947, 1991 and 1996 census reports', *People and Place*, vol 5, no 3 (http://elecpress.monash.edu.au/pnp/free/pnpv5n3/bouma.htm, 25/05/05).

Bouma, G. (2002) 'Globalization and recent changes in the demography of Australian religious groups: 1947 to 2001', *People and Place*, vol 10, no 4, pp 17-23.

Bouma, G. (2006) *Australian soul: Religion and spirituality in the 21st century*, Port Melbourne: Cambridge University Press.

Broom, D. (1995) 'Masculine medicine, feminine illness: gender and health', in G.M. Lupton and J.M. Najman (eds) *Sociology of health and illness: Australian readings* (2nd edn), South Yarra: Macmillan Education Australia, pp 99-112.

Cannold, L. (2005) *What, no baby?*, Fremantle: Curtin University Press.

Carmichael, G.A. and McDonald, P. (2003) 'Fertility trends and differentials', in S.-E. Khoo and P. McDonald (eds) *The transformation of Australia's population: 1970–2030*, Sydney: University of New South Wales Press, pp 40-76.

Coleman, D. (2000) 'Book review of *Demographic methods* (Hinde 1998)', *Population Studies*, vol 54, no 3, p 357.

Day, L.H. (1965) 'Family size and fertility', in A.F. Davies and S. Encel (eds) *Australian society: A sociological introduction*, Melbourne: Cheshire, pp 156-67.

Greenhalgh, S. (1996) 'The social construction of population science: an intellectual, institutional and political history of twentieth-century demography', *Comparative Studies in Society and History*, vol 38, no 1, pp 26-66.

Howard, D. and Hopkins, P.E. (2005) 'Editorial: Race, religion and the census', *Population, Space and Place*, vol 11, no 2, pp 69-74.

Hugo, G.J. (2004) *Recent fertility trends in South Australia*, Report to Planning SA, Adelaide: Department of Geographical and Environmental Studies, The University of Adelaide.

Inglehart, R. (1977) *The silent revolution: Changing values and political styles among Western publics*, Princeton, NJ: Princeton University Press.

Inglis, K.S. (1965) 'Religious behaviour', in A.F. Davies and S. Encel (eds) *Australian society: A sociological introduction*, Melbourne: Cheshire, pp 43-75.

Lehrer, E.L. (2004) 'The role of religion in union formation: an economic perspective',   *Population Research & Policy Review*, vol 30, no 4, pp 1-25.

Lesthaeghe, R. (1977) *The decline of Belgian fertility 1800-1970*, Princeton, NJ: Princeton University Press.

Lesthaeghe, R, (1998) 'On theory development: applications to the study of family formation', *Population and Development Review*, vol 24, no 1, pp 1-14.

Lesthaeghe, R. and Willems, P. (1999) 'Is low fertility a temporary phenomenon in the European Union?', *Population and Development Review*, vol 25, no 2, pp 211-28.

McDonald, P. and Kippen, R. (1999) *Population futures for Australia: The policy alternatives*, Research Paper No 5, 1999-2000 (www.aph.gov.au/library/pubs/rp/1999-2000/2000rp05.htm, 25/07/05).

McQuillan, K. (2004) 'When does religion influence fertility?', *Population and Development Review*, vol 30, no 1, pp 25-56.

Meyer, R. (1999) 'Which Australians are having three or more children?', *People and Place*, vol 7, no 3, pp 31-8.

Newman, L.A. (2006) 'Images and impacts of parenthood: explaining fertility and family size in contemporary Australia', Unpublished PhD thesis, Adelaide: Department of Geographical and Environmental Studies, The University of Adelaide.

Newman, L.A. and Hugo, G.J. (2006) 'Women's religion, fertility and education in a low-fertility setting: evidence from South Australia', *Journal of Population Research,* vol 27, no 3, pp 41-66.

Presser, H.B. and Sen, G. (eds) (2000) *Women's empowerment and demographic processes: Moving beyond Cairo*, Oxford: Oxford University Press.

Ruzicka, L.T. and Caldwell, J.C. (1982) 'Fertility', in United Nations, *Population of Australia,* Country Monograph Series no 9, Bangkok: Economic and Social Commission for Asia and the Pacific, pp 119-229.

Southworth, J.R. (2005) 'Religion in the 2001 Census for England and Wales', *Population, Space and Place*, vol 11, no 2, pp 75-88.

Thurer, S.L. (1994) *The myths of motherhood*, Boston, MA: Houghton Mifflin Co.

UN (United Nations) Secretariat (2000) *Replacement migration: Is it a solution to declining and ageing populations?*, New York, NY: Population Division, UN Department of Economic and Social Affairs.

van de Kaa, D.J. (1996) 'Anchored narratives: the story and findings of half a century of research into the determinants of fertility', *Population Studies*, vol 50, no 3, pp 389–432.

Westoff, C.F. and Potvin, R.H. (1967) *College women and fertility values*, Princeton, NJ: Princeton University Press.

Weston, R., Qu, L., Parker, R. and Alexander, M. (2004) *It's not for lack of wanting kids: A report on the fertility decision making project*, Melbourne: Australian Institute of Family Studies.

EIGHT

Turning the world upside down

Caroline Humphrey

Introduction

The metaphor of 'turning the world upside down' is deployed in this chapter to examine differences between world-views and their implications for research in the social sciences and practice in the caring professions. The first section sketches out the contours of four world-views – that is, secular, scientific, spiritual and religious – with reference to their philosophical premises. It will be shown that the scientific world-view often inverts the secular world-view insofar as scientists uncover deeper truths and realities of human beings and planet earth, while spiritual and religious world-views involve an inversion of both secular and scientific world-views insofar as they invoke meta-physical truths and realities beyond human beings and planet earth.

The rest of the chapter considers how the contemporary co-existence of world-views generates dilemmas for researchers and practitioners. The social sciences were incubated within the womb of a secular and scientific world that divested the meta-physical realm of any reality, but they are now inhabiting multicultural societies in an era of globalisation, where spiritual and religious world-views jostle alongside secular and scientific ones. Caring professionals have been schooled in the sciences and regulated by a secular state, but they have often been required to occupy the vacuum left by the demise of spiritual professionals when dealing with death, disability, depression and domestic violence, and they are now being exhorted to develop 'cross-cultural competences' in dealing with citizens who harbour diverse world-views.

The metaphor of 'journeying' is invoked to suggest fruitful ways forward. On the one hand, there is a journeying between world-views that can be found among some scholars. When they are able to sojourn in other life worlds as well they can acquire an insider appreciation of other world-views and open up a dialogue between world-views. On the other hand, there is a journeying deeper into one's own faith that can be found among some practitioners. When they are able to share the inner workings of faith-based practices in public forums, the differences made by spiritual and religious world-views can be appreciated by secular and scientific audiences. If both kinds of journeying are quite rare, it is because they require extraordinary care, courage and conviction.

World-views

Secular world-views

The secular world-view revolves around the facticities of everyday life on earth. The term 'secular' actually derives from the Middle Ages when everyone was socialised into a religious world-view (Christianity in Europe). The distinction was between the religious clergy who devoted their lives to God's work and the secular congregation who devoted their lives to everyday survival on earth. An umbilical cord united clergy and congregation, since the former supplicated for the souls of their parishioners in the hereafter, while the latter supplied the clergy with the necessities of life on earth. During the long transition to modernity this umbilical cord was severed, and the terms 'secular' and 'religious' became antithetical, so that those who adhere to a secular world-view are those whose view of the world is limited to the everyday world around them, with a disinterest in any other world(s) or a denial of the possibility of any other world(s). In other words, secularism is now associated with agnosticism or atheism (Walter, 1997).

The philosophical premises of secularism are summarised in the motto 'life on earth is the measure of all things'. In terms of ontology there is a naïve realism whereby being is what it appears to be, that is, here we all are on earth, going about our everyday lives of surviving, struggling, reproducing, childrearing, dying. The eschatology follows on from this – death defines the destiny for each and every one of us, and once we are burned or buried we are as dead as we appear to be. In terms of epistemology and methodology there is an optimism that we can discover whatever we need to know for our survival and sense-making from the world around us insofar as we are endowed with faculties for sense perception, reflection and communication. Secularism may be both self-evident and self-sufficient for everyday life in modernity. Nevertheless, sophisticated philosophies have also been built on secular premises, ranging from existentialism which laments the absurdity of the human condition with death built into its destiny (Camus, 1951) to postmodernism which plays with the aporias of human reflection as self-created systems devoid of external referents (Sarup, 1993).

Scientific world-views

Science emerged from the 16th century onwards in Europe and became the cultural laboratory in which the institutions associated with modernity were developed. As the sciences proliferated in every sphere they transcended secular ways of knowing and eclipsed all other ways of knowing. The motto is that 'science is the measure of all things' since knowledge only counts if it has been theorised and tested within the paradigm of Western science. The result of such scientism is that the world-views of the majority of people may be discounted (Beck, 1992). This elitism and ethnocentricity has caused great consternation, yet the elitism is not entirely unwarranted insofar as science reveals that the world is not what it appears to be.

In other words, science turned the world upside down by revealing its hidden depths. Its ontology is depth realism, as it takes the world we all inhabit and digs deeper into it. The realm of being is multilayered – each phenomenon has layer-upon-layer of reality as a result of its complexity and history (transphenomenality) – the inner core of a phenomenon often contradicts its surface appearance (counterphenomenality), and it is this unseen inner core which harbours causal significance in producing the world (Collier, 1994). Astronomers discovered that the apparently flat and static earth was a sphere revolving around the sun; physicists demonstrated that the solid objects around us are all comprised of atoms and molecules in perpetual motion; psychologists showed that scary sensory experiences are routinely relegated to an unconscious realm (Gribbin, 2002). Its epistemology renders all things potentially knowable but nothing is ever definitively known since there may be exceptions to 'laws of nature' in the future. Its methodological tree has theoretical, experimental and statistical branches, and the fruits of this tree are fed into the databases of governments, businesses and professions. Science has its own eschatology – each science was a beacon of light, and collectively they were dubbed 'The Enlightenment' for they promised encyclopaedic knowledge about all that exists, which was to be harnessed to the end of progress. At the turn of the 21st century ventures into the cosmos are causing another revolution in scientific world-views (Greene, 2004).

Spiritual world-views

Spiritual world-views have been prevalent throughout human history and have survived the rise of secularism and scientism. The everyday world is once again turned upside down, but this time in the service of exploring other dimensions of existence beyond those which are tangible to human senses or recordable by scientific instruments such as microscopes, telescopes or inter-galactic probes. In other words, it is a meta-physics, that which goes beyond physics, even beyond astro-physics. The motto is that 'the spirit of the cosmos is the measure of all things'. The nature of spirit has been conceptualised in different ways by different people, as testified by a brief overview of animism, ancestralism and Buddhism. Animism is when all that exists is endowed with its own life force that partakes of the cosmic spirit. This is an important strand in modern paganism, where trees, rocks and planets are regarded as living creatures which human beings should be listening to and learning from (Harvey, 1997). Ancestralism lives on in African and Aboriginal cultures where the spirits of dead ancestors continue to play a vital role in overseeing the worldly affairs of families and communities. Entreaties to the ancestors serve the dual function of helping their spirits to 'move on' from the earth-plane into higher realms of spirit, and ensuring that whatever ongoing influence they exert on their progeny is a benevolent one (Rees, 2001). Buddhism is associated with an elaborate meta-physics whereby all beings experience multiple re-births in a cycle governed by karma, the moral and meta-physical law of cause-and-effect. The wheel of life on earth spins off in many directions – for example, we could have arrived from or be heading towards the realms of demi-gods, hungry ghosts, bodhisattvas or demonic creatures (Hodge and Boord, 2000). While paganism and Buddhism could be construed as polytheistic and non-theistic religions respectively, their practitioners tend to cultivate an openness to the spiritual dimension of existence as it unfolds in their lives that takes precedence over scriptural authority, unlike other world religions.

In terms of ontology there is a web of existence whereby all beings are interconnected and different realms of being can have causal influence on one another, which has immediate implications on the level of eschatology. In other words, the choices we make during our earthly existence can change our cosmic destinations, just as the benevolent or baleful influences of gods, demons or ancestral spirits can affect our fate on earth. There is a similar link between epistemology and methodology – we can only come to know this web of existence through cultivating a seventh sense, since the web of existence is sutured together by spiritual forces beyond secular and scientific modes of knowing. In communities with a shared spiritual world-view, everyday life will itself yield regular confirmation of supranatural realities. In countries where secular and scientific world-views are hegemonic, supranatural realities are typically accessed by individuals in extreme situations such as encounters with death, and they may then be locked away in a closet of privatised (un)consciousness (Rees, 2001).

Religious world-views

Religious world-views also involve meta-physical reversals of secular and scientific ones. Although they are incubated in the womb of spiritual cultures, their coming-of-age has often culminated in a repudiation of these other cultures. The religious motto is that 'the Creator is the measure of all things' since it is the Creator who creates and sustains all life on planet earth, and who rules over the entire cosmos. World religions such as Judaism, Christianity and Islam owe their birth to the arrival on earth of a leader who is believed to have been sent by the Creator – for Jews there is a line of descendants from Abraham to Moses who were chosen by Yahweh to reveal His word and lead His people; for Christians it is Christ the Son of God who embodies the mystery of resurrection into eternal life; for Muslims it is the prophet Mohammed who was sent by Allah. The force of these divinely inspired leaders has been such that entire nations have undergone conversion experiences, and worldwide organisations have endured for millennia (see Partridge, 2005).

The hallmark of a religion lies in a certain closure around its philosophy. At the level of ontology there are typically three realms of being, that is, earth, heaven and hell. The earth is represented as a battlefield between the forces of good and evil where human beings have a capacity for conscious choices in their conduct and convictions. The eschatology follows on from this – each choice lends weight to the cause of good or evil in the world; all our choices will be weighed by our Creator after our death on the Day of Judgement; and our destiny will be decided accordingly. At the level of epistemology it is only the Creator who is all-seeing and all-knowing; the Creator endowed us with our capacity for sense perception and scientific investigation; but the Creator cannot be directly seen or known by any creature. The methodology of science is still intact for making sense of the physical reality of the cosmos, but the religious person must rely on revelations and scriptures to make sense of its underlying meta-physical reality. How can we accommodate to the diversity of religions? Gandhi's proclamation that 'God has no religion' and that he was as much a Jew, a Christian and a Muslim as a Hindu signposts a way forward (Gandhi, 2007). In other words, the constructions of creatures cannot circumscribe their Creator, who may appear to them in different ways in different eras.

These world-views are ideal-types to be found in their purity only in relatively insular communities and they increasingly co-exist within individuals in (post)modernity. However, they serve a heuristic purpose in clarifying the trajectories of the social sciences and caring professions to date, as well as the journeying of some practitioners.

Social sciences

The social sciences emerged from the mid-19th century onwards across Europe. Since their task was to make sense of 'the social' in terms of 'science', spiritual and religious traditions were subjected to a secular-scientific gaze. This can be illustrated by reference to the works of Émile Durkheim, Karl Marx and Sigmund Freud, who were among the founding fathers of anthropology, sociology and psychology respectively.

Durkheim (1915) studied the available literature on the Aboriginal peoples in Australia and claimed that their 'primitive' practices contained the essence of all religion. In the schema presented here, the Aboriginal world-view is a spiritual one characterised by animism and ancestralism. Each clan is named after an animal or bird or ancestor that is represented on its totem, and the totem is the centrepiece of collective worship. Durkheim adopted a positive attitude towards religion insofar as it is an expression of the 'conscience collective' and operates as a socialising and moralising force to prevent and/or remedy transgressions that could be harmful to the community. However, he was adamant that the only thing that could ever be sacred is society itself and concluded that the clan was essentially worshipping itself. When the social becomes sacred by virtue of itself, this is tantamount to the death of the spiritual *qua* supranatural.

Marx (1963) argued that all meta-physics involve an inversion of the real world that is harmful to humanity: that is, there is only life on earth; any vision of life beyond earth is a delusion; and delusions undermine the evolution and enlightenment of humanity. In societies where the material infrastructure reproduces economic exploitation, it is elites who have perpetuated ideologies to sustain the status quo, and religions have operated to persuade the masses to acquiesce to their subordination (for example, the virtue of humility) while offering them the olive branch of a hereafter (that is, rewards in heaven). For critical theorists the only thing that matters is that their work should nurture the education and emancipation of the people in the tangible world around us, which has all too often entailed the suppression of spiritual and religious traditions by communist regimes (cf McLellan, 1979; Held, 1980; Fay, 1987).

Freud's (1964) hypothesis was that religion is a universal human neurosis and an ineradicable part of the human condition. It is an illusion since there is nothing beyond our embodied existence, but it is an enduring one since it is rooted in the origin of our species. Freud regarded all spiritual and religious phenomena as byproducts of primitive psychic drives that have been repressed to the unconscious. For example, an inability to countenance our own death generates the idea of an after-life as a wish fulfilment; child-like needs and desires create the image of a Father-God to protect us; and the ambivalent feelings we harbour towards significant others are projected onto the phantasmagoric figures of ancestors in a spirit realm.

Scientific and religious world-views were mutual enemies in early modernity since each of them claimed to represent the whole truth of humanity. By late modernity there were signs of a rapprochement, that is, the Roman Catholic church apologised for its persecution of Galileo; some natural scientists acknowledged that their own hypotheses about evolution were speculative and that science had no way of accessing the truth about our ultimate origin or end; and some social scientists entertained the notion of multiple realms of reality (Macionis and Plummer, 1997). There has also been an intermingling of secular and spiritual world-views in grassroots communities. Practices such as yoga and meditation that had been nurtured for millennia within the womb of Eastern spiritual traditions have been popularised among secular publics, notably by the Friends of the Western Buddhist Order (Vishvapani, 2001). Yet this intermingling of world-views is not unproblematic. The Enlightenment of Eastern wisdom is antithetical to that paraded in Western sciences, states and societies. Eastern Enlightenment is a Tao-Enlightenment; it cultivates a non-attachment to the earth-plane – a letting go of all that binds us and a letting be of all that is around us. Western Enlightenment is an Ego-Enlightenment; it seeks to comprehend the world in order to control and change the world.

What are the implications for research and scholarship in the 21st century? Those who already inhabit a fixed position in the schema of world-views need to appreciate that this places limitations on their comprehension. As a general rule, scientists *qua* scientists can only provide an 'outsider' account of faith-based societies or sacred works which are likely to be mis-representations from the vantage point of the faithful. As a general rule, adherents of a particular faith can provide deep 'insider' accounts of their own faith, but this can skew their perception of other faiths. Dewi Rees (2001) synthesised medical science and Christian faith in his work as a hospice director but in his research into death and dying across cultures there are occasional lapses in his portrayal of other spiritual and religious world-views. For example, ancestralism is defined as 'a cult' (Rees, 2001, p 36), which is typically a pejorative term, and Buddhists are said to believe that being born as a human being is 'the supreme evil' (p 23) in a strange reversal of the *dharma* (the teachings of the Buddha).

Multicultural societies are sorely in need of people who are prepared to journey between world-views. Those who sojourn among a different people have an opportunity to acquire an insider appreciation of another world-view to minimise the risks of mis-representation. A famous example in anthropology is in the work of Evan-Pritchard (1976), who lived among the African Azande tribe and who surprised himself and his scientific peers by revealing that witchcraft made such perfect sense in this community that he ran his own affairs by reference to its norms, such as consulting oracles and performing magic rituals. An example in theology is in the writings of Johnston (1978), a Jesuit priest who lived among Zen Buddhists in Japan, and experienced for himself the deep union between Eastern and Western faiths on a mystical and meta-physical plane.

Such journeying opens up novel territories for research and reflection and may pave the way towards new world-views. Bentz and Shapiro (1998) have drawn on the insights and practices of Buddhism to promote 'mindful inquiry', since meditation can free the mind of its fixed concepts and predetermined goals and free up the spirit of inquiry. Peter Reason and John Heron founded the Centre for Action Research in Professional Practice in the UK in order to promote 'humanistic inquiry'. The spiritual dimension of our existence is acknowledged and the result is that social science is reconfigured. Researchers are co-inquirers who respect the indigenous knowledges of their community, including those rooted in poetry, painting and prayer, and who work towards healing the suffering in the world, where healing is 'making whole' which in turn is 'making holy' (Reason, 1994). Subsequently their attention was directed towards the spiritual realm itself. Heron established the International Centre for Co-operative Inquiry in Italy where groups of co-inquirers from diverse faith and non-faith backgrounds undertake a variety of sacred practices in an attempt to re-discover the subtle and the spiritual and to create theoretical and methodological parameters for a new 'sacred science' (Heron, 1998).

Caring professions

The caring professions were originally spiritual professions – in antiquity medicine-men were shamans steeped in alchemy (Helman, 2001); in medieval Europe many midwives were pagan women dispensing herbal and magical remedies (Marland, 1993); and the first generation of modern social workers were Christians doing God's work on earth (Woodroofe, 1961). Care and cure for our bodies, psyches and communities, along with the earth which sustains us from below and the heavens that sustain us from above, were indivisible.

The ascendancy of secular and scientific world-views in the 19th and 20th centuries, along with the increasing regulation of caring professions by secular states, operated to erase these origins. Since erasure always leaves traces of that which preceded it, and since these traces will be re-activated within individuals and communities, particularly in times of trauma or transition, professionals are now in a conundrum. This can be depicted by reference to modern social work. The state-prescribed curriculum for social workers contains no references to spirituality, but law and policy specifies that they must take account of 'culture', including 'religion', when undertaking statutory duties such as providing substitute families for children, and recent practice guidance exhorts them to assess the 'spiritual needs' of service users and carers facing disease, disability and death (Moss, 2005). Educators are keen to promote 'cross-cultural competencies' (O'Hagan, 2001) but practitioners are apprehensive about its religious and spiritual dimensions (Crompton, 1998). At one extreme there are practice teachers who have treated faith among students as evidence of a fundamentalism incompatible with anti-oppressive practice, as if only agnostics or atheists can be open-minded and anti-oppressive (Gilligan, 2003). At the other extreme there are practitioners from a variety of religious backgrounds who engage in faith-based practices such as praying with and for clients, debating life-after-death and performing the laying on of hands (Furman et al, 2004). Their faith is akin to a 'skeleton in the closet': it is alive in the professional practices of public servants conducted in quasi-private spaces, but many dare not speak its name, except in anonymous surveys.

This conundrum is replicated in research and policy-making circles. During the 1990s social workers in the UK investigated cases of organised sexual abuse of children that appeared to involve occult elements, but the government commissioned research that repudiated the notion of 'satanic abuse' and rationalised away the religious dimension by claiming that professionals had misinterpreted children's stories (La Fontaine, 1995). Silence reigned in respect of the unsolved cases that transgressed the boundaries of the secular-scientific imagination (Crompton, 1998). In the government inquiry into the murder of Victoria Climbié the report mentions that the pastor of her church had concurred with her carer-abuser that the child was possessed by a demonic spirit which needed to be 'beaten out' of her. None of the professionals had paid any attention to the religious community of this African family, and none of the recommendations advised them to do so in future (Laming, 2003). 'The spiritual and religious dimension of abuse is also akin to a 'skeleton in the closet': if this other skeleton is alive, it will be dangerous if we dare not speak its name.

If we want to explore further these spiritual and religious dimensions of practice, we have to turn to the works of therapists in the independent sector. They include Barbara Ann Brennan, who is an ex-physicist who became a shamanic healer; M. Scott Peck and Brian Thorne, who incorporate Christian theology into their work in psychiatry and counselling respectively; and David and Caroline Brazier, who developed Zen therapy as a Buddhist approach to psychotherapy.

These paradigms reveal that spiritual and religious world-views can literally turn the world upside down, that is, in these schema the root causes of both suffering and healing reside in meta-physical realms. Brennan (1988) regards diseases as the end-product of disturbances in the universal energy field which have been internalised by a person or carried over from past lives. She claims supranatural powers of perception whereby she detects diseases in the energy field surrounding an individual person and in their energy centres (chakras), and supranatural powers of healing whereby diseases are dissipated by the laying on of hands and meditation-visualisation practices under the direction of a 'spirit guide'. Brazier (1995) regards the self-actualisation associated with Western psychotherapy as symptomatic of the problem of Ego-Enlightenment; Zen therapy involves a Tao-Enlightenment with the ultimate self-overcoming of selfhood itself.

The synthesis of Christian theology with Western psychology has generated some extraordinary theoretical frameworks that can fruitfully expand our other-worldly horizons, as well as some extraordinary case studies which can offend our this-worldly ethics. Thorne (1998) regards Jesus as the incarnation of the ideal of 'the fully functioning person' that underpins person-centred counselling, and as his spiritual guide in his profession. Both counsellors and clients are sons and daughters of God, using language and touch as the sacred medium of healing, 'waiting on God' for those crucial breakthroughs, and striving to become Christ-like. In one case this mystical union with the other in the presence of God became a physical union between a naked therapist and client, as sexuality and spirituality were reconciled and mortal bodies encountered immortal souls (Thorne, 1998, pp 81-5). The other side of spirituality has been explored by Scott Peck in his book *People of the lie* (Scott Peck, 1990). Here the cosmos is ultimately a battleground between God and Satan, and disturbed people are often caught up in this battle, as God and Satan each bid for their souls. The diagnostic category of 'evil' is applied to 'people of the lie' who continually perpetrate harm on others while parading their own innocence, a category he developed initially in relation to parents who subjected their offspring to severe and sometimes fatal abuse. 'Evil' is defined as 'live written backwards': it is that which destroys life while denying its deeds. 'Satan' is named as 'the Father of all lies', and Scott Peck has also been involved in exorcisms, although Satanic possession is said to be rare, unlike everyday encounters with evil. The question is whether the widening of our conceptual horizons by the incorporation of notions such as the 'Christ-like counsellor' and 'people of the lie' necessarily entrains the widening of concrete practices that will leave us wide open to accusation of malpractice insofar as we could venture *ultra vires* (that is, beyond the remit of our professions)? But these independent therapists do publicise their spiritual orientation and their clients have specifically chosen therapists whose world-views are congruent with their own.

Conclusion

In this chapter a fourfold schema of world-views has been presented as a heuristic device to examine the ways in which the world can revolve in tandem with our world-views. To circumvent the question of world-views is not an option for social scientists and caring professionals: if you are an atheist, ancestralist, Buddhist or Christian it will make a world of difference in how you understand life and death and it has always already impacted on your teaching, research and therapeutic interventions. An open-minded and open-hearted approach can help to dissolve the antagonisms between world-views. Indeed, a global history of world-views might show that each world-view when developed to its limits actually gives birth to another world-view as if making sense of the universe requires such a kaleidoscope of world-views. For example, ancient alchemy was the incubator of chemistry (Marshall, 2001) just as 21st-century astro-physics is engendering a new cosmology (Greene, 2004).

It has been suggested that the future of the social sciences may hinge on the capacity of its scholars to journey between life worlds and world-views, and that this journeying may herald a deconstruction of the antinomies between science and spirituality, selfhood and scholarship, Western and Eastern Enlightenment (Heron, 1998). Such work may also be beneficial to caring professionals and their clients where spirituality and religion are akin to a 'skeleton in the cupboard'. We have this quandary in relation to social work, but similar observations apply to nursing (McSherry, 2006). Therapists in the independent sector have pioneered spiritual conceptions of counselling and healing, but some of their casework examples would breach codes of ethics in the statutory sector, suggesting that pondering on spirituality is much safer than practising under its auspices. In any event, it is high time that wider publics of clients and citizens alike were engaged in these debates.

Note
[1] Interestingly, the government has recently issued practice guidance with reference to this issue (DfES, 2007).

References

Beck, U. (1992) *Risk society: Towards a new modernity*, London: Sage Publications.

Bentz, V.M. and Shapiro. J.J. (1998) *Mindful inquiry in social research*, Thousand Oaks, CA: Sage Publications.

Brazier, D. (1995) *Zen therapy: A Buddhist approach to psychotherapy*, London: Constable & Robinson.

Brennan, B.A. (1988) *Hands of light: A guide to healing through the human energy field*, New York, NY: Bantam Books.

Camus, A. (1951) *L'homme révolté,* Paris: Gallimard.

Collier, A. (1994) *Critical realism: An introduction to Roy Bhaskar's philosophy*, London: Verso.

Crompton, M. (1998) *Children, spirituality, religion and social work*, Aldershot: Ashgate.

DfES (Department for Education and Skills) (2007) *Safeguarding children from abuse linked to a belief in spirit possession*, London: DfES.

Durkheim, É. (1915) *The elementary forms of the religious life*, London: Allen & Unwin.

Evan-Pritchard, E.E. (1976) *Witchcraft, oracles and magic among the Azande*, Oxford: Clarendon Press.

Fay, B. (1987) *Critical social science: Liberation and its limits*, Oxford: Polity Press.

Freud, S. (1964) 'The future of an illusion', in *The standard edition of the complete psychological works of Sigmund Freud. Volume 21*, Toronto: Hogarth, pp 18-44.

Furman, L.D., Benson, P.W., Grimwood, C. and Canda, E. (2004) 'Religion and spirituality in social work education and direct practice at the millennium: a survey of UK social workers', *British Journal of Social Work*, vol 34, no 6, pp 767-92.

Gandhi, M. (2007) Entry in Wikipedia (http://en.wikipedia.org/wiki/Mahatma_Gandhi, 4/01/07).

Gilligan, P. (2003) '"It isn't discussed". Religion, belief and practice teaching: missing components of cultural competence in social work', *Journal of Practice Teaching*, vol 5, no 1, pp 75-95.

Greene, B.R. (2004) *The fabric of the cosmos: Space, time and the texture of reality*, London: Penguin.

Gribbin, J. (2002) *Science: A history 1543-2001*, London: Penguin.

Harvey, G. (1997) *Listening people, speaking earth: Contemporary paganism*, London: Hurst & Co.

Held, D. (1980) *An introduction to critical theory: Horkheimer to Habermas*, London: Hutchinson.

Helman, C.G. (2001) *Culture, health and illness*, London: Arnold.

Heron, J. (1998) *Sacred science: Person-centred inquiry into the spiritual and the subtle*, Ross-on-Wye: PCCS Books.

Hodge, S. and Boord, M. (2000) *The illustrated Tibetan book of the dead*, London: Godsfield Press.

Johnston, W. (1978) *The inner eye of love: Mysticism and religion*, London: Collins & Co.

La Fontaine, J. (1995) *The nature and extent of organised and ritual sexual abuse of children*, London: HMSO.

Laming, Lord (2003) *The Victoria Climbié Inquiry*, London: The Stationery Office.

McLellan, D. (1979) *Marxism after Marx*, Basingstoke: Macmillan.

McSherry, W. (2006) *Making sense of spirituality in nursing and health care practice*, London: Jessica Kingsley.

Macionis, J.J. and Plummer, K. (1997) *Sociology: A global introduction*, Upper Saddle River, NJ: Prentice Hall.

Marland, H. (ed) (1993) *The art of midwifery: Early modern midwives in Europe*, London: Routledge.

Marshall, P. (2001) *The philosopher's stone: A quest for the secrets of alchemy*, London: Pan Macmillan.

Marx, K. (1963) *Early writings*, London: Watts.

Moss, B. (2005) *Religion and spirituality*, Lyme Regis: Russell House.

O'Hagan, K. (2001) *Cultural competence in the caring professions*, London: Jessica Kingsley.

Partridge, C. (ed) (2005) *The world's religions*, Oxford: Lion Hudson Plc.

Reason, P. (ed) (1994) *Participation in human inquiry*, London: Sage Publications.

Rees, D. (2001) *Death and bereavement: The psychological, religious and cultural interfaces*, London: Whurr Publishers.

Sarup, M. (1993) *An introductory guide to post-structuralism and postmodernism*, Hemel Hempstead: Harvester Wheatsheaf.

Scott Peck, M. (1990) *People of the lie: The hope for healing human evil*, London: Arrow Books.

Thorne, B. (1998) *Person-centred counselling and Christian spirituality: The secular and the holy*, London: Whurr Publishers.

Vishvapani (2001) *Introducing the friends of the Western Buddhist Order*, Birmingham: Windhorse.

Walter, T. (1997) 'Secularisation', in C.M. Parkes, P. Laungani and B. Young (eds) *Death and bereavement across cultures*, London: Routledge, pp 166–88.

Woodroofe, K. (1961) *From charity to social work in England and the United States*, London: Routledge and Kegan Paul.

NINE

Spirituality and gender viewed through a global lens

Ursula King

Introduction

The contemporary cross–disciplinary interest in spirituality is a phenomenon of global proportions that belies the process of secularisation so normatively believed and proclaimed in the West. Western women's and gender studies have largely operated within a dominant secular framework whose blindness to religion is now increasingly recognised and critiqued. Not only has religion been a contributing factor in the rise of the women's movement, but also a wide range of religious ideas has impacted on feminism/gender thinking and practice, so that a large body of literature on women's spirituality, feminist spirituality, and spirituality and gender has emerged. While comparatively few secular feminist voices explicitly engage with religion and spirituality, there nonetheless exists a strong implicit spiritual dimension within modern feminism (King, 1993a; King and Beattie, 2005). Moreover, several feminist theorists draw on religious ideas from widely different sources; best known for this are French writers like Irigaray, Kristeva, Cixous and Clément (Joy et al, 2002, 2003).

The Pakistani scholar, Durre S. Ahmed (2002), who works in psychology, communications and cultural studies, has created the striking formulation *Gendering the Spirit* for a collection of essays primarily concerned with women and religion in South and South East Asia, but they also reveal some of the commonalities in the globally emerging narratives of women and spirituality. Ahmed convincingly argues that in a globally postmodern world the subject of women and religion 'remains postcoloniality's last frontier' (2002, p 27) which has to be contested and transcended. In the past, women and religion were often colonised through a combination of cultural, religious and sociopolitical forces that used and exploited them for their own particular ends. Differently expressed, one could say that in most previous historical periods women were *defined* and also largely *confined* by religious teachings and institutions. Now, by contrast, women are actively *redefining* religion and spirituality for themselves, in their own voices and categories. Thus with ever greater urgency the challenging question arises as to how women's past situation of unfreedom and dependency, experienced in so many religions, can be replaced by a newly gained autonomy and freedom reached through newly articulated and experienced spiritualities.

The complexities of religion, spirituality and gender

In many discussions on spirituality, including some sociological studies, scant attention is paid to gender. Although gender is a widely contested concept, it has proved most helpful for analytical purposes and has influenced an amazingly large range of disciplines from the social sciences to the humanities, arts and the history of the pure sciences. Gender perspectives arrived later in the study of religions than in most other disciplines. Although the gender concept is by no means used universally, a remarkable paradigm shift has occurred, especially among younger religion scholars, so that gender-critical analyses have globally spawned an impressive range of new research in a relatively short time (Hawthorne, 2005; King, 2004a, 2005a).

These intellectual developments are marked by considerable theoretical sophistication with the result that debates about religion and spirituality have become more complexified and nuanced, but also thoroughly pluralised. Both religion and spirituality are widely ramified concepts with multiple definitions that are vigorously debated among scholars, and their relationship to each other is very controversial. Are religion and spirituality interdependent and closely related, or are they totally independent from one another?

Modernity and postmodernity have led to an increasing privatisation of religion, so that long established religious institutions have lost much of their social and political power held earlier. This is most evident in European societies, but the processes of globalisation now affect the religious attitudes and practices of urban populations all over the world, especially through the powerful influence of global media and communications networks. Thus one can observe at the same time the marginalisation and loss of influence of traditional religious institutions but also a rise in religious fundamentalisms and a remarkable rise in the interest in spirituality. Some of this occurs within or at the margin of traditional religions, but there also exists a growing trend toward alternative spiritualities completely independent from any religious institutions, as is the case with new religious movements studied by many sociologists (Wessinger, 1993; Puttick, 1997), goddess and Wicca spirituality (Christ and Plaskow, 1979; Plaskow and Christ, 1989; Eller, 1993), ecofeminist and ecological spirituality (Adams, 1993; Mies and Shiva, 1993; Barnhill and Gottlieb, 2001; King, 2004b) or even the revival of traditional forms of spirituality, such as Celtic spirituality (Meek, 2000; Bowman, 2002), that cut across different religions or exist quite independently outside them.

Many contemporary spiritualities, even alternative ones, draw on certain traditional religious elements or historical precedents mixed with new secular and global concerns, such as the pressing environmental and ethical issues affecting the whole planet; other forms of spirituality are primarily geared to the discovery and development of the personal self. Most of these are strongly influenced by current psychological thinking and psychotherapeutic practices. It is particularly these forms of spirituality that are now often seen as alternatives to religion, more healing and wholesome than the oppressive hierarchical and dualistic religious institutions that so often seem to represent the shadow side of religion. It therefore comes as no surprise that some vehemently argue for the complete independence of spirituality from religion, and postulate that spirituality must be kept entirely distinct from institutional religion (Ó Murchú, 1998; Tacey, 2004). Some researchers even set up a sharp, dualistic opposition between spirituality and religion. Spirituality is then understood as consisting of those spiritual orientations and practices that are found *outside* religious institutions whereas religion is restricted to what happens in churches, temples, synagogues, mosques and other religious circles (Heelas et al, 2005).

There can be no doubt that the understanding of spirituality has radically changed in the West under the impact of modernity, but it is nonetheless doubtful whether spirituality can be seen as entirely, and permanently, divorced from religion. Historically and structurally, religions still possess a spiritual core and still nurture much spirituality, although the traditional relationship between spirituality and religion may now be inverted and very different from what it was in the past (King, 1996, 2001). Spirituality has come to be seen as more open, inclusive and important than religions as traditionally defined. Religions are undergoing radical processes of reinterpretation and transformation in the contemporary world, but that does not mean that they are completely cut off from spirituality. It is thus unhelpful to separate religion and spirituality too sharply from each other since the two remain interrelated in many different ways. Their relationship is dialectic and dynamic, so that they react and respond to each other in their mutual transformations (van Ness, 1996).

To catch something of the dynamic fluidity of religious and social transformations, Eileen Barker has developed ideal-typical models that relate spirituality to religiosity and secularism rather than religions. These models demonstrate that the characteristics of religiosity and spirituality can partly or wholly overlap, or develop independently from each other (2004, p 28). Barker's approach provides a more multilayered, nuanced orientation towards social and religious dynamics than the sharp separation between spirituality and religion. For many, spirituality is the central essence of religion but, conversely, spirituality can be taken as so all-encompassing that religion, or rather religiosity, becomes a subsection of spirituality.

Numerous definitions of spirituality have been suggested, but given the vast array of meanings attached to this word, it has also been argued that spirituality escapes definition altogether (Tacey, 2004). In the widest sense, spirituality can be linked to all human experiences but has a particularly close connection with the imagination, with human creativity and resourcefulness, with relationships, whether with oneself, others, or a transcendent reality, often called Divine, God or Spirit. It is important that spirituality is not understood in an essentialist manner but is perceived as rooted within a thoroughly historicised and contextualised framework. Thus it makes more sense to speak of *spiritualities* in the plural than of spirituality in the singular. I propose an open-ended, general definition whereby spiritualities quite simply connote those ideas, practices and commitments that nurture, sustain and shape the fabric of human lives, whether as individual people or communities. A wide exploration of spirituality is of considerable interest today, not only to people of religious faith but also to those working in psychotherapy and the human potential movement, to adherents of new religious movements, to supporters of the ecological and peace movement as well as the women's movement.

Many contemporary understandings capture the dynamic, transformative quality of spirituality as lived experience linked to our bodies, nature and our relationships with others and society. At the same time traditional stereotypes still subtly influence people's attitudes when thinking about spirituality. Most pervasive are the customary associations with masculinity and femininity still deeply rooted in Western culture. Masculinity is often perceived as linked to reason, transcendence and divinity, whereas femininity is associated with body, immanence and humanity. Male philosophers and religious thinkers have conceptualised the Sacred, the Absolute, the Spirit, God, or whatever other word is used, mostly as wholly 'Other' – an ultimate Reality or Being that is very different from the world of matter, flesh and human action. In traditional societies women are much more immersed in the latter, in the world of the immediate, the physical and material, not least through physically giving birth to other human beings, and through numerous family and domestic duties. Thus their world is one of immanence rather than transcendence, but it is above all the latter that is closely associated with religion, spirituality and the realm of the Divine. It is not only feminists who now question these lifeless, static dichotomies of classical theism, but some contemporary male theologians and process philosophers also call these binaries much into question in favour of more integral, dynamic and fluid categories that are closer to life and human experience (Eller, 1999; Christ, 2003).

Such traditional, stereotypical gender associations provide some, although not all, explanations of why women were often deemed unable to reach the exalted, transcendent heights of the spirit. This is not only true in Christianity and Judaism, but also in most other religions. The widespread perception of women as inferior to men, characteristic of so many religious teachings, has meant that women were for a long time excluded from the realms of spiritual authority and the spiritual hierarchies of established religious institutions. As Julie Clague has written: 'It has been men who, on the whole, have held positions of authority, and have been described as authorities and have been said to speak with authority. Women, on the whole, have been ruled and have obeyed, have been denied their own voice, and have been denied the opportunity to become authorities in their own right' (1996, p 13). But this is changing fast, not only in the secular, social realm but also in religion and spirituality, where attentive observers and participants get drawn into the remarkable process of 'gendering the spirit' (Ahmed, 2002; King, 2006), so that a great variety of women's spiritualities has emerged.

Varieties of women's/feminist spiritualities

Women's spiritualities express themselves in multiple varieties and contexts in the contemporary world. Depending on location, adherence or non-adherence to a specific religious tradition and level of critical self-reflexivity, preference may be given to speaking about women's spirituality or the women spirit movement rather than feminist spirituality, especially where feminism connotes an exclusive, radical secular stance that is completely opposed to any religious expression or institution. The multiple, complex links and respective interactions between feminism and secularism, and between feminism and religion, vary enormously and 'must be evaluated on a case-by-case basis and with careful attention to historical and cultural content' (Jakobsen and Pellegrini, 1999, p 334). To many, modern feminism and spirituality seem at first to have little in common, especially when understood in a narrow, exclusive way (King, 1993a). When both are approached from a wider, more inclusive perspective, then all sorts of connections are discovered; there can be no doubt that what has been called 'spiritual feminism' – as distinct from social, political or other kinds of feminisms – is now a trend of global diffusion that can be perceived in most religions and cultures.

For analytical purposes three major strands can be distinguished in the contemporary development of women's spiritualities, each covering a wide variety of phenomena. These are the growth of feminist spirituality, goddess spirituality and ecofeminist spirituality. They represent three distinctive, yet closely interrelated, developments linked to a widespread quest for personal, social and planetary transformations. Differently expressed, they search for a new sense of self, a new sense of community, and a new relationship to the whole web of life and all living beings on planet earth.

Feminist spirituality

In its widest sense this term refers to the spiritual quest and creativity of contemporary women, whether pursued in more traditionally religious or non-traditional, secular ways. In a more specific sense it means a new movement arisen out of second-wave feminism and existing outside traditional religious institutions. It articulates the reclaiming by women of the reality and power designated by 'spirit', but it is also a reclaiming of female power, of women's partaking in the Divine, and their right to participate in shaping the realm of spirit by fully participating in religion and culture (Christ and Plaskow, 1979; Spretnak, 1982; King, 1993a).

Feminist spirituality is rooted in women's experience and oriented towards bonding among women. It believes in the inherent goodness of matter, body and the world, thrives on ecological sensitivity, and re-imagines the Divine. It has created new rituals and liturgies, drawn from Wicca and folk traditions celebrating especially life and nature cycles, but it is also based on the imaginative reinterpretation of traditional religious rites and texts. Women's spirituality groups, whether inside or outside specific faith communities, have created new symbols, prayers, songs, feasts and liturgies (Christ and Plaskow, 1979; Plaskow and Christ, 1989; Harris, 1991; Starhawk, 1999 [1979]).

Prominent themes of feminist spirituality are women's discovery of their own self and agency, the experience of networking and sharing, the new awareness of empowerment from within to work collaboratively for personal, social and political changes. Many of these themes are reflected in contemporary women's culture that, through poetry and fiction, songs, music, film, art and theatre, explores different aspects of women's spiritual quest. This includes their experience of loss and pain, oppression and freedom, intimacy and mutuality with others, and the multiple connections between sexuality and spirituality (Zappone, 1991; Nelson and Longfellow, 1994; Raphael, 1996).

Women's spiritual quest and discovery of self is vividly described in the works of contemporary writers such as Margaret Atwood, Doris Lessing, Adrienne Rich and Ntozake Shange. Carol Christ (1980) first mapped the stages of this discovery as a series of steps moving from initiation to awakening, then to insight, transformation and wholeness. Of immense influence among women in the US and elsewhere was Carol Christ and Judith Plaskow's edited collection *Womanspirit Rising: A Feminist Reader in Religion* (1979), followed 10 years later by *Weaving the Visions: New Patterns in Feminist Spirituality* (1989). Equally influential was Charlene Spretnak's *The Politics of Women's Spirituality* (1982), with contributions by many founding mothers of feminist spirituality. These demonstrate beyond doubt that women's search for wholeness and integration requires a radical transformation of traditional patriarchal attitudes to gender, sexuality, work and society. In other words, the profoundly empowering spirituality of women has important political implications for both women's life in society and their participation in religious life. This, in turn, will have a potentially revolutionary impact on the transformation of the whole social fabric, with global implications for women, men and children.

Discussions about the possibility and necessity of a feminine Divine, accompanied by a new re-evaluation of the body and maternal experience, have a central place in feminist thinking and spirituality, leading to wider debates in contemporary philosophical and theological thought (Jantzen, 1998; Anderson and Clack, 2004; Joy, 2006). Among Christian and Jewish feminist theological writers, the greatest effort has gone into re-imagining the Divine by developing more inclusive metaphors for God that are not uniquely male. Central to this is the recognition of the power of the Goddess, and the rediscovery of many very ancient goddess traditions around the world (Baring and Cashford, 1993; Eller, 1993; Christ, 1997).

Goddess spirituality

The most significant feature of contemporary feminist spirituality is probably the (re)discovery and contemporary worship of the goddess in Western societies, described as 'the rebirth of the goddess' (Christ, 1997), best documented for the US (Eller, 1993; Salomonsen, 2002). Because of this rebirth, feminist spirituality is sometimes simply seen as 'goddess spirituality', yet these two spiritualities are not identical, even though they overlap considerably. Some women reject all anthropomorphic approaches that link representations of the Divine to either male or female forms, preferring instead an androgynous or monistic understanding of ultimate reality.

Goddess spirituality draws on traditional and non-traditional religious sources and has produced many new religious rituals and practices. The Great Goddess, manifest in myriad historical and cultural forms, is seen as immanent rather than transcendent, and is strongly connected with body and earth. Thus she can be experienced within oneself, within other human beings, within nature. Systematic reflections on the goddess are now called *thealogy* after Naomi Goldenberg, who first suggested this expression in order to distinguish new feminist approaches from traditional Jewish and Christian *theology,* so much concerned with God-talk in exclusively male terms. Instead, goddess thealogy uses female images and metaphors largely drawn from goddesses of the ancient Mediterranean world (Baring and Cashford, 1993), but less so from goddesses of other cultures and religions, whether African, Asian, Central or South American.

For example, Hinduism is one of the historically richest traditions regarding female perceptions of the Divine; it probably possesses the most vibrant living goddess worship in the contemporary world (Hawley and Wulff, 1996). Yet very few Indian goddesses figure in Western feminist spiritual practice. Moreover, the relationship between female symbolism of the Divine and the real lives of women is very ambivalent. Many religions that worship goddesses do not necessarily empower women's actual lives, as is evident in many countries around the world.

The greatest contribution of *thealogy* probably consists in the reaffirmation of female sacrality by seeing the life-giving powers of women's bodies linked to divine creative activity (Raphael, 1996). This has led to a new 'spiritual feminism' that has contributed to contemporary transformations of religious practice. The (re)discovery of the goddess is also linked to women's reclamation of witchcraft and the practice of Wicca, originally meaning 'wisdom'.

Wicca is a goddess-centred religion that forms part of the wider goddess-worshipping community, but it is not a separate religion. It is organised in covens that can consist of both women and men. Followers of Wicca have created their own rituals, dances and chants, and one of the most influential practitioners and teachers of feminist witchcraft is the North American Starhawk, sometimes described as the high priestess of the modern witchcraft movement. Her ideas have been widely diffused through her writings, workshops and covens, which have created distinct communities, especially the *Reclaiming Collective* in and around San Francisco (Salomonsen, 2002). Starhawk's book *The Spiral Dance* (1999 [1979]) is a classic of feminist spirituality with many invocations, chants, blessings and spells.

Contemporary feminist spirituality is widely influenced by psychological writings about the goddess, primarily based on Jungian thought. Much use is made of Jung's archetypal theory about the feminine and masculine that coexist within every human being (Jung, 1986, 1989). However, Jung's ideas about the harmonious complementarity of the feminine and masculine, of *anima* and *animus* in each human being, often unfortunately reinforce traditional sexual archetypes and gender hierarchies, since even in an androgynous approach to humans and the Divine the male still seems to be given priority over the female.

Ecofeminist spirituality

One of the most exciting developments is the growth of ecofeminist spirituality. Similar to feminist spirituality in many ways, it focuses more explicitly on ecological issues. It also puts a far stronger emphasis on women's connection with the earth and all forms of life. Ecofeminist spirituality grew out of ecofeminism, a word first coined in 1974 to describe a new movement based on the close connection between ecology and feminism. One of the principal ecofeminist insights consists in the belief that the oppressive exploitation of women and nature are closely interrelated, and both are equally destructive to the wholeness of life, the well-being of people and the planet. One can distinguish between political and spiritual ecofeminism (Mies and Shiva, 1993), philosophical reflections on women, culture and nature (Warren, 1997) and multiple approaches to the sacred, including a wide variety of ecofeminist spiritualities (Adams, 1993).

From a critical ecofeminist perspective, there exists a disconnection between humans, the earth and the Divine – a deep split that must be healed. Women can make an essential contribution to this earth healing, for earth and women are linked through their birthing activities, through weaving the fabric of life in continuous renewal, creating a multistranded web of which all are part. This is a very creation–centred spirituality where nature itself is experienced as hierophany, revealing the presence and beauty of spirit. The world is seen as the body of god/dess, or simply as *Gaia* (adopting the name of the Greek earth goddess), and therefore humans must honour and revere the earth (Ruether, 1992, 1996; Rae, 1994; Primavesi, 2000).

Ecofeminism thus has a strong orientation towards the sacred. It seeks the revisioning of traditional religions through the development of new ecofeminist spiritualities, but also draws on alternative religions and spiritualities as well as on the spirituality of the land, found among indigenous and native peoples. Significant themes of ecofeminist spirituality are the connections between the bodies of women and the earth; the alignment with the seasons of nature; the dynamism and energy of life; and the interconnectedness of the web of life. This spirituality aims at an alternative culture that is more peace loving and non-hierarchical, breaking down the boundaries between nature and culture.

Like ecofeminism itself, ecofeminist spirituality is a movement involved in global activism committed to global social and planetary change. These cannot happen without a spiritual change nor without the indispensable, essential contribution of women from all parts of the world. 'Women healing earth' is an integral part of the activism of many women's groups in the so-called third world (Ruether, 1996). However, it is not only in the two thirds of the developing world or the South, but all over the globe that women and their spirituality are necessary to promote sustainable development, ecological integrity and a more just and peaceful world. The widely ramified themes of ecofeminism and ecofeminist spirituality are also dealt with in works on ecofeminist theologies (Grey, 2003; Eaton, 2005). Each of these overlapping areas contains a number of similar elements, while each also offers its own distinctive emphasis and focus.

By now the literature on women's spiritualities, whether feminist, ecofeminist, Wicca, pagan, goddess-oriented or grounded in traditional religious sources, has grown to almost unmanageable proportions. However, from a critical perspective it must be emphasised that in spite of the global diffusion of some of these ideas, the overall focus remains predominantly Western, since the re-reading, deconstruction and re-construction of religious traditions has mainly been undertaken by women from Christian, Jewish or secular backgrounds in Europe or North America. This Western-centred perspective applies also to most feminist theorists. It is therefore important to give space to the generally less well-known processes of radical transformation that at present are also taking place in predominantly non-Western religions such as Hinduism, Buddhism and Islam. Many comparable developments of the critical resifting of traditional religious teachings and practices are taking place without achieving the same publicity and notoriety as Western feminist writing, so that these transformations among women are sometimes described as the occurrence of a silent revolution.

Gender and spirit: global transformations

For women's full participation in all aspects of religion and spirituality it is essential that women are as fully trained and qualified in their intellectual and spiritual attainments as men. This was already recognised at the 1893 Chicago World's Parliament of Religions, the first global interfaith meeting, which had numerous women participants and plenary speakers who stressed the new opportunities for women in religion, but also the need to study the sacred languages and scriptures for themselves (King, 1993b). Since that remarkable event over a century ago, an ever-growing number of highly educated Jewish women rabbis, Christian women ministers, female theologians and religion scholars are playing their part in shaping contemporary religious practice and scholarship in the West.

Similar developments can now be observed in Hinduism, Buddhism, Islam, Sikhism, and other religions in Asia, Africa and elsewhere in the world. Women around the globe are fast acquiring both scholarly and spiritual competences; they are gaining new knowledge, agency, authority and public visibility, sometimes only reluctantly acknowledged or even strongly resisted within their own communities. Contemporary Muslim, Buddhist and Hindu women, and many others who have acquired a critical feminist awareness, often also possess an activist inclination to work for change in their own communities and in wider society. This transformative process can only happen when women gain full access to literacy and education at all levels. With regard to the religious heritage this not only means the ability to read and write, but to understand and interpret religious thought, offer spiritual advice with discernment, authority and wisdom, and to acquire what I call the full *spiritual literacy* of women.

A surprising cross-cultural development is the discovery of the global spiritual heritage of women. So many spiritual 'foremothers', female saints, mystics, women's religious communities and practices are now being discovered that our knowledge about women in world religions has greatly increased in recent years. A comparative historical enquiry provides much evidence, however, that most religions have validated women's lives more in terms of domestic observances and family duties than they have encouraged women's search for religious enlightenment, holiness or liberation. Imprisoned by the daily tasks of *immanence*, by the recurrent demands of immediacy that the maintenance and nurture of personal and community life requires, women have usually been so much equated with immanence that the realms of *transcendence* remained largely out of their reach, even forbidden to their desire (Eller, 1999). Thus one must ask whether women really possessed a spiritual space of their own in the past, and how far they were able to pursue the same spiritual disciplines as men.

In spite of numerous social obstacles and interdictions from families, friends and religious authorities, many women of different religions have struggled throughout history to pursue a spiritual path of their own. The comparative history of nuns in the Indian religions of Jainism and Buddhism (Batchelor, 2005) and of Christian nuns, which still remains to be written, provides ample proof of women following extraordinary paths of spiritual devotion and attainment and exercising wide social influence (King, 2005b). Women often had the greatest difficulties in rejecting their prescribed social roles as wives and mothers by following a path of renunciation and asceticism, and creating their own religious communities. Since their gender always provoked male resistance to female claims to autonomy, independent power and spiritual authority, women's activities remained in most cases constrained and controlled by male religious hierarchies, and this is still predominantly the case today. Nowhere is this struggle more evident than in the richly documented history of Christian nuns and sisters, in whose cloisters and convents appeared countless women scholars, mystics, artists, activists, healers and teachers over many centuries of Western history (McNamara, 1996).

One of the most striking examples of the innovative process of 'gendering the spirit' is *Sakyadhita,* the global women's movement for Buddhist nuns and lay women inaugurated in 1987 in Bodhgaya, India. Its aims include the creation of a global network of communication among Buddhist women; the education of women as teachers of Buddhism; research on Buddhist women; and the full ordination of Buddhist nuns. So far, *Sakyadhita* has organised eight international conferences in different Asian countries. Much effort goes on education and the reinterpretation of texts, but also on reforming unjust, non-egalitarian practices and the development of socially engaged Buddhism, where the issues for Buddhist women in Asia are different from those of Buddhist women in the West (Findly, 2000; Tsomo, 2000, Part II, 'Women in compassionate social action'; Tsomo, 2006).

In most, but not all, Asian countries the number of Buddhist nuns is less than that of monks. In Taiwan, however, there are two thirds more nuns than monks; Korea also possesses a large number of nuns whose experiences, like those of other nuns, have rarely been recorded in Buddhist texts nor have they been much investigated by scholars (Tsomo, 1999, 2000 ; Goonatilake, 2002; Batchelor, 2005; Cheng, 2007; Lindberg Falk, 2007). This is changing now that Buddhist women have organised themselves to study their own history and activities, as can be seen from *Innovative Buddhist women: Swimming against the stream* (Tsomo, 2000). The contemporary controversy over the higher ordination of Buddhist nuns in Theravada (or southern Buddhist) countries illustrates well how women from one major non-Western religious tradition are pressing for spiritual and practical equality.

Among the Mahayana (or northern and eastern Buddhist) countries, the strongest resurgence of Buddhism is found in Taiwan, where over 60% of all ordained Buddhists are women. No other *Bhikkhuni Sangha* is as strong as that of Taiwan. In China, where Buddhism was repressed between 1949 and 1980 by the communist regime, some Buddhist monasteries have been reopened since 1980 (Bianchi, 2000; Batchelor, 2005). So far, however, Buddhist training and ordination have attracted more women than men, in fact more than the government-regulated nunneries can accommodate.

A new ground-breaking empirical study comparing the lives and thoughts of Buddhist nuns in Sri Lanka and Taiwan (Cheng, 2007) reveals the gap between Western feminist discourse on Buddhism and the actual lives of Asian Buddhist women, but also the quite different social, political and historical contexts of Buddhist nuns in Taiwan and Sri Lanka, and the different role that Buddhism plays in these two countries. The rich data document the profound processes of transformation among Buddhist women in hitherto unknown detail, while revealing the regrettable lack of communication between the different branches of Buddhism. The relatively recent foundation of *Sakyadhita* as a global Buddhist women's movement with many cross-tradition connections between the different branches of southern Theravada and northern and eastern Mahayana branches of Buddhism will no doubt help to change this situation. Its president, Karma Lekshe Tsomo, speaks of 300 million Buddhist women in the world (only 1% are Western women) who must work for their social and spiritual liberation. According to her, the meeting of Buddhist and feminist prspectives is fertile ground for innovation and mutual enrichment on many levels (Tsomo, 1999, p 32).

Women's asceticism, based on traditional spiritual practices and the reinterpretation of religious traditions within a modern, postcolonial context, have become a fascinating focus for investigation by women scholars. This is evident from several studies on Hindu women ascetics and gurus (Hallstrom, 1990; Denton, 2004; Khandelwal, 2004). Contemporary women's ashrams, ascetics, gurus and new religious communities provide important examples of women's initiative and spiritual agency in appropriating traditional Hindu religious practices while reinterpreting and transforming them in the context of modernity and postmodernity (Sinclair-Brull, 1997). Indian women possess a wealth of symbolic resources in terms of female religious imagery, mythical narratives and socioreligious practices, and these include several other religions than Hinduism (Jakobsh, 2003). However, the profound ambivalence of this rich heritage is apparent in the contradictory ways in which the same symbols, beliefs and practices are appealed to as sources of legitimation by Hindu women reformers on the one hand, and the Indian secular feminist movement or extreme Hindu fundamentalists on the other. The same goddesses, practices and beliefs can be appealed to as sources of women's agency, empowerment and resistance or, by contrast, they can be politically used to reinforce gender divisions, traditional social roles and malpractices such as sati and dowry abuses (King, 2004c).

Much has been written on Islam and gender, especially by secular feminists, but the complex attitudes held towards the re-reading of classical religious texts and their ambiguities among secular, Muslim and Islamist feminists in different Islamic countries are probably less well known. All groups seem to agree that women's greatest challenge in Islam is their lack of religious expertise and training (van Doorn-Harder, 2005: see her analysis of secular feminism, Muslim feminism and Islamist feminism). An exceptional counter-example is provided by Indonesia, with the largest Muslim population in the world, where thousands of institutions train both women and men as specialists in Islamic knowledge. Women can move into positions of religious authority by becoming scholars of Islam and judges. By re-reading the Qur'an, Indonesian Muslim women leaders are thus 'shaping Islam' (van Doorn-Harder, 2006) and utilising its resources as a significant force for social change.

The impact of gender thinking on women in the Muslim world expresses itself in social, legal and educational developments, but also in the area of spirituality. Depending on the sociohistorical context of different countries and cultures, Muslim women are actively involved to different degrees in reinterpreting Islamic thought and practices, and by claiming more mosque space for themselves. Separate women's mosques continue to exist in communist China now, but have a tradition of 400 years, a fact hardly known even among Muslims (Jaschok, 2000). Muslim women in the US met considerable opposition to a first mixed gender prayer meeting led by a woman in a New York mosque in March 2005. This meeting also announced a 10-point 'Islamic Bill of Rights for women in the mosque', first formulated by the US Muslim feminist and journalist Asra Q. Nomani in her newly published book *Standing Alone in Mecca* (2005). The New York event attracted much media attention around the world (*Japan Times*, 2005), but was denounced by most male Muslim authorities except in Egypt. Progressive Muslim women in different countries feel encouraged by these developments and will no doubt develop further initiatives in the future.

Conclusion

Education and literacy open up new, hitherto unknown pathways for women that produce an empowering spiritual literacy through which, in a movement of critical self-reflexivity, emerges a new dynamic that leads to active transformation and innovation in the fields of religion and spirituality in different societies.

Changes in religious practice include the adoption of gender-inclusive language in religious readings and prayers, and institutional changes which give women access to official religious positions. Women's new opportunities also include taking up many traditional religious choices that were unavailable in the past. In spite of revolutionary changes in global gender consciousness and practices during relatively few decades, it will still require considerable effort and time before the full equality of women and men is achieved in all religions of the globe, or even before women's new spirituality groups are fully accepted in Western secular societies.

For the first time in human history an increasing number of women from different religious and secular backgrounds are articulating their own spiritual experiences, reflections and quests not simply as individuals, but as a social *group* of worldwide outreach. This phenomenon is a genuine *novum* in human history whose transformative impact on religion and spirituality in global society cannot yet be fully assessed with certainty, but opens up promising perspectives for future research.

References

Adams, C.J.(ed) (1993) *Ecofeminism and the sacred*, New York, NY: Continuum.

Ahmed, D.S. (2002) *Gendering the spirit: Women, religion and the post-colonial response*, London and New York, NY: Zed Books.

Anderson, P.S. and Clack, B. (eds) (2004) *Feminist philosophy of religion: Critical readings*, London and New York, NY: Routledge.

Baring, A. and Cashford, J. (1993) *The myth of the goddess: Evolution of an image*, London: Arkana (Penguin Books).

Barker, E. (2004) 'The church without and the god within: religiosity and/or spirituality', in D.M. Jerolimov, S. Zrinscak and I. Borowik (eds) *Religion and patterns of social transformation*, Zagreb: Institute for Social Research, pp 23-47.

Barnhill, D.L. and Gottlieb, R. (eds) (2001) *Deep ecology and world religions: New essays on sacred grounds*, Albany, NY: State University of New York Press.

Batchelor, M. (2005) 'Nuns: Buddhist nuns', in L. Jones (ed) *The encyclopedia of religion* (2nd edn), Detroit, MI and New York, NY: Macmillan Reference USA, Thomson Gale, vol 10, pp 6759-63.

Bianchi, E. (2000) 'Tiexiangsi: a Gelugpa nunnery in contemporary China', in K.L. Tsomo (ed) *Innovative Buddhist women: Swimming against the stream*, Richmond: Curzon Press, pp 130-41.

Bowman, M. (2002) 'Contemporary Celtic spirituality', in J. Pearson (ed) *Belief beyond boundaries: Wicca, Celtic spirituality and the New Age*, Milton Keynes/Aldershot: The Open University/Ashgate, pp 55-102.

Cheng, W.-Y. (2007) *Buddhist nuns in Taiwan and Sri Lanka: A critique of the feminist perspective*, London and New York, NY: Routledge.

Christ, C.P. (1980) *Diving deep and surfacing: Women writers on spiritual quest* (2nd edn 1986), Boston, MA: Beacon Press.

Christ, C.P. (1997) *Rebirth of the goddess: Finding meaning in feminist spirituality*, Reading, MA: Addison-Wesley Publishing Company.

Christ, C.P. (2003) *She who changes: Re-imagining the divine in the world*, New York, NY, and Basingstoke: Palgrave Macmillan.

Christ, C.P. and Plaskow, J. (eds) (1979) *Womanspirit rising: A feminist reader in religion*, San Francisco, CA: Harper & Row (1992 edn: New York, NY: HarperSanFrancisco).

Clague, J. (1996) 'Authority', in L. Isherwood and D. McEwan (eds) *An A to Z of feminist theology*, Sheffield: Sheffield Academic Press, pp 12-14.

Denton, L.T. (2004) *Female ascetics in Hinduism*, Albany, NY: State University of New York Press.

Eaton, H. (2005) *Introducing ecofeminist theologies*, London and New York, NY: T & T Clark International (Continuum).

Eller, C. (1993) *Living in the lap of the goddess: The feminist spirituality movement in America*, Boston, MA: Beacon Press.

Eller, C. (1999) 'Immanence and transcendence', in S. Young (ed) *Encyclopedia of women and world religion*, New York, NY: Macmillan Reference USA, vol 1, pp 465-6.

Findly, E.B. (ed) (2000) *Women's Buddhism, Buddhism's women: Tradition, revision, renewal*, Boston, MA: Wisdom Publications.

Goonatilake, H. (2002) 'The forgotten women of Anuradhapura: "Her story" replaced by "History"', in D.S. Ahmed, *Gendering the spirit*, London and New York, NY: Zed Books, pp 91-102.

Grey, M.C. (2003) *Sacred longings: Ecofeminist theology and globalization*, London: SCM Press.

Hallstrom, L.L. (1990) *Mother of bliss: Anandamayi Ma (1896-1982)*, New York, NY, and Oxford: Oxford University Press.

Harris M. (1991) *Dance of the spirit: The seven steps of women's spirituality*, New York, NY: Bantam Books.

Hawley, J.S. and Wulff, D.M. (eds) (1996) *Devi: Goddesses of India*, Berkeley, CA: University of California Press.

Hawthorne, S. (2005) 'Gender and religion: history of study', in L. Jones (ed) *Encyclopedia of religion* (2nd edn), New York, NY: Macmillan Reference USA, Thomson & Gale, vol 5, pp 3310-18.

Heelas, P. and Woodhead, L. with Seel, B., Tusting, K. and Szerszynski, B. (2004) *The spiritual revolution: Why religion is giving way to spirituality*, Oxford: Blackwell Publishing.

Jakobsen, J.R. and Pellegrini, A. (1999) 'Feminisms', in S. Young (ed) *Encyclopedia of women and world religion*, New York, NY: Macmillan Reference USA, vol 1, pp 334-6.

Jakobsh, D.R. (2003) *Relocating gender in Sikh history: Transformation, meaning and identity*, Delhi: Oxford University Press.

Jantzen, G.M. (1998) *Becoming divine: Towards a feminist philosophy of religion*, Manchester: Manchester University Press.

Japan Times (2005) 'Woman leads US Islamic prayer service – an Islamic Bill of Rights for women in the mosque', 20 March.

Jaschok, M. (2000) *The history of women's mosques in Chinese Islam: A mosque of their own*, Richmond: Curzon Press.

Joy, M. (2006) *Divine love: Luce Irigaray, women, gender and religion*, Manchester: Manchester University Press.

Joy, M., O'Grady, K. and Poxon, J.L. (eds) (2002) *French feminists on religion: A reader*, with a foreword by Catherine Clément, London and New York, NY: Routledge.

Joy, M., O'Grady, K. and Poxon, J.L. (eds) (2003) *Religion in French feminist thought: Critical perspectives*, with an introduction by Luce Irigaray, London and New York, NY: Routledge.

Jung, C.G. (1986) *Aspects of the feminine*, London: Ark Paperbacks (Routledge imprint) (1982 edn: Princeton University Press).

Jung, C.G. (1989) *Aspects of the masculine*, London and Princeton, NJ: Ark Paperbacks (Routledge) and Princeton University Press.

Khandelwal, M. (2004) *Women in ochre robes: Gendering Hindu renunciation*, Albany, NY: State University of New York Press.

King, U. (1993a) *Women and spirituality: Voices of protest and promise* (2nd edn), Basingstoke: Macmillan.

King, U. (1993b) 'Rediscovering women's voices at the World's Parliament of Religions', in E.J. Ziolkowski (ed) *A museum of faiths: Histories and legacies of the 1893 World's Parliament of Religions*. Atlanta, GA: Scholars Press, pp 325-43.

King, U. (1996) 'Spirituality', in J. Hinnells (ed) *A new handbook of living religions*, Oxford: Blackwell, pp 667-81.

King, U. (2001) 'Spirituality, society and the millennium – wasteland, wilderness, or new vision?', in U. King (ed) *Spirituality and society in the new millennium*, Brighton and Portland, OR: Sussex Academic Press, pp 1-18.

King, U. (2004a) 'Religion and gender: embedded patterns, interwoven frameworks', in T.A. Meade and M.E. Wiesner-Hanks (eds) *A companion to gender history*, Malden, MA, and Oxford: Blackwell Publishing, pp 70-85.

King, U. (2004b) 'Feminist and eco-feminist spirituality', in C.H. Partridge (ed) *Encyclopedia of new religions*, Oxford: Lion Publishing, pp 379-84.

King, U. (2004c) 'Hinduism and women: uses and abuses of religious freedom', in T. Lindholm, W.C. Durham, Jr and B. Tahzib-Lie (eds) *Facilitating freedom of religion or belief: A deskbook by the Oslo Coalition on Freedom of Religion or Belief*, Leiden: Martinus Nijhoff Publishers, pp 523-43.

King, U. (2005a) 'Gender and religion: an overview', in L. Jones (ed) *Encyclopedia of religion* (2nd edn), New York, NY: Macmillan Reference USA, Thomson & Gale, vol 5, pp 3296-310.

King, U. (2005b) 'Nuns: an overview', in L. Jones (ed) *Encyclopedia of religion* (2nd edn), New York, NY: Macmillan Reference USA, Thomson & Gale, vol 10, pp 6756-9.

King, U. (2006) '"Gendering the spirit". Reading women's spiritualities with a comparative mirror', *Religion och Existens. Årskrift för Teologiska föreningen i Uppsala*, pp 37-54.

King, U. and Beattie, T. (eds) (2005) *Gender, religion and diversity: Cross-cultural perspectives*, London and New York, NY: Continuum.

Lindberg Falk, M. (2007) *Making fields of merit: Buddhist female ascetics and gendered orders in Thailand*, Copenhagen: Nordic Institute of Asian Studies (NIAS) Press and Washington, DC: University of Washington Press.

McNamara, J.A.K. (1996) *Sisters in arms: Catholic nuns through two millennia*, Cambridge, MA, and London: Harvard University Press.

Meek, D. (2000) *The quest for Celtic Christianity*, Edinburgh: Handsel.

Mies, M. and Shiva, V. (1993) *Ecofeminism*, London and New Jersey, NJ: Zed Books.

Nelson, J.B. and Longfellow, S.P. (eds) (1994) *Sexuality and the sacred: Sources for theological reflection*, Louisville, KY: Westminster/John Knox Press.

Nomani, A.Q. (2005) *Standing alone in Mecca: An American woman's struggle for the soul of Islam*, San Francisco, CA: HarperSanFrancisco.

Ó Murchú, D. (1998) *Reclaiming spirituality: A new spiritual framework for today's world*, New York, NY: Crossroad.

Plaskow, J. and Christ, C.P. (eds) (1989) *Weaving the visions: New patterns in feminist spirituality*, San Francisco, CA: Harper & Row.

Primavesi, A. (2000) *Sacred Gaia: Holistic theology and system science*, London and New York, NY: Routledge.

Puttick, E. (1997) *Women in new religions: In search of community, sexuality and spiritual power*, Basingstoke and New York, NY: Macmillan Press and St Martin's Press.

Rae, E. (1994) *Women, the earth, the divine*, Maryknoll, NY: Orbis Books.

Raphael, M. (1996) *Thealogy and embodiment: The post-patriarchal reconstruction of female sacrality*, Sheffield: Sheffield Academic Press.

Ruether, R.R. (1992) *Gaia and God: An ecofeminist theology of earth healing*, London: SCM Press.

Ruether, R.R. (ed) (1996) *Women healing earth: Third world women on ecology, feminism, and religion*, Maryknoll, NY: Orbis Books.

Salomonsen, J. (2002) *Enchanted feminism: The reclaiming witches of San Francisco*, London and New York, NY: Routledge.

Sinclair-Brull, W. (1997) *Female ascetics, hierarchy and purity in an Indian religious movement*, Richmond: Curzon.

Spretnak, C. (ed) (1982) *The politics of women's spirituality: Essays by the founding mothers of the movement* (1994 edn), New York, NY: Doubleday.

Starhawk (1999 [1979]) *The spiral dance: A rebirth of the ancient religion of the Great Goddess*, San Francisco, CA: Harper.

Tacey, D. (2004) *The spirituality revolution: The emergence of contemporary spirituality*, Hove and New York, NY: Brunner-Routledge.

Tsomo, K.L. (ed) (1999) *Buddhist women across cultures: Realizations*, Albany, NY: State University of New York Press.

Tsomo, K.L. (ed) (2000) *Innovative Buddhist women: Swimming against the stream*, Richmond: Curzon Press.

Tsomo, K.L. (ed) (2006) *Out of the shadows: Socially engaged Buddhist women*, Delhi: Sri Satguru Publications.

van Doorn-Harder, P. (2005) 'Gender and religion: gender and Islam', in L. Jones (ed) *The encyclopedia of religion* (2nd edn), Detroit, MI, and New York, NY: Macmillan Reference USA, Thomson Gale, vol 5, pp 3364-71.

van Doorn-Harder, P. (2006) *Women shaping Islam. Reading the Qur'an in Indonesia*, Urbana and Chicago, IL: University of Illinois Press.

van Ness, P.H. (ed) (1996) *Spirituality and the secular quest*, New York, NY: The Crossroad Publishing Company, vol 22 of *World Spirituality: An encyclopedic history of the religious quest*.

Warren, K.J. (ed) (1997) *Ecofeminism: Women, culture, nature*, Bloomington and Indianapolis, IN: Indiana University Press.

Wessinger, C. (ed) (1993) *Women's leadership in marginal religions outside the mainstream*, Chicago, IL: University of Illinois Press.

Zappone, K. (1991) *The hope for wholeness: A spirituality for reminists*, Mystic, CT: Twenty-Third Publications.

TEN

Reading spiritually: transforming knowledge in a new age

Natassja Smiljanic

> Four thousand volumes of metaphysics will not teach us what the soul is. (Voltaire)

Imagine a scene some time in the not too distant future, the world is in a new era of spiritual consciousness. A legal theorist sits and surveys legal thinking as it has flowed through the latter part of the 20th century through the early 21st. What critiques of law do they find? Feminist, critical legal studies, Marxist critiques, critical race theory, psychoanalytical theory....What do they do with this information? Notice the labels, the boxes, the schools. My question would be, as they sift and review this work, how do they feel about the work of legal theorists? What were legal theorists interested in during this time? During the latter part of this 'era' sexual, social and racial inequality, discrimination and human rights are dominant themes. The desire to change the world – a political motive yes, but is an emotional desire possible to discern? What drove these legal theorists? What emotions – pain, anger, love – or was this desire only in the mind?

What if this legal theorist was then comparing a new paradigm of knowledge in which we were now frequenting? What if there had been a revolution in thinking, maybe subtle, perhaps not? One where thinking, reading as an academic, a student, a teacher, was now more balanced with feeling? What if there were no clinical boxes anymore, no labels, no categories? Does knowledge feel different, does it have a sensation rather than purely a feeling? What would academic life look like in this different state of consciousness? Academics, students able to speak and not be cautious of speaking from the heart as well as the mind, to freely express feeling and personal experience in their work, not having to detach their feelings from their subject matters of research. How does that vision seem? Unsettling? Would academic life be unpredictable, spontaneous, messy, difficult, ecstatic, real? Would we all be running off to psychotherapists to deal with having to cope with emotions or would we be fully embracing and working with knowledge in a different way?

These questions have been presented due to a personal mystery that I have long been trying to work out – why is it that emotions are kept hidden as part of our lives within the university and working with knowledge? In this chapter I attempt to forge out the possibilities of different ways of approaching knowledge as we approach a new era of spiritual awareness, and examine the possibilities of transforming consciousness in our roles as academics, teachers, thinkers.... I am not good with labels but for ease will situate myself as a legal theorist, in the sense that throughout researching and thinking about law my project has been the typical one of a legal theorist, which is not just to look at what the law is (positivism), but the justice of the law and how we can critique it. And whether law can save the world or whether it is part of the problem. Legal theory occupies a place within the social sciences in the sense that law is a social phenomenon. The juncture where it distances itself from other social science disciplines such as criminology or psychology is the absence of examining human behaviour – the root of law's alienation.

Law is surely structured around our experiences, our sufferings as human beings. Law is created to protect, to honour rights and obligations, to punish those who have committed a crime, or so the simple story goes. Despite this, legal education and most legal research are based not on people and their experiences of law, but purely on the study of legal rules. For teachers, researchers and students of law, we focus on learning and regurgitating *what* the law is, with an occasional foray into criticising law and what reforms could be made to the rules or the institutions. For legal theorists, we have seen a development throughout the 20th century where positivism has given way to critiques of law grounded in social theories, such as Marxism and feminism through to psychoanalytical and literary theory. Despite the crisis in legal theory, a never-ending journey of finding new theories to jazz up the tasteless brew of law continues. Yet if we think for one moment perhaps the answers could be found not in the mind but in the soul, we may be able to feel something for legal theory at last.

Academic life, from my perspective, has always been striking for the absence of emotion – the need to stay calm and detached and not to engage in a personal or emotional way with the subject matter, and to be very guarded with colleagues and with students. For me this has always been a very difficult situation, which has an inherently emotional context. Throughout my years of studying and researching law, it was clear that the academic discipline of law, despite the fact that it usually involved real people and suffering, would be presented as clinical and detached, in order for it to be studied and assimilated 'correctly'. Morrison (1995, p 45) describes the situation perfectly:

> ... real life is blood and guts, sex and vomit, hope and depression, oppression and profit – all outside the materials discussed in law schools.

Keeping emotion and the pain of reality out of legal learning was something I did unconsciously as a law student and I did not realise how dissatisfied I was until I discovered critical race theory. I was instantly captured by the theory; intellectually it drew me in as critical race theorists do not work within the clinical tradition of all the other legal theories I had come across. Emotionally, their passion and desire to expose law and change the world was something I was able to feel. It was so different from reading other theorists who were just names on a page and who I could not view as real people. Critical race theorists write about who they are, there is an autobiographical tone to their words on the page. The energy of their emotions enraptured me, I would feel their anger and pain at the state of injustice, and be moved by the desire and practise to change the world. Working with stories, analogies, to imagery, music, I could feel the pain and the joy of what they wished to commune. I felt I had a relationship with their feelings, words, ideas.... It gave me a sanctuary within the standard conditioning of learning legal rules, a place to escape where legal academics wrote about the agony of legal discourse and the hope for change.

Despite the fact that I knew such perspectives would not be popular (most students dislike legal theory for not providing knowledge about what the law 'is'), I took the view that teaching critical race theory was absolutely essential. However, due to its 'emotional context' it would be challenging, as many students are thrown into disarray. Some of those blindfolds created by thinking like a lawyer start to become displaced and it becomes uncomfortable. I always taught law like an outsider, like an alien speaking a truth to a group, many of whom were not sure if they wanted to be taught, and I was uncomfortable about encouraging them to look at something so alive and visceral when the detached general world of law could be so clean and tidy. I always remember footnoting Toni Morrison's *Beloved* in a handout and feeling uncomfortable stating what the novel is about ('it's the story of a slave woman who murders her baby so it does not have to grow up in slavery'), and leaving little opportunity for students to respond. It was a book I struggled to read, such was the impact it had on me, and here I was recommending others to try that experience; I could not reconcile how difficult I found it to discuss the subject openly, hence the footnote.

I have often wondered how others deal with what I perceived to be this necessity in academic life – this absence of emotion, which I read to be the need for impersonality, the denial of the self, having to hide who you really are in order to work with secular presentations of knowledge. Being otherwise feels uncomfortable, not 'right'. This point has been echoed by many critical race theorists, for example Patricia Williams. In discussing her experiences of being criticised for being 'too personal' in her writing for a legal academic audience, Williams looks at the relationship between writing impersonally and empowerment, arguing that in doing so, we may be empowered and work within common values and understandings, but there is a price to pay:

> I suppose there's nothing wrong with that attempt to empower, it generates respect and distance and a certain obeisance to the sleekness of a product that has been skinned of its personalized complication. But in a world of real others, the cost of such exclusive forms of discourse is empowerment at the expense of one's relation to those

others; *empowerment without communion.* (Williams, 1992, p 92; emphasis added)

Williams' work is underpinned by a critique of the law that is seen as limited by its impassiveness to real people's experiences and sufferings under artificial legal constructions. This phenomenon means that legal education and research by its very essence, through instituting value-neutral analysis and detachment, encourages a silencing of the self. Surely, then, this will naturally remove a person from the need to examine themselves and their relationship to their subject of study? This is the norm within which academics work. Writers such as Williams and bel hooks are perturbed by a universal or 'essentialised world-view' (Williams, 1992, p 9), and how that distracts us from promoting and privileging the perspective of the individual and their experiences; this dominant view is a worrisome tendency to disparage anything that is non-transcendent (temporal, historical) or contextual (socially constructed) or non-universal (specific) as 'emotional', 'literary' or just 'not true'. This is particularly emblematic of legal study due to the worry that anything emotional or personal will endanger the objective of seeing something 'fairly' (translated as 'justice' in legal practice) – as the subject matter must be viewed from a detached and clinical perspective in order for the truth to be seen; the point that truth can only be seen from an individual perspective is largely ignored. This is reflected in the personality of academic life where discussing anything emotional is unprofessional and even dangerous – it is not 'real knowledge'. As hooks points out, this is 'not being scholarly enough' (hooks, 1994, p 71). It goes without saying that the institutional patriarchy (for want of a better expression) of university life privileges the male 'rational' view of the world, evaluative as contrasted with feelings, emotions, the classic public/private dichotomy which has been well established by feminist theorists (for example, Pateman, 1998).

The lack of personal engagement with the subject matter within legal theory and critiques of the law has been a phenomenon challenged by critical race theorists. hooks discusses how theory for her is 'most meaningful when it invites readers to engage in critical reflection and to engage in the practice of feminism'. She talks of how 'theory emerges from the concrete', from making 'sense of everyday life experiences…'; this makes feminist transformation all transformation possible (hooks, 1994, p 70). We look at our relationship with knowledge, and how we feel about it. We have a responsibility as academics to change society through our work – to 'be the change you want to be in the world' (Gandhi). Educating students is part of that, but foremost there is a responsibility to be reflective in our own work about who we are and how we feel about our ideas, to feel comfortable about sharing these ideas with colleagues, students and even the structures of power, including the 'gatekeepers of knowledge'.

The problem is that there is little space for this kind of work within universities, and no doubt many would like to be able to be different, the role precludes this. How can we allow for space to change?

I believe that this involves a difficult personal project – that of self-actualisation and even transformation. hooks discusses the importance of teachers as self-actualised. She wrote of her deep disappointment that in her experience as a student this was not found to be the case and how it was something that was out of place within the university. She points out that 'teachers must be actively committed to a process of self actualisation that promotes their well being if they are to teach in a manner that empowers students' (hooks, 1994, p 15). In discussing teachers as healers, acknowledging the discomfort that this may bring, she examines the Buddhist Thich Nhat Nanh's idea of 'teachers as healers' and our responsibility to heal ourselves first. Our 'healing' is intrinsic to our lives as spiritual beings, it informs our path of awareness and means that we can 'read differently'.

I am framing my exploration of reading differently by suggesting a space to work with 'spirituality' within academic discourse. But what do I mean by spirituality? For me, it is an individual experience, not definable, uniquely described – we can all say something about it. Spirituality is about my relationship with myself and involves a connection to a higher power, although that higher or greater power is not outside of myself – it is, but is also within, blended. And what does it mean to work with our spiritual nature as thinkers, readers, academics, researchers or students? It means knowing yourself, and how this manifests is individual. For me, it means working with feelings. I do not think I can truly understand my spiritual nature unless it is connected through feeling, and academic work must be informed by that. Essentially, and very simply, spirituality is working with the self. The project of working with the self involves examining ourselves and redefining our relationship to what we do.

I have found that the mention of the word 'spiritual' generally provokes a defensive reaction in many people, particularly where it is immediately associated with religion. The notion of discussing 'spirituality' on a public level, let alone within our own praxis, is viewed with great discomfort and inappropriateness, and worse than with emotions, the danger of dogma? Grof describes it as 'the S word or spirituality.... It is often hidden, unspoken, but a central quality of life that is often surrounded by more taboos than the more obvious areas of sexuality and money' (Grof, 1993, p 21).

The result of this has been denial of spirituality within our Western society and this is echoed strongly within academia, perhaps due to the fear that anything more personal would adversely affect the production and teaching of knowledge. Therefore, we are not able to express ourselves and our understandings of the deeper meaning of existence and how that informs our work, to share our experiences and allow for students to do the same.

The drive for spiritual knowledge is an innate one; it is difficult to argue against the notion that most people would like to know or understand themselves better. Grof discusses our restless souls searching for a deeper meaning of life: 'this intense and at times painful craving is a deep thirst for our own wholeness and our spiritual identity, our divine Source or God' (1993, p 15). I am sure that if many academics and teachers were asked, they would on reflection say that there is a spiritual dimension to their work, that they are aware of it and quite possibly, for some, for many or even for all, it drives them to continue with their work, to look for wholeness, satisfaction, answers, maybe even love.

Secular, Western notions of experiencing knowledge are centred narrowly on the physical body and what is tangible – this is the basis of the empiricist tradition. The mind is viewed as an instrument to perceive that what can be seen. Eastern spiritual traditions and indigenous perceptions of knowledge see existence very differently. It has only really been in the past decade or so (linked to the vastly growing 'New Age' literature and practice underpinned by a growing awareness of a 'non-religious' spirituality) that greater awareness has developed in the West towards viewing the body and the human experience in a broader way. Eastern spiritual and indigenous traditions work not just with the physical tangible human body – the 'home' of the soul – but view the human as an energy field, a physical body surrounded and intertwined with several layers. These energetic layers are commonly known to us as the aura, or the subtle bodies (that is, not perceptible with the ordinary five senses). On a simple level, the human energy field can be perceived as consisting of emotional, mental and spiritual bodies, which exist alongside the tangible physical body, and all together form our consciousness, our being. Healers who work with complementary systems of healing work with the energy not just in the physical body but with the other bodies, to rebalance, the idea being that all illness has its roots or reflections in a disturbance in the other subtle bodies, and this area must also be worked with in order to bring the person back into balance.

A detailed examination of the human energy field has been represented by Barbara Brennan, a renowned Western healer and writer on this subject, although this 'methodology' is an ancient one, practised by the Ancient Egyptians in their healing temples. It is the system which all 'energy workers' and healers are trained within, West and East (see Brennan, 1987, p 29, for a discussion of how the energy field has been viewed by, for example, Indian and Chinese spiritual traditions, the Kabbalah, Buddhism and Native American Indians to name a few).

Western thinking has difficulties with what cannot be perceived by the immediate ordinary senses, the idea of the human energy field as a 'luminous body that surrounds and interpenetrates the physical body' (Brennan, 1987, p 41). Despite the fact that we all think and feel, in our minds and bodies, those energies are not just situated within the physical body and the brain but also within the subtle bodies – to make us what we are – *physical, emotional, mental and spiritual beings.*

Therefore, our knowledge, personal experiences, the conscious and the subconscious, and to push out the boundaries of knowledge even further, the collective unconscious, past lives and the entire history of human and multidimensional existence, are stored within the human energy field (known as the 'Akashic record' or cosmic consciousness). To quote a favourite philosopher of mine, Yoda, 'luminous beings are we, not this crude matter' (in 'Star Wars 5:

The Empire Strikes Back'). And further, we are all interconnected, linked to each other, and to the ultimate source, God, however defined or experienced.

I am writing about the human energy field to reintroduce the idea underpinning my thoughts here, which is our denied yet overflowing consciousness that needs to break out and make itself known. I visualise our tradition of academic thinking rather like a body, a corpus of knowledge, unlike the Western tradition of privileging the physical body and a neglect of what is 'invisible' – the subtle bodies – to bring in a new era of consciousness where we work with our obvious although neglected gifts of perception and knowing.

To take things further, perhaps it is time that we accepted reading spiritually – to use a metaphor, to 'read shamanically' – to 'shamanise' means to access other states of consciousness, to see the worlds in different ways (indeed to visit other worlds to obtain information, guidance, healing for use in this world – 'ordinary reality'). This metaphor is used here as a way to open up our consciousness so that we do not just read with the mind, but with the heart, the soul, the spirit, to access knowledge not just through what can be perceived physically, but more broadly, using all our senses.

I am not working here with the concept of being a shaman (documented, for example, in the classic works of Eliade, 1989, and Harner, 1980), but as a spiritual practice or tradition, working with the energy of shamanising – opening up our consciousness to its limitless 'end', to feel our emotional and spiritual selves and to use those 'bodies' to help us open up our experiences of how we perceive knowledge. Indigenous knowledge sees beings as physical, emotional, mental and spiritual, and crucially, all knowledge is made up of all of these elements, not just what can be physically perceived but what is felt. On a more personal level we can draw on R.E. Ryan (2002), who, in his striking work, *Shamanism and the psychology of C.G. Jung*, draws clear parallels between the practice of shamanism and the methodology of Jung – human experience as a process of individualisation and self-actualisation, basically the objective of knowing oneself as a spiritual journey. I use the metaphor 'reading shamanically' as a description of being, doing our work differently in the academy – this process involves the realisation of oneself as a spiritual being, that we are not just a mind. When someone reads shamanically they read with their whole being.

Being in this way is a process, a journey, a lifetime's work, something that we are doing both consciously and unconsciously. There is no prescription here and each one of us sets our own path – and the path of awareness is the first step. Can we expand ourselves to feel comfortable with feeling and communicating our larger selves, emotionally and spiritually within the academy? How do we deal with the stigma attached to doing this within a traditional intellectual and impersonal environment?

I can only speak of my experiences here and hope some of this resonates. Looking back over my experiences in university, a deep unhappiness of having to totally hide my real self was always apparent, and this is evident in my writing and research – the danger of expressing myself was too much of a risk and hiding behind the impersonality of legal knowledge seemed to be easier. For some reason I thought I could learn more about myself by researching law, to understand human suffering and pain, not realising that the more I hid within theory the more in denial I became. 'And the day came when the need to remain closed became more painful than the risk to bloom' (Anais Nin). I had to look at this pain and acknowledge who I was and why I did the work that I did: 'The drive to know our true selves elicits a kind of divine discontent within' (Grof, 1993, p 15).

Reading spiritually demands the desire to want to 'know thyself'. We live in times of great spiritual emergency and to function partially is no longer an option. This way of being means that we have to see ourselves not just through the mind and body; we have to deal with our emotions and healing. This can involve very painful, frightening and difficult experiences. As spiritual initiations and journeys unfold, the death of the old self begins and the new enters within. Ryan writes of how deep-set psychological transformation is within our mind source, relaying Jung's notion of 'its archetypal and universal creative and spiritual foundation' (Ryan, 2002, p 113).

The journey is not an easy one; there is pain in thinking about change and reflection, in seeking awareness. There is journeying through the dark night of the soul, uncovering what lies beneath, who we are and dealing with the dark side. It involves the stripping of the self and the death of the ego, 'divest[ing] oneself of the false trappings of the persona ... that acquired identity by which we define ourselves in terms of socially accepted categories of reality and identity, and to begin the process of individuation which has its goal the creation of a psychic centre beyond the ego' (Ryan discussing Jung's observation, 2002, p 115).

Going 'beyond the ego' is quite possibly one of the most difficult challenges to set up for oneself, particularly as we are brought up to situate our identity largely within the ego mirroring an ego-based society, which mainly seeks to keep individuals in fear and disempowerment. Going back to the broader theme of the academy here, I have always felt that universities are sites where development has risen little above that of the ego. I have felt this from the institutional fear of the power plays of politics in departments, the fears (beyond the normal personal ones of rejection) in relation to publishing (especially in journals), the experiences of academics giving papers in conferences where the ego of an audience member envelopes any constructive criticism let alone support of what the speaker may be saying. I learned quite early to depress my surprise and rejection of finding that very few feminist legal theorists whom I met with great enthusiasm were actually interested in talking and sharing their work and ideas with me, preferring to be polite and continue with their work in private. In essence, my ego has limited me in innumerable ways, to put it succinctly now, that as I write there is always a voice at my shoulder that hates each word and tells me I am not good enough – and as I write with shaking hands I keep awareness and tell my mind not to listen, but to ask the heart how it feels. However, once we can start to move beyond the ego, that takes us to our true self, the place of great transformation and creativity.

When we see (and free) ourselves from beyond the mental body, we can view ourselves as vast multidimensional beings – emotional, spiritual, connected to our soul purpose and our source of being. This is a spiritual reading of a theory encapsulated by critical race theorists who have had to understand identity through different levels of consciousness and experience, through race and gender. In identifying critical race theory writers who work with these concepts, Wing (2003) summarises these levels of experiences as concepts such as 'multiple consciousness … holism … interconnectivity and multidimensionality'. Wing uses the concept of 'multiplicative identity' in examining the different identities that women of colour possess, discussing how 'identities must be multiplied together to create a holistic One when analysing the nature of discrimination against them' (Wing, 2003, p 7). This kind of analysis reflects the phenomenon of all of us as multiplicative beings – our gender, race, economic, religious social identities, but as spiritual beings.

There is, in essence, a political call here – for us to work in relationship to our subject matter, to our readers, to our colleagues and students. It may not be comfortable and it will be something that some may not wish to do … ever. But many of us do feel differently and want to create a new way of working, not to be afraid of feeling and communicating a way which may at times be difficult, disruptive, strange even, but which is real.

My call is to encourage an opening up of academic discourses, spaces, relationships, to break out of its controlled consensus reality of thinking and to create with the awareness that we are spiritual beings involved with many things deeper than we have been allowed to express. To fear not the confines of the rigidity of directed thinking but to be creative, fearless, emotional, unstructured – to be emissaries of new ways of thinking, feeling, being – what we are all trying to do already, but realised, actualised and, ultimately, to set ourselves and the world free.

References

Brennan, B. (1987) *Hands of light: A guide to healing through the human energy field*, New York, NY: Bantam Books.

Eliade, M. (1989) *Shamanism: Archaic techniques of ecstasy*, Harmondsworth: Penguin.

Grof, C. (1993) *The thirst for wholeness: Attachment, addiction and the spiritual path*, New York, NY: HarperCollins.

Harner, M. (1980) *The way of the shaman*, New York, NY: HarperCollins.

hooks, b. (1994) *Teaching to transgress: Education as the practice of freedom*, New York, NY: Routledge.

Morrison, W. (1995) *Jurisprudence: From the Greeks to postmodernism*, London: Cavendish.

Pateman, C. (1998) *The sexual contract*, Cambridge: Polity Press.

Ryan, R.E. (2002) *Shamanism and the psychology of C.G. Jung: The great circle*, London: Vega Books.

Williams, P. (1992) *The alchemy of race and rights: Diary of a law professor*, Cambridge, MA: Harvard University Press.

Wing, A.K. (2003) *Critical race feminism: A reader*, New York, NY: New York University Press.

'Star Wars 5 – The Empire Strikes Back' (1980).

Part 3
Reflections on social science research methodologies

For many researchers engaged in social science research involving dimensions of religion and spirituality, the range of methodologies available to them in a Western context are often inadequate for, or unable to allow, the respectful analysis of data that include aspects of the religious or the spiritual. Researchers who wish to pursue such analyses have been forced to reflect critically on the ways in which social scientific tools of analysis have been constructed to marginalise religion and spirituality. For instance, Leslie J. Francis's contribution to this Part (Chapter Eleven) explores how quantitative social science research has downplayed the importance of self-assigned religious affiliation in favour of the more independently verifiable category of 'religious practice'. Francis's work demonstrates that the neglect of self-assigned religious affiliation in social science research has reduced the understandings of subtle and nuanced differences and similarities within and between religious groups. His contribution emphasises the importance of exploring individuals' expressions and experiences of faith within quantitative studies as these provide a richer portrait of social contexts.

In their important contribution to this Part, Miguel Farias and Elisabeth Hense (Chapter Twelve) agree with Francis's position that social science methodologies have largely ignored the importance of religion and spirituality, but they also argue that social science research has not paid due attention to the distinctions between 'religion' and 'spirituality'.

The third chapter in this Part explores how specific religious traditions (in this instance, Islam) can offer crucial tools for the analysis of the life experiences of adherents. Muzammil Quraishi, in Chapter Thirteen, provides a number of important examples that demonstrate that social science methodologies across a number of disciplines are able to elicit richer data when faith perspectives are embedded in the research frameworks and procedures. For Quraishi, the hegemonic urge to expunge religious identity from the research relationship is impossible to fulfil and, furthermore, is unhelpful in understanding the importance of religion and spirituality in particular social contexts.

While Quraishi draws on his own religious identities to reflect on his engagements with social science research, Maree Gruppetta, in Chapter Fourteen, argues that those involved in researching religious identities must be cognisant of individualised interpretations of religiosity so as not to cause offence.

All contributions in this Part argue that mainstream social science methodologies should heed the call from critical researchers to widen the lens of analysis to include religion and spirituality.

ELEVEN

Self-assigned religious affiliation: a study among adolescents in England and Wales

Leslie J. Francis

Introduction

Religious affiliation is both the most readily available and least understood indicator of religiosity within the social scientific literature. It is readily available because religious affiliation is regarded as an aspect of personal and social identity (like sex, age and ethnicity), properly included within public enquiries like the national Census. In this sense, 'religious affiliation' is regarded as belonging to the public and social domain, in marked contrast to 'religious beliefs' and 'religious practices' which are generally regarded as belonging to the private and personal domain, properly protected from public scrutiny. It is poorly understood because both conceptually and empirically religious affiliation seems to function quite differently from the ways in which other indicators of religiosity (like beliefs and practices) function. As a consequence, religious affiliation acts as a relatively poor predictor of other religious indicators.

The debate about the usefulness of religious affiliation as an indicator in social research was brought into particular prominence in England and Wales in the six-year period prior to the 2001 national Census, when the introduction of a religious affiliation question within the Census was seriously debated for the first time (Francis, 2003; Weller, 2004). The major argument against accepting religious affiliation as a useful variable in the Census in England and Wales was based on a failure to understand affiliation as a serious social indicator in its own right, but to see it only as a poor predictor of other religious dimensions. Similar debates have occurred in other countries such as New Zealand (Statistics New Zealand, 1998).

For a question on religious affiliation to be included as a valid social indicator in the national Census, affiliation needed to be understood in its own right and not merely as a poor approximation for other dimensions of religion. An important and powerful attempt to rehabilitate self-assigned religious affiliation as a theoretically coherent and socially significant indicator has been advanced by Fane (1999), drawing on Bouma's (1992, p 110) sociological theory of religious identification, according to which religious affiliation is defined as a 'useful social category giving some indication of the cultural background and general orientating values of a person'. Bouma (1992) then posits a process through which cultural background and general orientating values are acquired and which consists of meaning systems and plausibility structures. He describes meaning systems as 'a set or collection of answers to questions about the meaning and purpose of life' (Bouma, 1992, p 106), and plausibility structures (borrowed from Berger, 1967, 1971) as 'social arrangements which serve to inculcate, celebrate, perpetuate and apply a meaning system' (Bouma, 1992, p 107). He maintains that people possess meaning systems from which they derive their existential purpose. Although self-assigned religious identity might also imply commitment to a plausibility structure (practice) and adherence to its relating meaning system (belief), Bouma (1992) suggests that it might be equally, perhaps more, significant in terms of the exposure to the particular cultural background that it represents. Crucially, this alternative conceptualisation avoids the difficult terrain of religious affiliation as proxy for practice and belief by recognising that even non-churchgoers and non-believers 'may still show the effect of the meaning system and plausibility structure with which they identify' (Bouma, 1992, p 108).

The value of Bouma's (1992) sociological theory of religious identification is that it allows self-assigned religious affiliation to be perceived, and thus analysed, as a key component of social identity, in a way similar to age, gender, class location, political persuasion, nationality and ethnic group (Zavalloni, 1975). Religious affiliation informs our attitudes and, in turn, our modes of behaviour by contributing to our self-definition, both of who we are, but equally importantly, of who we are not. This type of analysis is especially advantageous when interpreting Census data, because it is inclusive of all those who claim a religious affiliation, not only of the minority who also attend a house of worship.

Alongside Bouma's (1992) theory of religious identification, Fane also draws on Bibby's (1985, 1987) theory of 'encasement' developed from his empirical surveys in Canada. Bibby argues that Canadian Christians are 'encased' within the Christian tradition. In other words, this tradition has a strong influential hold over both its active and latent members from which affiliates find it extremely difficult to extricate themselves. Contrary to the claims of secularisation theorists that low levels of church attendance are indicative of the erosion of religion's social significance (Wallis and Bruce, 1992), Bibby (1985, 1987) would argue that this trend is actually a manifestation of the re-packaging of religion in the context of late 20th-century consumer-orientated society. Consumers are free to select 'fragments' of faith, and they are encouraged to do this by the way in which the churches have simulated the marketing strategies of the wider society.

The central point made by Bibby's (1985, 1987) analysis is that the potential for religion (in this case Christianity) to be a socially significant attitudinal and behavioural determinant has not necessarily disappeared. If anything, the Christian 'casing' may have been strengthened, because the accommodationist stance adopted by the Christian churches has, according to Bibby (1985, 1987), reduced the need for affiliates to look elsewhere. The flaw in the question eventually introduced to the

2001 Census in England and Wales was that religious affiliation was conceptualised only in terms of the major faith traditions (Christian, Buddhist, Hindu, Muslim, Jewish, Sikh). The government at Westminster remained unconvinced that any further relevant information would be generated by subdividing the Christian category into the component denominations. The aim of the present study is to expose the flaw in this position, specifically in respect of the world-view of young people. Building on Fane's development of Bibby's encasement theory, the thesis of the present chapter is twofold. Stage one of the argument tests the extent to which information about affiliation with faith groups predicts significant individual differences in the world-views of young people living and growing up in England and Wales. Stage two of the argument tests the extent to which additional information subdividing the Christian category into denominational affiliation is also significant in understanding individual differences in the world-views of these young people.

In spite of the potential importance of religious affiliation in shaping the world-views of young people living in the contemporary multicultural and multifaith society of England and Wales, relatively little research has been published in this area. One major study has recently been published by Smith (2007) comparing the attitudes of Christian, Hindu, Muslim and Sikh young people living in Walsall with the attitudes of their non-affiliated peers. For example, Smith found that, overall, young people affiliated to a faith group adopted a significantly more positive attitude towards law and order in comparison with their non-affiliated peers, although there were significant variations from one faith group to another. While 39% of non-affiliated young people rated the police as doing a good job, the proportions rose to 50% among Muslims and 52% among Christians, but stood at 39% among Hindus and fell to 33% among Sikhs. Like the Census data, Smith's study did not differentiate between Christian denominations.

A couple of studies by Francis (2001a, 2001b), however, have provided some relatively recent evidence that Christian denomination may be far from irrelevant in predicting individual differences in the world-views of adolescents living in England and Wales. These two studies profiled differences according to the categorisation of four Christian groups: Anglican, Catholic, Protestants, and the smaller and stricter sects that emphasise their discontinuity from contemporary society. For example, drawing on a sample of 29,124 13- to 15-year-old pupils, Francis (2001a) gave particular attention to ways in which affiliation to these four Christian groups predicted individual differences in moral values. Interesting patterns emerged. Thus, 44% of young people affiliated to Christian sects maintained that it is wrong to become drunk, compared with 26% of Protestants, 19% of Anglicans and 18% of Catholics; 65% of young people affiliated to Christian sects maintained that abortion is wrong and so did 50% of Catholics, compared with 38% of Protestants and 31% of Anglicans.

Against this background the aim of the present study is to build on the initial findings presented by Francis (2001a, 2001b), delineating a fuller profile of the adolescent world-view and distinguishing both between major faith groups and between individual Christian denominations (rather than groups of denominations). These new analyses draw on the Religion and Values Today database (see Francis, 2001c), which provides a reliable and representative sample of nearly 34,000 Year 9 and Year 10 pupils (13- to 15-year-olds) across England and Wales. In view of space restrictions, the analyses will concentrate on female pupils only, obviating the need to take sex differences into account.

Method

Sample

A sample of 33,982 Year 9 and Year 10 pupils participated in the project from schools throughout England and Wales, including a proper mix of urban and rural schools, and independent and state-maintained schools. Pupils were assured of confidentiality and anonymity. Although all pupils were given the choice not to participate, very few decided not to take part in the survey.

Instrument

In addition to a number of background questions, the questionnaire included 128 well-focused and easily understood statements, to which the pupils responded on a five-point Likert-type scale (Likert, 1932): 'Agree strongly', 'Agree', 'Not certain', 'Disagree' and 'Disagree strongly'. Although presented in a thoroughly randomised fashion, the items were designed to profile the adolescent world-view through 15 themes.

Analysis

In order to clarify the analysis, this study is based on the responses of 16,581 female pupils. Religious affiliation was assessed by the question 'Do you belong to a church or other religious group?' followed by a list beginning with 'No', identifying the major Christian denominations and the major world faiths, and ending with 'Other (please specify)'. Responses to this question then allowed five main 'faith' groups to be identified, namely those who self-identified as: No religious affiliation (7,132), Christian (8,650), Muslim (257), Sikh (136) and Hindu (92). The numbers of self-identified Jews (42) and Buddhists (18) were too low to allow stable analyses. Within the Christian category, there were seven sufficiently well-represented groups to sustain independent analysis by denomination, namely those who self-identified as: Anglican (4,996), Baptist (438), Jehovah's Witnesses (91), Methodist (480), Pentecostal (102), Presbyterian (119) and Roman Catholic (1,698). A number of other established Christian denominations were represented by insufficient pupils to sustain independent analysis.

From the large quantity of information within the database the relationship between self-assigned religious affiliation and the adolescent world-view was tested by selecting items from six themes: personal well-being, worries, school, social concern, sex and morality, and substance use. In the following tables responses are presented in the following order: No religious affiliation (None), Christian, Muslim, Sikh and Hindu; No religious affiliation (None), Anglicans (Ang), Roman Catholics (RC), Methodists (Meth), Baptists (Bapt), Pentecostals (Pent), Presbyterians (Pres) and Jehovah's Witnesses (JW). Multiple chi-square tests have been employed to test the statistical significance of the difference between the endorsement of the non-affiliates and the endorsement of each faith group or each denominational group in turn. Endorsement has been calculated as the sum of the 'Agree strongly' and 'Agree' responses compared with the sum of the ''Disagree strongly', 'Disagree' and 'Not certain' responses on the five-point Likert scale. In view of the complexity of the data, statistical significance tests have not been employed to compare the responses of the seven denominational groups. In interpreting the levels of probability, it needs to be recognised that statistical significance is highly dependent on the sample size and that in the present study, there is a wide discrepancy between the strength of the different groups, from the two extremes of 4,996 Anglicans to 91 Jehovah's Witnesses.

Results and discussion

Tables 11.1 and 11.2 present the item endorsement for the five faith groups and for the eight Christian denominational groups of young females in respect of four aspects of personal and social life (personal well-being, worries, school and social concern). Two items have been selected to illustrate each of these four areas.

In terms of personal well-being, affiliation with a faith group is significantly associated with an enhanced sense of purpose in life among Christians, Muslims and Sikhs, but not among Hindus. At the same time, there are significant variations among the Christian denominations, with Pentecostals and Jehovah's Witnesses recording higher purpose-in-life scores than the other denominational groups. In terms of negative well-being, affiliation with a Christian denomination (any denomination) is significantly associated with a lower level of suicidal ideation, but this significant difference is not the case among other faith groups.

In terms of personal worries, fear about being bullied at school casts a shadow over the lives of far too many young people. Being affiliated to a faith group (any faith group) increases the likelihood of such anxiety. While 29% of non-affiliates were worried about being bullied at school, the proportions rose to 32% among Christians, 39% among Muslims, 39% among Hindus and 45% among Sikhs.

Anxiety about getting AIDS varies significantly from one faith group to another, with significantly lower levels of anxiety being expressed by Muslims and by Sikhs. There are also highly significant differences from one Christian denomination to another, with much lower levels of anxiety regarding AIDS among the more conservative denominations (Pentecostals and Jehovah's Witnesses). Such variations may well reflect the influence of different teachings regarding sexual relationships.

Table 11.1: Views on personal and social life by faith group (%)

	None	Christian	Muslim	Sikh	Hindu
Personal well-being					
I feel my life has a sense of purpose	50	60***	63***	52	64*
I have sometimes considered taking my own life	32	28***	34	36	23
Worries					
I am worried about getting AIDS	63	62	53***	56	49**
I am worried about being bullied at school	29	32***	39**	45***	39*
School					
School is boring	37	30***	24***	33	26*
Teachers do a good job	40	49***	58***	50*	50
Social concern					
I am concerned about the risk of pollution to the environment	63	70***	57*	58	71
I am concerned about the poverty of the third world	60	72***	57	62	79***

Note: * = *p*<0.05; ** = *p*<0.01; *** = *p*<0.001

In terms of attitude towards school, affiliation with a faith group (any faith group) is associated with a more positive approach. While 40% of non-affiliates regarded teachers as doing a good job, the proportions rose to 49% among Christians, 50% among Sikhs, 50% among Hindus and 58% among Muslims. While 37% of non-affiliates dismissed school as boring, the proportions fell to 30% among Christians, 26% among Hindus and 24% among Muslims, although remained at 33% among Sikhs.

In terms of social concerns, affiliations with all the Christian denominations were associated with greater concern about the risk of pollution to the environment, but Muslims and Sikhs tended to show less concern than the non-affiliated. Affiliations with all the Christian denominations were associated with greater concern about the poverty of the third world. Muslims and Sikhs displayed the same level of concern about the poverty of the third world as the non-affiliates, but a higher level of concern was displayed by Hindus.

Tables 11.3 and 11.4 present the item endorsement for the five faith groups and for the eight denominational groups of young females in respect of views on sexual morality and substances. Four items have been selected to illustrate each of these two areas.

Table 11.2: Views on personal and social life by Christian denomination (%)

	None	Angl	RC	Meth	Bapt	Pent	Pres	JW
Personal well-being								
I feel my life has a sense of purpose	50	58***	63***	64***	65***	75***	59	73***
I have sometimes considered taking my own life	32	28***	29*	27*	28	28	17***	24
Worries								
I am worried about getting AIDS	63	64	64	54***	59	41***	62	33***
I am worried about being bullied at school	29	32**	33***	32	36**	29	32*	28
School								
School is boring	37	28***	35	26***	28***	30	33	32
Teachers do a good job	40	48***	48***	55***	53***	60***	55***	56**
Social concern								
I am concerned about the risk of pollution to the environment	63	71***	67**	78***	72***	71	83***	80**
I am concerned about the poverty of the third world	60	71***	77***	73***	75**	75**	79***	74**

Note: * = *p*<0.05; ** = *p*<0.01; *** = *p*<0.001

In respect of views on sexual morality, some very clear delineations take place between the different faith groups. While 9% of non-affiliates believed that it is wrong to have sexual intercourse outside marriage, the proportions rose to 15% among Christians, 17% among Muslims, 33% among Sikhs and 35% among Hindus. A somewhat different pattern emerged in respect of homosexuality: 42% of Muslims believed homosexuality to be wrong, compared with 21% of Hindus, 21% of Christians, 20% of non-affiliates and 18% of Sikhs. Young Muslims also took a distinctively more conservative view on abortion and divorce. Thus, 58% of Muslims maintained that abortion is wrong, compared with 43% of Sikhs, 40% of Christians, 38% of non-affiliates and 34% of Hindus. Similarly, 39% of Muslims took the view that divorce is wrong, compared with 24% of Sikhs, 21% of Hindus, 16% of Christians and 13% of non-affiliates.

Table 11.3: Views on sex and substances by faith group (%)

	None	Christian	Muslim	Sikh	Hindu
Sex					
It is wrong to have sexual intercourse outside marriage	9	15***	17***	33***	35***
Homosexuality is wrong	20	21*	42***	18	21
Abortion is wrong	38	40**	58***	43	34
Divorce is wrong	13	16***	39***	24***	21*
Substances					
It is wrong to smoke cigarettes	35	39***	54***	44*	47*
It is wrong to become drunk	15	20***	69***	30***	29***
It is wrong to use marijuana	49	56***	38***	38*	54
It is wrong to use heroin	74	78***	67*	64**	78

Note: * = $p<0.05$; ** = $p<0.01$; *** = $p<0.001$

Table 11.4: Views on sex and substances by Christian denomination (%)

	None	Ang	RC	Meth	Bapt	Pent	Pres	JW
Sex								
It is wrong to have sexual intercourse outside marriage	9	12***	14***	16***	23***	54***	12	70***
Homosexuality is wrong	20	19	20	21	27***	59***	18	81***
Abortion is wrong	38	34***	53***	37	45**	68***	36	82***
Divorce is wrong	13	14*	19***	7**	24***	40***	11	61***
Substances								
It is wrong to smoke cigarettes	35	40***	35	47***	43***	54***	52***	78***
It is wrong to become drunk	15	18***	17	24***	29***	47***	32***	59***
It is wrong to use marijuana	49	58***	52*	59***	54*	69***	69***	76***
It is wrong to use heroin	74	79***	77*	82***	75	89***	87**	87**

Note: * = $p<0.05$; ** = $p<0.01$; *** = $p<0.001$

In respect of views on sexual morality, some very clear delineations also take place along denominational lines. Anglicans, Presbyterians, Roman Catholics and Methodists are slightly more conservative in their approach to sexual intercourse outside marriage than young people who claim no religious affiliation. While 9% of the non-affiliates believed that it is wrong to have sexual intercourse outside marriage, the proportions rose to 12% among Anglicans, 12% among Presbyterians, 14% among Roman Catholics and 16% among Methodists. The proportions rose further to 23% among Baptists, 54% among Pentecostals and 70% among Jehovah's Witnesses. Similar contours are followed in respect of attitude towards homosexuality. The view that homosexuality is wrong was taken by 20% of non-affiliates, 18% of Presbyterians, 19% of Anglicans, 20% of Roman Catholics and 21% of Methodists. The proportions rose, however, to 27% among Baptists, 59% among Pentecostals and 81% among Jehovah's Witnesses. A somewhat different pattern emerges in respect of attitude towards abortion in light of the clear stance of the Roman Catholic church on this issue. The view that abortion is wrong was taken by 38% of non-affiliates, 34% of Anglicans, 36% of Presbyterians and 37% of Methodists. The proportions rose, however, to 45% among Baptists, 53% among Roman Catholics, 68% among Pentecostals and 82% among Jehovah's Witnesses. The view that divorce is wrong was taken by 13% of non-affiliates, and rose to 14% among Anglicans, 17% among Methodists, 19% among Roman Catholics and 24% among Baptists. The proportions then rose more steeply to 40% among Pentecostals and 61% among Jehovah's Witnesses.

In respect of views on substances, some very clear delineations take place between the different faith groups. While 35% of non-affiliates believed that it is wrong to smoke cigarettes, the proportions rose to 39% among Christians, 44% among Sikhs, 47% among Hindus and 54% among Muslims. While 15% of non-affiliates believed that it is wrong to become drunk, the proportions rose to 20% among Christians, 29% among Hindus, 30% among Sikhs and 69% among Muslims.

In respect of views on substances, once again some very clear delineations also take place along denominational lines. A more liberal position was generally taken by Roman Catholics, and a more conservative position was generally taken by Jehovah's Witnesses. In terms of tobacco use, 35% of non-affiliates believed that it is wrong to smoke cigarettes, and so did 35% of Roman Catholics. Then, in ascending order, this view was taken by 40% of Anglicans, 43% of Baptists, 47% of Methodists, 52% of Presbyterians, 54% of Pentecostals and 78% of Jehovah's Witnesses. In terms of alcohol use, 15% of non-affiliates believed that it is wrong to become drunk. The proportion rose marginally to 17% among Roman Catholics and 18% among Anglicans. The proportion rose further to 24% among Methodists, 29% among Baptists, 32% among Presbyterians, 47% among Pentecostals and 59% among Jehovah's Witnesses.

Conclusion

Drawing on a large dataset of 16,581 female secondary school pupils, between the ages of 13 and 15 years, the present chapter set out to test two hypotheses: that young people who self-identify with a faith group (Christian, Muslim, Sikh, Hindu) differ in significant ways in terms of their world-view from young people who self-identify with no religious group; and that within the Christian tradition the nature of this difference varies greatly from one denomination to another. Both hypotheses have been supported by the data. Two main conclusions follow from these findings.

First, the considerable variations between the world-views of young people who self-identify with a faith group and the world-views of young people who identify with no faith group provide clear support for the view that self-assigned religious affiliation is of social significance within England and Wales. The 2001 Census was clearly wise to have included the religious affiliation question. In terms of a range of socially significant aspects of the young person's world-view, Muslims, Sikhs and Hindus clearly project distinctive profiles. Among all the faith groups, young Muslims display the most positive attitude towards school and a high sense of purpose in life. Young Muslims are the most likely to reject abortion, homosexuality and divorce. They are also the most likely to reject alcohol and tobacco. Affiliates to all the faith groups appear more vulnerable than non-affiliates to bullying at school, and young Sikhs emerge as the most vulnerable of all.

Second, the considerable variations between the different Christian denominations clearly highlight the inadequacy of the religious operationalisations included in the national Census for England and Wales in 2001. In terms of a range of socially significant aspects of the young person's world-view, knowledge about denominational affiliation is of considerably greater use than the broad-brush grouping of all Christian denominations together.

Considering the seven denominational groups together, there is broad evidence that, compared with young females whose families hold no religious affiliation, those who claim Christian affiliation (in whatever form) tend to enjoy a greater sense of purpose in life and are less likely to entertain suicidal ideation. They are likely to hold a more positive attitude towards school, and espouse a higher level of social commitment. They are more likely to take a conservative stance on issues concerning sexual morality and the use and abuse of substances. Behind this global summary, however, there are considerable variations from one denomination to another. Each denomination will be reviewed in turn to highlight distinctive features.

On many issues young Anglicans stand closer to the non-affiliates than young people belonging to other denominations. Nonetheless, there are clear distances between the young Anglicans and the young non-affiliates. Anglicans are likely to take a slightly more conservative view on sex outside marriage, on getting drunk and on smoking cigarettes.

In many ways young Methodists stand quite close to the young Anglicans. On the other hand, young Methodists take a more conservative stand than young Anglicans on alcohol and on tobacco, positions consistent with the historic roots of Methodism. Young Methodists also display greater concern than young Anglicans for environmental issues, a position consistent with current national programmes in the Methodist church in the UK.

Young Presbyterians stand a little further away from the non-affiliates than either Anglicans or Methodists. They take a somewhat more conservative view on substances, but not on sexual morality. They show a higher level of social concern, but not a higher sense of purpose in life.

Compared with the three mainline reformed denominations (Anglicans, Methodists and Presbyterians), the young Catholics project a distinctive profile. In terms of the use of alcohol and tobacco, young Catholics take a more permissive view than young Anglicans, Methodists and Presbyterians. In terms of sexual morality, young Catholics are much more likely than Anglicans, Methodists and Presbyterians to reject abortion. In terms of social concerns, young Catholics show more concern than young Anglicans and Methodists for world development issues, but less concern for environmental issues.

Young Baptists seem to occupy a position midway between the mainline reformed denominations (Anglicans, Methodists and Presbyterians) and the more sectarian groups (Pentecostals and Jehovah's Witnesses). Compared with the mainline reformed denominations, young Baptists are more inclined to take a conservative view on areas of sexual morality (sex outside marriage, homosexuality, abortion and divorce) and on the use and abuse of alcohol.

Young Pentecostals appear to be inhabiting a very different world-view from that adopted by Anglicans, Methodists, Presbyterians and Catholics. Young Pentecostals are much more likely to take a conservative view on areas of sexual morality (sex outside marriage, homosexuality, abortion and divorce) and on the use and abuse of substances (tobacco, alcohol, marijuana and heroin). They benefit from a much higher sense of purpose in life and are significantly less likely to be worried about getting AIDS, since their lifestyle seems to protect them from the transmission of such diseases.

Like young Pentecostals, young Jehovah's Witnesses inhabit a highly distinctive world-view. Their world-view is highly committed to moral absolutes. The vast majority also reject sex outside marriage, homosexuality, abortion and divorce. The vast majority also reject tobacco and alcohol as well as other substances.

For young Jehovah's Witnesses there seems comparatively little fear from AIDS. The findings generated by the present study provide important new data that support the overall contention advanced by Fane (1999), drawing on ideas formulated by Bibby (1985, 1987) and Bouma (1992). Fane (1999, p 122) summarised her conclusion as follows:

> Self-assigned religious affiliation may also be useful as a predictor of social attitudes and behaviours, particularly when sub-divided by denomination.... In analyses of census data, it may prove helpful to conceptualise self-assigned religious affiliation as a component of social identity, rather than as an inadequate indicator of religious practice and belief.

In terms of this chapter, this conclusion is consistent with the view that for adolescents self-assigned religious affiliation conveys really important information about the context in which their family life is nurturing their world-view, with or without additional information about their religious beliefs and their religious practices. In light of studies of this nature social science research would be wise to include religious affiliation as a routinely collected demographic variable.

References

Berger, P. (1967) *The sacred canopy: Elements of a sociology of religion*, New York, NY: Doubleday.

Berger, P. (1971) *A rumour of angels: Modern society and the rediscovery of the supernatural*, Harmondsworth: Penguin Books.

Bibby, R.W. (1985) 'Religious encasement in Canada: an argument for Protestant and Catholic entrenchment', *Social Compass*, vol 16, pp 287–303.

Bibby, R.W. (1987) *Fragmented gods: The poverty and potential of religion in Canada*, Toronto: Irwin Publishing.

Bouma, G.D. (1992) *Religion: Meaning, transcendence and community in Australia*, Melbourne: Longman Cheshire.

Fane, R.S. (1999) 'Is self-assigned religious affiliation socially significant?', in L.J. Francis (ed) *Sociology, theology and the curriculum*, London: Cassell, pp 113–24.

Francis, L.J. (2001a) 'Religion and values: a quantitative perspective', in L.J. Francis, J. Astley and M. Robbins (eds) *The fourth R for the third millennium: Education in religion and values for the global future*, Dublin: Lindisfarne Books, pp 47–78.

Francis, L.J. (2001b) 'The social significance of religious affiliation among adolescents in England and Wales', in H.-G. Ziebertz (ed) *Religious individualisation and Christian religious semantics*, Münster: Lit Verlag, pp 115–38.

Francis, L.J. (2001c) *The values debate: A voice from the pupils*, London: Woburn Press.

Francis, L.J. (2003) 'Religion and social capital: the flaw in the 2001 Census in England and Wales', in P. Avis (ed) *Public faith: The state of religious belief and practice in Britain*, London: SPCK, pp 45–64.

Likert, R. (1932) 'A technique for the measurement of attitudes', *Archives of Psychology*, vol 140, pp 1–55.

Smith, A.G.C. (2007) *Growing up in multi-faith Britain: Explorations in youth, ethnicity and religion*, Cardiff: University of Wales Press.

Statistics New Zealand (1998) *2001 Census of population and dwellings: Preliminary views on content*, Wellington: Statistics New Zealand.

Wallis, R. and Bruce, S. (1992) 'Secularization: the orthodox model', in S. Bruce (ed) *Religion and modernization: Sociologists and historians debate the secularization thesis*, Oxford: Clarendon Press, pp 8-30.

Weller, P. (2004) 'Identity, politics, and the future(s) of religion in the UK: the case of the religious question in the 2001 decennial census', *Journal of Contemporary Religion*, vol 19, pp 3-21.

Zavalloni, M. (1975) 'Social identity and the recording of reality: its relevance for cross-cultural psychology', *International Journal of Psychology*, vol 10, pp 197-217.

TWELVE

Concepts and misconceptions in the scientific study of spirituality

Miguel Farias and Elisabeth Hense

We all seem to be in favour of spirituality these days.
But what are we in favour of? (Chatterjee, 1989, p xvii)

Introduction

In one of her last public interventions at a British Academy symposium on neo-evolutionary views of religion, anthropologist Mary Douglas argued that modern Man was not mentally more complex than 2,000 years ago; he was simply more confused. This thought is well illustrated by the recent history of the term 'spirituality', which is now widely used in an astonishing variety of ways and almost invariably with a positive connotation, although very few people seem to know what they are referring to. Central to the matter is a construction of spirituality as a universal feature of human experience addressing a feeling of a transcendent force or presence, which need not be framed within any particular theological or belief system but can instead rely solely on the individual's experience.

Many academics have embraced the popular understanding of spirituality as distinct from the religious, notwithstanding the very flaky historical grounds on which to base this differentiation. We can think of several reasons why the idea of spirituality has become socially agreeable and detached from that of religion. These include a sense of distrust and disenchantment with institutions, a search for meaning that appeals to our modern 'homeless' minds and sensitivities (Berger et al, 1974), and an awareness of commonalities in the different human cultures, expressed in terms like 'global consciousness' (Chatterjee, 1989). Spirituality is seen as addressing something deep and private within each one of us but which is also envisioned to be potentially shared by the whole humankind beyond racial, national and cultural distinctions.

However, the term elicits ambiguity, subjectivity and is read in a variety of ways within academia. The first part of the chapter discusses the major ways in which spirituality is constructed by academics. After this we move on to discuss the empirical attempts to assess spirituality as a universal experience. Our analysis of the literature, with a special focus on psychological studies, sheds a very different light on our understanding of spirituality. We suggest that the most statistically reliable measures of spirituality to date are simply assessing a human capacity to experience non-ordinary states of consciousness, a capacity which largely overlaps with partly inheritable personality traits of schizotypy or psychoticism. While not ascribing any pathological meaning to this argument, we suggest that a natural tendency to experience unusual perceptions and ideas should not be considered valuable as such and need not be regarded as a significant common attribute of humanity.

Spirituality concepts

The enigmatic phenomenon of spirituality, first studied in the humanities, has increasingly attracted the attention of social scientists. The different disciplines approach spirituality in a variety of ways, and each has focused on different aspects of the phenomenon. As a result, each line of research has developed its own concept of spirituality. In the following section, we will briefly describe and examine three important concepts in use today.

Universal categories and historical manifestations

Contemporary spirituality research generally distinguishes between (1) spirituality as a universal category and (2) the many specific manifestations of spirituality (see Baier, 2006).

Spirituality as a universal category refers to an experience believed to be common to all human beings, one that lies at the core of the person. In the view of Ewert Cousins, editor of the *World spirituality* series, spirituality encompasses everything that is connected with this shared human experience: 'This spiritual core is the deepest centre of the person. It is here that the person is open to the transcendent dimension: it is here that the person experiences ultimate reality' (Cousins, 1986, p xiii). This understanding of spirituality is mainly intuitive and relies on an emphasis on one's inner experience of the transcendent, rather than an analytical attempt to describe what its characteristics are.

One other view stresses *spirituality as a social and culturally constructed form*. Only by looking at different spiritual traditions, such as Buddhist, Jewish, Christian, Islamic or even non-religious, can we attempt to describe the core experience of a particular tradition. For example, the union with the divine bridegroom (for example, Bernard de Clairvaux and John of the Cross) is a central experience in Christianity; by way of contrast, in the Buddhist tradition, *Śūnyatū* (emptiness) is a focal experience in the Mahāyāna and Zen schools. Under this pluralistic perspective, one can also consider forms of spirituality that are located outside of the established religious spiritualities, such as esoteric and New Age groups (Bochinger, 1995; Hanegraaf, 1996; van Ness, 1996; Faivre, 2000; von Stuckrad, 2004; Heelas et al, 2005). The essays contained in the aforementioned reference work on *World spirituality* provide an overview of the archaic and great spiritual traditions of all continents, including extinct spiritualities like those of the

Egyptians, Sumerians, Greeks and Romans, and finally the esoteric and secular movements. Since the scholars who contributed to this work studied these many spiritualities from very different perspectives, Ewert Cousins decided not to offer a definition of spirituality, for the 'term "spirituality", or an equivalent, is not found in a number of the traditions' (Cousins, 1986, pp xii–xiii), thereby emphasising a subjective and pluralistic view. This explains the inclusion of nihilistic and atheistic movements in this encyclopaedia, alongside religious traditions.

Spirituality as ethnocategory and social-scientific construct

From a sociological point of view, exemplified in the work of Hubert Knoblauch, spirituality may be approached as an ethnocategory, that is, a category that is used by the subjects of sociological analysis to describe themselves (Knoblauch, 2006). Based on the semantic field associated with the ethnocategory, social scientists may then develop a construct, or an empirically grounded theoretical understanding of spirituality.

Spirituality as *ethnocategory* serves to define the field of study: the actors who apply this category to themselves. According to Knoblauch (2006), these are mainly people who consider themselves part of the 'neo-religious scene'. This refers to experientially oriented Christian movements such as Pentecostals and Charismatics, or to the alternative spirituality movement, which has also been referred to as New Age, esotericism, cultic milieu or invisible religion.

Spirituality as a *construct* that builds on the interpretations of the actors, but incorporates them into a scientific frame of reference, compares the phenomenon of spirituality with other phenomena in the social world. The result of this comparison, in Knoblauch's (2006) understanding, is a communitised form (*Vergemeinschaftung*) of religion that is concerned with an inner experience or experience of transcendence articulated in terms of its contrast with or distance from the major organisational forms of religion. The content of these experiences resists rational communication or intersubjective corroboration. Spiritualities, writes Knoblauch (2006), are profoundly subjective: they lack an institutional and dogmatic core and lead to a generalisation of charismas or spiritual gifts. The view upheld by most social scientists studying spirituality as a construct is that whereas religions are, above all, systems of knowledge, spiritualities must be considered first and foremost systems of experience.

Knoblauch's (2006) framing of spirituality ensures that new spiritual movements inside or outside the established traditions are taken into account. However, his notion of spirituality as either an ethnocategory or a construct could be considered too broad as it allows spirituality to be defined as anything that is characterised as such by the subjects of the phenomenon. At the same time, this notion of spirituality is also too narrow, as it ignores the long history of spirituality that exists – albeit with a different semantic connotation – within the established religions. These classic spiritualities of the established religious traditions, which demand self-critical rationality and intersubjective verifiability of their practitioners, do not fit into this construct. We will further examine other limitations of this view of spirituality as a subjective and experiential phenomenon below, providing examples from empirical measurements of spirituality.

Theological definitions and theologies of spirituality

Theological discussions of spirituality are concerned with defining spirituality and defining theologies of spirituality. Definitions of spirituality generally encompass both the material object (what is being studied) and the formal object (the point of view from which it is being studied). One of the most influential definitions currently in academic use is surely that of Sandra Schneiders (1998). She describes the material object as 'the experience of conscious involvement in the project of life-integration through self-transcendence towards the ultimate value one perceives' (Schneiders, 1998, p 42). The formal object, on the other hand, refers to the various methodological approaches that should ideally be used in a combined interdisciplinary manner.

The diverse religious or world-view traditions produce different datasets – aesthetic, kinematic, material, social and literary – that are relevant to spirituality studies. Taking Christianity as an example, Schneiders (1998) argues that the theology of spirituality is characteristically hermeneutical in its effort to interpret the experience it studies and make it understandable, without violating its historical reality. In this hermeneutic approach, exegesis and history can be seen as constitutive disciplines, as both are concerned with basic symbols, the religious matrix and the 'meta-story into which each individual and communal Christian story is integrated and by which it is patterned' (Schneiders, 1998, p 43).

What we have described above regarding the theology of Christian spirituality can be applied, *mutatis mutandi*, to other theologies of spirituality. This broad, anthropologically and interreligiously oriented definition of spirituality and a theology specific to a particular spiritual tradition corresponds to the general view that spirituality is a phenomenon common to all human beings, but that it is expressed and interpreted within a variety of hermeneutic horizons. The question of whether spiritual experiences that take place within the context of different religious traditions are comparable poses a special problem. Although contemporary interreligious research does consist of extensive interreligious negotiation, it is not clear to what extent basic symbols, meta-narratives or underlying patterns of spirituality are truly translatable, or whether ultimately they have to be simply presented in juxtaposition.

Measuring spirituality: limitations and misconceptions

After this brief description of three major conceptual perspectives on spirituality, we will now focus on the problems arising from the social scientific study of the concept, with special attention to the construction of measures of spirituality. Thus, we will attempt to provide an answer to the question: what are social scientists *really* measuring when they construct and use a scale to assess spirituality?

As reviewed above, spirituality can be understood both as a universal category of human experience and as culturally idiosyncratic attempts at creating meaning. This entanglement is central in the scientific assessment of spirituality, where diverse conceptual understandings have been employed (see Cook, 2004). The somewhat ambiguous and indiscriminate use of the term 'spirituality' has been criticised in both religious and non- or anti-religious quarters. For example, the education officer of the British Humanist Association has found the term 'superfluous', 'sentimental' and 'muddy', arguing for its exclusion from the education system (Mason, 2000). Traditional religious sources (for example, the Roman Catholic church) have issued similar criticisms, being particularly concerned about the attempt to empty religion of its existential and spiritual depth.

In popular modern usage religiousness is seen to concern doctrine and the institutional, ritual aspects of a tradition, while spirituality concerns a personal experience of the sacred or transcendent. The religious individualism which gave rise to this division is also reflected in the social sciences, primarily via William James' (1902/1929) highly influential work which focused on religion as a personal emotional experience, but neglected the social and institutional aspects of religious experience. We do not take this division for granted, and we are not alone in this. This split has been addressed as an unfortunate anti–institutional bias (Pargament, 1997), and it does not stand up to close scrutiny: people searching for individual religion or spirituality are influenced and supported by literature, groups and practices which are socially embedded and adapted or inspired from historical religious sources. Furthermore, empirical research on the religion–spirituality division has shown that there is in fact a major overlap between the two (Zinnbauer et al, 1997). Nonetheless, it is this popular understanding, which tends to treat spirituality as a universal – even if personal and subjective – category of human experience, that is used in most empirical studies. Thus, although there is no consensus about what spirituality consists in, there is a tendency to see spirituality as a common core of experiences related to the transcendent. This tendency is particularly prominent in psychology, a discipline with a tradition of studying religious experience (James, 1902/1929) and of discriminating between the extrinsic (institutional) and intrinsic (personal) aspects of religion (Allport, 1951). In what follows, we will first criticise the assumption of a common core experience or the universality of spirituality as a scientific construct. We will then propose an alternative explanation of what the various measures of spirituality tap into.

The heterogeneity and non-universality of spirituality: empirical findings

One of the first empirical studies of how spirituality was understood reported a large overlap in the use of the terms 'religious' and 'spiritual' (Zinnbauer et al, 1997): 74% of participants across several religious and New Age groups (*n*=343) rated themselves both as religious and spiritual, and only 19% considered themselves to be spiritual but not religious. Similar results were subsequently reported by Marler and Hadaway (2002). Zinnbauer and colleagues (1997) accordingly argued for keeping the study of spirituality *within* a broad understanding of religion.

Zinnbauer et al (1997) also found that Roman Catholic participants tended to rate themselves as moderately religious and spiritual, while people from the New Age group thought of themselves as highly spiritual but not very religious. Similar findings have been reported in other studies contrasting New Age and Roman Catholic participants (for example, Farias, 2004). These findings suggest that separating the spiritual from the religious is not common practice, and that traditionally religious people find aspects of spiritual fulfilment in their faith.

Before the above-mentioned studies were conducted, some ground-breaking research *unsuccessfully* attempted to construe spirituality as a universal value type. Schwartz (1992) hypothesised that spirituality would emerge as one of a set of universal value types that also included benevolence, universalism, power, tradition, conformity, hedonism, security, self-direction, stimulation and achievement. He saw spirituality as a motivation towards finding meaning and inner harmony through the transcendence of everyday reality and defined it primarily as having a spiritual life, inner harmony, meaning in life and detachment. He also considered unity with nature, accepting one's portion in life, and being devout. Schwartz (1992) used a large cross-cultural sample, consisting mainly of students and school teachers, that included both atheists and adherents of eight religious groups from 20 countries. In this study, a value type was considered universal if it emerged in at least 70% of the samples, in statistical smallest space analysis. Spirituality was the sole hypothesised value type that failed to reach this criterion: a distinct statistical region for spirituality only emerged for 8 of the 40 samples.

In line with these results, Schwartz (1992) argued that although there is a human need to find meaning and transcendence in life, this need may find expression through other value types rather than through spirituality as such. Supporting this argument, the values 'detachment' and 'accepting my portion in life' appeared in the statistical region of the tradition value types. Likewise, the values 'a spiritual life', 'meaning in life', 'unity with nature' and 'inner harmony' tended to lie within the statistical regions of the benevolence and universalism value types. Schwartz (1992) also argued that there may be a number of distinct types of spirituality, each one with its own subset of values.

In the studies just reported, the attempts to empirically establish spirituality as a homogeneous and universal construct have clearly failed. They show that it is dubious to distinguish religion from spirituality, and that spirituality cannot be universally defined as a set of particular values or motivations, in the same way that other value types can. However, despite lacking a consensual definition of spirituality, there are a number of studies which have assessed either a particular kind of spirituality (for example, New Age) or a more abstract type in relation to psychological characteristics. These studies allow us to look at the ways in which people who score high on spirituality scales may be psychologically different from those scoring lower. We suggest that it is the psychological differences observed in relation to spirituality that will afford us a better understanding of what spirituality scales in fact measure.

Individual differences in spirituality

Are some people innately more spiritually gifted than others? Religious traditions generally accept this may be the case, while offering such divergent explanations for the origin of these individual differences as accumulated experience in previous lives or God's grace. There are many accounts according to which such spiritual giftedness is not present from birth but arises at a certain point in adult life – the lives of the Christian saints, rich in accounts of deep conversion, display this pattern, and the New Age milieu represents an interesting modern example. Many of the New Age's ideas have become culturally mainstream from belief in reincarnation as a positive experience of learning to an understanding of spirituality as a personal inner experience different from institutionalised religion. People interested in the New Age favour an active search for experiences in which everyday senses of self and reality are transformed, and thus tend to employ a great variety of techniques and practices (for example, hypnotherapy, hyperventilation, visualisation) to trigger these experiences.

Recent psychological research on New Age spirituality has found its practices and beliefs to be significantly associated with a particular set of cognitive and personality factors that include magical thinking, cognitive loose associations (for example, seeing patterns in a random display of dots), schizotypy and thin boundaries (Farias et al, 2005). Farias and colleagues (2005) suggest that people drawn to New Age spirituality are psychologically prone to having unusual ideational and perceptual experiences, such as paranormal occurrences and altered states of consciousness, and to be emotionally hypersensitive. They also suggest that the New Age offers these individuals a way of explaining and expanding their experiences. Interestingly, traditional religiosity was found not to be associated with these cognitive and personality factors.

Research on New Age spirituality has also uncovered differential patterns in parental attachment when comparing people adhering to the New Age to individuals involved in traditional Christianity. Using standardised questionnaires and interviews with New Age participants in Sweden, this research has shown New Age spirituality to be particularly associated with an insecure pattern of parental attachment, where people find their childhood relationship to one or both parents to lack emotional care and support (Granqvist and Hagekull, 2001; Granqvist et al, 2007).

The research reviewed above suggests that some forms of spirituality, such as the New Age, are associated with cognitive, personality and early environmental factors which may dispose the person to be particularly interested in certain spiritual ideas and practices (see also Farias and Granqvist, 2007). On the other hand, these factors are not associated with religion. A purely descriptive examination of the type of unusual ideational and perceptual experiences reported by New Age adherents has led some researchers to see in them genuine expressions of self-transcendence achieved by the practice of certain techniques (for example, Rose, 1996). The psychological research, however, suggests otherwise. The type of 'spiritual' experiences reported is more likely to be the result of cognitive, personality and early environmental factors that dispose individuals with such characteristics to perceive events in an unusual way, or to attribute particular significance to them. This means that the reported experiences are not the result of a spiritual transformation willed by the individual, but more likely the outcome of psychological features with deep biological and early environmental roots, of which one is usually unaware and over which one can exert little influence. However, our focus in this chapter is not on a particular type of spirituality, even if it is something as broad as the New Age, but on what we could call mainstream or unaffiliated spirituality. Can we observe similar individual differences as those found for New Age individuals when looking at mainstream spirituality?

The answer is yes. Although the evidence is still patchy, it is nonetheless revealing. A behavioural-genetic study conducted in Australia, with a large sample of monozygotic (identical) and dizygotic (fraternal) Australian twins over 50 years of age (n=3,116), is particularly interesting in this respect (Kirk et al, 1999). This study employed measures of personality, psychological well-being, physical health and religiosity, as well as a spiritual self-transcendence scale that was taken from a larger temperament and character inventory (Cloninger et al, 1993). The 15 items of the self-transcendence scale asked about strong spiritual/emotional experiences or an unusual sense of connection (for example, "I often feel a strong spiritual or emotional connection with all the people around me"). No significant association between spirituality and health status was found, but there were small significant associations between spirituality and optimism, extraversion, fatigue, anxiety and depression for both sexes. There was also a small significant association between spirituality and neuroticism for men and between spirituality and psychoticism for women. Interestingly, church attendance emerged as the strongest correlate of spirituality (r=0.41 for men and r=0.30 for women), showing an overlap between spirituality and religiosity, as in other studies mentioned above. However, when contrasting the results found between monozygotic and dizygotic twins, the outcomes were very different for genetic and environmental influences on spirituality and religiosity. The genetic factor for spirituality was estimated to be approximately 41% in women and 37% in men, while the shared environment factor contributed very little (only about 8%). In contrast, shared and unique environmental factors played a much larger role in determining church attendance (about 50%), while genetic factors were non-significant.

The results of this study indicate that: (1) there is a significant inheritable biological disposition to spirituality (as measured by the particular scale employed in this research), which is stronger for women than for men; (2) the frequency of spiritual experiences is little influenced by social-cultural learning; (3) being a religious churchgoer is mostly determined by what you learn from your family and social environment; and (4) spirituality is associated with different personality traits for men (neuroticism) and women (psychoticism). In a nutshell, these results suggest that there are highly significant individual differences (including gender) in the occurrence of spirituality, which are partly biologically driven, and associated with particular personality traits. This is just one study, which has not been replicated so far, and it is likely to raise suspicion among religious scholars, including social scientists. However, setting aside the genetic and personality component of the study for the moment, the main results have been observed before: women are more interested in spirituality than men (see Heelas and Woodhead, 2004), including New Age practices and beliefs (Farias et al, 2005); and religious affiliation and practice are known to be primarily influenced by family and educational background (see Hood et al, 1996). If the results regarding the genetic basis of spirituality are more difficult for us to accept, we have to ask ourselves what prevents us from doing so – whether scientific or ideological considerations. In what follows, we would like to further substantiate the biological thesis of spirituality, by addressing the nature of the scales being used to measure this construct, and how they are related to personality and cognitive dispositions.

What do spirituality scales measure?

There is little doubt about what the majority of spirituality scales are looking at. One needs only notice the description of items which generally portray experiences of *feeling* connected with the sacred or the world, *experiencing* altered states of consciousness or unusual perceptions – very much what Maslow (1964) called peak experiences. The measures also assess paranormal experiences such as clairvoyance (for example, "I seem to have a sixth sense that sometimes allows me to know what is going to happen") and telepathy. There is indeed evidence that belief in the paranormal is an aspect of spirituality and that the type of experiences described by New Age spirituality overlap with unaffiliated contemporary spirituality (Nasel and Haynes, 2005). Thus, the universal and innate aspect that spirituality scales are tapping into, we suggest, is a particular capacity to enter altered or non-ordinary states of mind and to be highly susceptible to interpreting physiological and environmental cues in an unusual way.

As described above, spirituality has been found to be associated with personality traits, particularly with schizotypy or psychoticism. People with such personality characteristics tend to report more unusual ideas and perceptions (including magical and paranormal) than others (see Claridge, 1997, 2001). In recent years, our knowledge of the cognitive and neural underpinnings of schizotypy has grown immensely. There have been studies reporting positive correlations between this personality trait and left temporal lobe dysfunction (Mohr et al, 2001), a loosening or disinhibition of semantic network functioning (Pizzagalli et al, 2001), and an overactivation of the right hemisphere (Pizzagalli et al, 2000). These correlations – which are not an indication of pathology but of a distinct cognitive and neural functioning – are evidence of what may underlie experiences of unusual ideas and perceptions, like those described in spirituality scales.

Psychologists have sometimes used more neutral expressions, such as transliminality, to describe individual differences in the extent to which ideas and affects are able to cross the threshold of conscious awareness. Transliminality is associated with reports of paranormal and spiritual experiences and better dream recall (Thalbourne and Delin, 1999). Other recent studies have shown spirituality scales to be correlated with personality and cognitive dispositions that fall under the general cluster of schizotypy. One study ($n=169$) has shown that a measure of spirituality which accounts for three different dimensions, including connectedness, universality and prayer fulfilment (Piedmont, 1999), was significantly correlated with a scale of delusional beliefs, while traditional religiousness was not (Rawlings et al, submitted). Another study ($n=217$) has shown that spirituality was significantly associated with suggestibility and absorption, magical thinking and experiences, and thin boundaries (including reports of paranormal experiences; see Farias et al, 2006). Both studies found a relationship between personality traits associated with reports of unusual experiences and spirituality, but no association between these personality factors and religiosity. We have already addressed our scepticism in separating religion from spirituality. The fact that the cited studies empirically differentiate between them only lends more weight to our argument: religion not only addresses the experience of non-ordinary states of mind which are reported in all traditions, but also includes daily worship, social service and communal relationships. Spirituality, on the other hand, is constructed as an individual and abstract experience that is emptied of its social-historical grounding.

In summary we believe that spirituality scales are measuring a susceptibility to experiencing unusual perceptions and ideas or non-ordinary states of mind – a susceptibility which varies considerably according to biological and early environmental influences, and that is addressed in the psychological literature in connection with personality traits like schizotypy or psychoticism. It is unlikely that these scales would be able to differentiate a holy or saintly figure, often described in various religious traditions as attaining 'elevated' states of mind, from a highly imaginative character prone to experience unusual states of consciousness.

Conclusion

Although, to our knowledge, no one had yet sought to provide a connection between empirical research on spirituality and the capacity to experience non-ordinary states of mind, this association had been made before at a conceptual level. In her work on spirituality concepts, Chatterjee (1989) notices the disembodied and individualistic character of our idea of spirituality and how it is often described in association with the occurrence of unusual experiences. She goes on to comment: 'That some people are able to attain unusual states of consciousness tells us something about human capacities, but is there any merit in such attainment per se? I have yet to be convinced that there is' (Chatterjee, 1986, p 101). It is well known that, from the viewpoint of some religious traditions, taking unusual experiences at face value can be misleading. The questioning and testing of such experiences is necessary and so-called spiritual experiences are not to be taken as absolute. The critical attitude displayed by John of the Cross (2000) is a good example:

> And I am appalled at what happens in these days – namely, when some soul with the very smallest experience of meditation, if it be conscious of certain locutions of this kind in some state of recollection, at once christens them all as coming from God, and assumes this is the case, saying: "God said to me…"; "God answered me…"; whereas it is not so at all, but, as we have said, it is for the most part they who are saying these things to themselves. (II, 29, 4)

In this chapter, we have argued that scientific constructs and measurements of spirituality should also not be taken uncritically. Conceptual and empirical attempts to define spirituality as a universal experience seem to be tapping into a natural capacity to experience unusual states of mind that varies across individuals, but are not necessarily addressing an 'elevated', deep or meaningful core of humanity. Our analysis has been generally based on psychological grounds, but this can be tackled at a sociological and cultural level as well. The erosion of religious traditions, with its elaborate systems of spiritual guidance and discernment, are being replaced with a vague sense of 'something out there', and an appetite to experiment with techniques that change our everyday sense of self. Underlying this is the social-historical context that praises the individual self and experience (Lukes, 1973), rather than collectively held goals. Within this social setting, it is not altogether surprising that a concept of spirituality that focuses on subjective individual experiences – while rejecting the historical and conceptual body of religious traditions – can flourish. The rise of our modern understanding of spirituality, as a collection of unusual experiences, manifests an impoverishment of the richness and density of the ways in which the spiritual life has been portrayed by the various religious traditions. Luckmann (1990) has spoken of this impoverishment in relation to the 'radically shrunken span of transcendence' (p 135) in modern religious consciousness. He suggests that in opposition to the great 'other-worldly' transcendences of religious traditions, with its focus on salvation and the after-life, today these are being replaced by small or minimal transcendences that speak to us of 'self-realisation', 'personal autonomy' and 'self-expression'. These are individual efforts that can hardly reach beyond oneself and lead towards solidarity, a sense of shared identity and community and the building of a meaningful structure that describes the nature and ways of approaching the transcendent.

We have spoken critically of the attempts to study spirituality. But can we think of ways of engaging in a study of religion and spirituality that is both conceptually grounded and empirically rigorous? We suggest two possible venues.

Firstly, empirical research should draw on a specific understanding of spirituality in the different traditions and not on vague generalisations or abstractions of putatively essential or common elements (see Hense, 2006). This is not to say that there are no commonalities between the experiences described in the various traditions, for we are bound to find similar emotive and cognitive expressions, as well as overlap between physiological and neural processes in diverse spiritual systems and phenomena (see d'Aquili and Newberg, 1999). However, if we are interested in scientifically understanding how an interest in spiritual ideas and practices makes a difference, our studies will profit from having clear groups of adherents, with a set of beliefs and practices that we can control for. Secondly, we urge the need for a systematic and wide-ranging phenomenological analysis of spirituality which includes not just non-ordinary states of mind but addresses changes in belief, affect, behaviours, as well as the universe of social relations which are intertwined in this process (for example, the religious community, a spiritual director, a fellow believer). Religious or spiritual experiences do not happen in a vacuum, and trying to strip out the inner subjective element from the whole may lead us further away from that which we are seeking to study, while giving us the illusion that we are nearing it.

Acknowledgements

We are grateful to Anna and David Newheiser for their careful reading of, and helpful comments on, a previous draft of this typescript.

References

Allport, G. (1951) *The individual and his religion: A psychological interpretation*, London: Constable and Company Ltd.

Baier, K. (2006) 'Spiritualitätsforschung heute', in K. Baier (ed) *Spiritualität. Zugänge, Traditionen, interreligiöse Prozesse, Handbuch Spiritualität*, Darmstadt: Wissenschaftliche Buchgesellschaft, pp 11–45.

Berger, P., Berger, B. and Kellner, H. (1974) *The homeless mind. Modernization and consciousness*, New York, NY: Vintage Books.

Bochinger, C. (1995) *New age und moderne Religion. Religionswissenschaftliche Analysen*, Gütersloh: Chr Kaiser.

Chatterjee, M. (1989) *The concept of spirituality*, New Delhi: Allied Publishers Private Limited.

Claridge, G. (ed) (1997) *Schizotypy: Implications for illness and health*, Oxford: Oxford University Press.

Claridge, G. (2001) 'Spiritual experience: healthy psychoticism?', in I. Clarke (ed) *Psychosis and spirituality: Exploring the new frontier*, London and Philadelphia, PA: Whurr Publishers, pp 90–106.

Cloninger, C., Svrakic, D. and Pryzbeck, T. (1993) 'A psychobiological model of temperament and character', *Archives of General Psychiatry*, vol 50, pp 975–90.

Cook, C. (2004) 'Addiction and spirituality', *Addiction*, vol 99, pp 539–51.

Cousins, E. (1986) 'Preface to the series', in M. McGinn and L. Meyendorf (eds) *Christian spirituality*, vol I, London: The Crossroad Publishing Company, pp xi-xiv.

Cross, J. of the (2000) *Ascent of Mount Carmel* (translated by William Whiston), Grand Rapids, MI: Christian Classics Ethereal Library Publisher.

d'Aquili, E. and Newberg, A. (1999) *The mystical mind: Probing the biology of religious experience*, Minneapolis, MN: Fortress Press.

Faivre, A. (2000) *Theosophy, imagination, tradition. Studies in Western esotericism*, New York, NY: State University of New York Press.

Farias, M. (2004) 'A psychological study of New Age practices and beliefs', Unpublished doctoral thesis, University of Oxford.

Farias, M. and Granqvist, P. (2007) 'The psychology of the New Age', in D. Kemp and J. Lewis (eds) *Handbook of New Age*, Leiden & Boston: Brill, pp 123-50.

Farias, M., Claridge, G. and Lalljee, M. (2005) 'Personality and cognitive predictors of New Age practices and beliefs', *Personality and Individual Differences*, vol 39, pp 979-89.

Farias, M., Newheiser, A., Wiech, K. and Kahane, G. (2006) 'The Oxford Centre for Science of the Mind (OXCSOM) religious belief scale: construction and validation', Unpublished manuscript and data.

Granqvist, P. and Hagekull, B. (2001) 'Seeking security in the New Age: on attachment and emotional compensation', *Journal for the Scientific Study of Religion*, vol 40, pp 529-47.

Granqvist, P., Ivarsson, T., Broberg, A.G. and Hagekull, B. (2007) 'Examining relations between attachment, religiosity, and New Age spirituality using the Adult Attachment Interview', *Developmental Psychology*, vol 43, no 3, pp 590-601.

Hanegraaf, W.J. (1996) *New Age religion and Western culture: Esotericism in the mirror of secular thought*, Leiden: Brill.

Heelas, P. and Woodhead, L. with Seel, B., Tusting, K. and Szerszynsky, B. (2004) *The spiritual revolution: Why religion is giving way to spirituality*, Oxford: Blackwell.

Hense, E. (2006) 'Reflection on "Conceptual definition and empirical validation of the spiritual sensitivity scale"', *Journal of Empirical Theology*, vol 19, pp 63-74.

Hood, R.W., Spilka, B., Hunsberger, B. and Gorsuch, R. (1996) *The psychology of religion: An empirical approach*, New York, NY, and London: Guilford Press.

James, W. (1902/1929) *The varieties of religious experience: A study in human nature*, New York, NY: The Modern Library.

Kirk, K., Eaves, L. and Martin, N. (1999) 'Self-transcendence as a measure of spirituality in a sample of older Australian twins', *Twin Research*, vol 2, pp 81-7.

Knoblauch, H. (2006) 'Soziologie der Spiritualität', in K. Baier (ed) *Handbuch Spiritualität*, Darmstadt: Wissenschaftliche Buchgesellschaft, pp 91-111.

Luckmann, T. (1990) 'Shrinking transcendence, expanding religion?', *Sociological Analysis*, vol 50, no 2, pp 127-38.

Lukes, S. (1973) *Individualism*, Oxford: Basil Blackwell Ltd.

Marler, P. and Hadaway, C. (2002) '"Being religious" or "being spiritual" in America: a zero-sum proposition?', *Journal for the Scientific Study of Religion*, vol 41, pp 289-300.

Maslow, A. (1964) *Religions, values and peak experiences*, Columbus, OH: Ohio State University Press.

Mason, M. (2000) 'Spirituality – what on earth is it?', Paper presented at the International Conference of Children's Spirituality, Roehampton Institute.

Mohr, C., Graves, R., Gianotti, L., Pizzagalli, D. and Brugger, P. (2001) 'Loose but normal: a semantic association study', *Journal of Psycholinguistic Research*, vol 30, no 5, pp 475-83.

Nasel, D. and Haynes, D. (2005) 'Spiritual and religious dimensions scale: development and psychometric analysis', *Australian Journal of Psychology*, vol 57, pp 61-71.

Pargament, K. (1997) *The psychology of religion and coping: Theory, research, practice*, New York, NY: Guilford Press.

Pizzagalli, D., Lehmann, D. and Brugger, P. (2001) 'Lateralized direct and indirect semantic priming effects in subjects with paranormal experiences and beliefs', *Psychopathology*, vol 31, pp 75-80.

Pizzagalli, D., Lehmann, D., Gianotti, L., Koenig, T., Tanaka, H., Wackermann, J. and Brugger, P. (2000) 'Brain electric correlates of strong belief in paranormal phenomena: intracerebral EEG source and regional omega complexity analyses', *Psychiatry Research: Neuroimaging Section*, vol 100, pp 139-54.

Rawlings, D., Hasseldine, P., Burton, C. and Zalewski, K. (submitted) 'Comparing delusional and religious belief in a normal sample'.

Rose, S. (1996) 'Transforming the world. An examination of the roles played by spirituality and healing in the New Age movement. "The aquarian conspirators revisited"', Unpublished PhD Thesis, Lancaster University.

Schneiders, S. (1998) 'The study of Christian spirituality', *Studies in Spirituality*, vol 8, pp 38-57.

Schwartz, S. (1992) 'Universals in the Content and structure of values: theoretical advances and empirical tests in 20 countries', in M. Zanna (ed) *Advances in experimental social psychology*, vol 25, San Diego, CA: Academic Press, Inc, pp 1-65.

Thalbourne, M. and Delin, P. (1999) 'Transliminality: its relation to dream life, religiosity and mystical experience', *The International Journal for the Psychology of Religion*, vol 9, no 1, pp 45-61.

van Ness, P.H. (1996) *Spirituality and the secular quest*, London: The Crossroad Publishing Company.

von Stuckrad, K. (2004) *Was ist Esoterik? Kleine Geschichte des geheimen Wissens*, München: C.H. Beck.

Zinnbauer, B., Pargament, K., Cole, B., Rye, M., Butter, E., Belavich, T., Hipp, A., Scott, A. and Kadar, J. (1997) 'Religion and spirituality: unfuzzying the fuzzy', *Journal for the Scientific Study of Religion*, vol 36, no 4, pp 549-64.

THIRTEEN

Religion, spirituality and social science: researching Muslims and crime

Muzammil Quraishi

Introduction

Criminological studies have not traditionally focused on faith groups per se. This is, in part, the outcome of the way in which official criminal statistics are classified, but it is also reflective of the traditional dominance of the race relations and subsequent ethnicity paradigm in social sciences more generally. The rapid recorded rise in the Muslim male prison population of England and Wales, coupled with global incidents such as 9/11, has resulted in the emergence of a faith paradigm within criminology (Beckford et al, 2005).

Such a paradigmatic shift has prompted increasing academic enquiry about Muslim people and communities within criminology (Webster, 1997; Wardak, 2000; Spalek, 2002). With the advent of new studies about traditionally under-researched people come accompanying methodological challenges.

This chapter explores some of the specific difficulties of crime research pertaining to Muslim populations while elucidating the significance of Islamic jurisprudence and culture to criminological enquiry. The chapter is presented in three parts. The first examines general issues pertaining to criminological research on Muslim populations and includes a brief overview of prominent studies in this area. The second part relates to my research in Pakistan and North West England, undertaken between 1997 and 2000. The third part evaluates my experiences of researching Muslim male prisoners in the UK (Quraishi, 2005, 2007).

Criminological research on Muslims in the UK

Although the latest focus on issues of faith and criminality pertains to Muslim populations in the UK, it must be acknowledged that the question of whether piety influences your propensity to commit deviant acts has been a well-established subject of criminological enquiry. The majority of these studies have been undertaken in the US with the faith in question being Christianity (Evans et al, 1995; Stark and Bainbridge, 1996; Baier and Wright, 2001; Clear and Sumter, 2002; Cretacci, 2003; Fernander et al, 2005).

The principal points of contention are how to measure 'religiosity' and which type of crime is being evaluated. This field has attracted less attention in the UK, partly due to the fact that official criminal statistics record ethnicity rather than faith. This has not prevented a small number of researchers from exploring the experiences of crime and victimisation among Muslim communities in the UK (Mawby and Batta, 1980; Webster, 1997; Wardak, 2000). Due to systems of demographic classifications, these early studies tended to concentrate on the descriptor of ethnicity (South Asian) rather than religion, but most certainly included respondents who were Muslim. These studies were undertaken within the context of relatively low levels of South Asian offending as compared to Black and White male populations (Fitzgerald, 1997; Quraishi, 2005). The studies also predate the counter-terrorism measures introduced via the 2000 Terrorism Act and corresponding over-representation of Asian people subject to Section 44 searches (Home Office, 2006).

However, since the 1952 Prison Act compelled the recording of religion a number of studies have initiated a focus on faith and criminal justice in relation to Muslim offenders in prison (Beckford and Gilliat, 1998; Spalek and Wilson, 2001; Beckford et al, 2005). The few studies mentioned complement well-established academic engagement with British Muslims in relation to issues of identity, citizenship, social exclusion and discrimination (Joly, 1995; Modood, 1996; Runnymede Trust, 1997; Home Office, 2004).

The criminological field regarding British Muslims is indeed undeveloped. This is partly due to the different forms of classification of populations in the respective parts of the criminal justice system. While we have a firm statistical record of Muslim populations in prison, other official statistics (police and court records) focus on categories of ethnicity rather than faith (Spalek, 2004). The limitations of official quantitative sources have prompted some researchers to undertake small-scale qualitative studies of Muslim offenders and victims (Macey, 1999; Quraishi, 2005). To avert the complications of homogenising diverse groups of people and the charge of essentialism regarding Islam, the concentration on locality and culturally specific 'communities' (such as Pakistanis in Bradford) is a prudent strategy, providing the findings of such research are placed within the culturally specific contexts of communities so identified rather than for the whole Muslim British population.

I have mentioned the academic neglect in this field among traditional British criminology. Scholars have asserted that the neglect may be partly due to the limited number of Muslim British criminologists (Spalek, 2002). A further factor could be that when assessing our national criminology we become blind to its culture-bound nature as well as its ethnocentrism (Sztompka, 1990). One strategy to challenge such ethnocentrism is to conduct comparative criminological enquiry that can prevent scholars resorting to stereotypes or denying differences between people and cultures (Nelken, 1997).

Classification and statistics

As mentioned, official criminal statistics such as court and police records record ethnicity and nationality but not religion. Prison populations, by contrast, have been recording statistics on religious affiliation since the 1952 Prison Act. Criminologists have to evaluate data on ethnicity and infer that since the majority of Pakistanis and Bangladeshis are also Muslims (although not exclusively), data on Pakistanis also refers to Muslims. The complications of aggregating populations under the assumed homogeneous categories of 'Asian', 'Black' or 'White' have been comprehensively articulated by commentators on race, ethnicity and criminal justice (Fitzgerald, 1997; Bowling and Phillips, 2002; Macey, 2002).

If we acknowledge that these complications are evident when discussing the broad categories of ethnic origin, they are of equal if not more concern when turning to issues of religious classification (Beckford, 1989). Therefore, any discussion of the terms 'Muslim' and 'Islam' warrants a caveat emphasising the diversity and heterogeneity the terms encapsulate. Nevertheless, with regard to ethnicity and country of origin, we can note that the majority of Muslims in the UK are South Asian. Of the estimated 1.6 million Muslims in the UK, Pakistani Muslims constitute 658,000, while there were 260,000 Bangladeshi Muslims who responded to the voluntary question about faith at the last census (Guessous et al, 2001). Furthermore, 13% of those declaring Indian ethnic origin registered Islam as their faith (Guessous et al, 2001). Therefore, it is no coincidence that all of the British criminological studies in this field to date have tended to concentrate on South Asian Muslims and that broader sociological research has explored issues of nationality, identity and culture among the Pakistani and Bangladeshi UK population (Eade, 1994; Webster, 1997; Macey, 1999; Wardak, 2000; Glynn, 2002). Furthermore, Akbar Ahmed captures the significance of South Asian Islam on global politics when he states:

> ... in some important senses South Asia is one of the most crucial and dynamic areas for Islam. Its population alone is almost 40 per cent of the total Muslim population. The region ... is a filter and store-house of diverse human knowledge. (Ahmed, 2002, p 5)

This is not to understate the diversity of class, culture, and language within the South Asian Muslim UK population or variance in interpretations of Islamic practices among the British Muslim population as a whole (Lewis, 1994; Joly, 1995; Küçükcan, 1999; Blakey et al, 2006).

Crime research on Muslims in Pakistan and Northern England

I was interested in the experiences of Muslims both as perpetrators and as victims of crime. The discussion below outlines some of the culture and faith-specific methodological considerations my fieldwork prompted between 1997 and 2000 in Pakistan and England.

The insider/outsider methodological debate within social sciences has been comprehensively articulated, particularly by researchers exploring issues of ethnicity and gender (Baca Zinn, 1979; De Andrade, 2000; Alexander, 2004). The terms of the debate essentially centre on the impact of insider or outsider status on the 'legitimacy' and 'authenticity' of the qualitative research undertaken. Among initial contributors to the debate were African American scholars of race who asserted that research on Black communities must rest on cultural awareness and therefore, in the words of Alford A. Young Jr:

> ... only African American scholars could discern the intricacies and complexities of African American culture and social organisation in ways that put black Americans on equal footing with others in American life. (Young, 2004, p 190)

It is important to note that the contemporary debate includes the potential benefits which outsider status may confer on qualitative researchers. Scholars have argued for more dynamic and fluid interpretations of these concepts whereby *outsider* status does not necessarily equate to *exclusion* and *illegitimacy*, or *insider* status to *inclusion* and *legitimacy* (Young, 2004).

As observed, this debate has principally centred on the gender, ethnic or racial category of the ethnographer. When evaluating issues of researcher faith identity, the canon of ethnographic literature is notably thin, despite the assertions that research participation is in itself a 'spiritual imperative' (Reason, 1998, p 162). When commencing fieldwork on Muslim communities in the UK and Pakistan, I was faced with the dilemmas outlined above with regard to how my biographical identity as a South Asian, British-born male Muslim would impact on the research I undertook (Quraishi, 2005).

The issue of classification has already been mentioned, but it is raised once more here in relation to how I positioned and viewed myself reflexively over the course of the ethnographic fieldwork undertaken. My parents were among the hundreds of thousands of Indians displaced by Partition in 1947 and arrived as refugees in Karachi in the newly founded Islamic Republic of Pakistan. Their story of migration from India, Pakistan and their subsequent arrival in England in the 1960s mirrors the life histories of many among the settled Muslim population in Britain (Lewis, 1994; Joly, 1995). Through the process of migration and the extended family nexus, Karachi occupied a paradoxical position in my life. It was familiar yet distant, it was where I went for family vacations, weddings and funerals and where I could become absorbed in speaking Urdu; yet it was also alien, unfamiliar and dangerous. I have never envisaged Pakistan as a present or future homeland, and here I echo the sentiments of young British-Pakistani men from Bradford articulated in a recent study (Alam and Husband, 2006). Therefore, my biographical profile both gave me access to a community of Muslims in

Pakistan and the UK and provided me with 'outsider' status when it was useful to distance myself from the ethnic and political sectarianism evident in Karachi (Quraishi, 2005).

Piety, religiosity and Islamic jurisprudence

One of my concerns was how to evaluate piety and religiosity among the Muslim respondents in both field locations. Part of the challenge for research in this field is to acknowledge the balance to be struck between globally articulated Islamic concepts and the divergence and anti-essentialist assertions within national and localised interpretations of Islam. Therefore, the difficulty presents itself as to which notions, concepts, views and ideas are applicable to Muslim communities wherever they may reside. Furthermore, does the assertion that some values are universally accepted by Muslims necessarily exclude and marginalise other equally worthy articulations? This has been rigorously debated within Islamic countries, among Muslim populations and within the historic Schools of *fiqh* (Islamic jurisprudence) (Coulson, 1964).

After careful consideration, my approach was to ask respondents whether they felt they were pious and to provide me examples of how they had arrived at this conclusion. Definitions of piety were therefore driven by the Muslim respondents themselves. Discussions tended to centre on the central tenets or five pillars of Islam,[1] with a particular focus on performing the obligatory five daily prayers and abstinence from consuming alcohol or prohibited sexual relationships (Quraishi, 2005). Therefore, any discussion about offending prompted respondents to evaluate all types of rule breaking, whether these were state-defined crimes or infractions of religious law. In Karachi, I found there were close parallels between what the state defined as criminal and what is declared illegal within *Sharia*. When the question was put 'Have you ever committed crime?', it yielded disclosure of activity prohibited within Islam, such as consumption of intoxicants, alongside confessions of offences against the criminal law such as fraud.

When speaking of Islam, respondents in both Karachi and England claimed it figured prominently in their lives, particularly as a provider of identity. In Karachi, youths spoke of how a 'Muslim identity' stood above any other notion of nationhood or national identity. Similarly, Bangladeshi youths interviewed in England expressed the view that religion was a way of life which was of prime importance and that any concepts of nationality came second to religious identity (Quraishi, 2005). Furthermore, in Karachi transgressions of *Sharia* were given priority over state law in the minds of some respondents. State law in Pakistan was viewed as corrupt but also crudely as a legacy of tainted oppressive colonialism. State law was considered incomplete and flawed since it was essentially the outcome of political subjectivity and secularism. By contrast, *Sharia*, in the eyes of some respondents, was irrefutable due to its divine origin. However, since *Sharia* lacked the official legal framework in which to operate it became subject to multiple interpretations among religious leaders in Pakistan (Quraishi, 2005).

I was particularly interested in the degrees to which Muslims in my study comprehended Islamic law (*Sharia*) or Islamic jurisprudence (*fiqh*) with a specific focus on Islamic criminal law (*al- 'uqūbāt*). The latter is divided into three categories: *hudūd*, *qisās* and *ta`zīr*. *Hudūd* offences are those specifically mentioned in the Qur`ān and hadīth (documentation of the practices of the Prophet Muhammad, SAW[2]) and include murder, fornication and theft. The second category, *qisās*, means the 'law of equality or just retaliation' and includes crimes such as murder, maiming and battery. Although *qisās* offences and corresponding punishments are specified in the Qur`ān, the decision to retaliate, accept compensation or pardon rests with the next of kin to the victim. The third category, *ta`zīr* (deterrence), includes all those crimes for which there are no specified penalties in the Qur`ān or hadīth and hence the definitions and corresponding punishments are the state's prerogative (Coulson, 1964; Quraishi, 2005).

Few of the Muslims I spoke with in Pakistan or England declared clear knowledge of *al- 'uqūbāt,* or of the three categories of criminal law. People tended to acknowledge *hadd* offences more easily than those within the categories of *qisās* or *ta`zīr* (Quraishi, 2005). In Pakistan, there was greater awareness of *hadd* offences over other categories, due to political educational programmes that have emphasised these offences following the *Hudūd* Ordinance in 1979 (Mehdi, 1994).

Researching Muslims in prison[3]

The qualitative data for this section originates from my work as researcher for the Muslims in Prison (MIP) project at the University of Warwick (see Beckford et al, 2005). The study was funded by the Economic Social Research Council (ESRC) and compared the experiences of a sample of Muslim prisoners in England and Wales against those of Muslim prisoners in France. The objectives of the study were to discover how Muslim prisoners were treated in French and English prisons; to examine how the category of Muslim was socially constructed and used in prison; and to evaluate whether Muslim prisoners were subjected to discrimination linked to their religious identity (Beckford et al, 2005). I undertook the main primary fieldwork in three male prisons in England and Wales, while a team at the Centre d'Analyse et d'Intervention Sociologiques (CADIS) in Paris carried out the fieldwork in France.

I worked full time in three prisons over a period of nine months, for approximately three months in each prison. The fieldwork commenced in July 2001 and concluded in June 2002. As a practising Muslim of Pakistani ethnicity, the ethnographic account of the project provides an insight into how I undertook complex research within a setting where I had to negotiate the expectations, suspicions and preconceptions of staff and prisoners around the particularly sensitive areas of faith, identity and discrimination.

The impact of 9/11 on the fieldwork

On 11 September 2001, I was on a prison wing undertaking interviews of officers when news broke of an attack on the Pentagon by terrorists. Prisoners were relaying the news across the wings and between the cells; I was later informed by a governor of the attacks on the World Trade Center. I anticipated greater restrictions on my access following 9/11 on learning that two of the Muslim researchers in France had been suddenly prevented access to the prisons where they had already commenced interviews. Fortunately, I was not refused access to the prison. However, on 27 September my passport was examined with greater detail and suspicion by Gate staff with particular attention to the many visas it contained for Pakistan. I had been security cleared in advance of the project and this had included a Criminal Records Bureau check. Despite this, from this point on, I noted that staff challenged the legitimacy of the research objectives more frequently. Furthermore, as a Muslim conducting the research, I was under more intense scrutiny. I also felt less confident about articulating the focus of the project on Muslim prisoner rights when public opinion was swinging significantly towards anti-Muslim rhetoric and a marked increase in physical attacks on Muslims in the UK (Smiljanic, 2002).

Protecting the vulnerable whilst negotiating a role

It was emphasised in the pre-interview disclosure and in talks to congregations that the broad aims of the research were exploratory but focused on finding out what the 'lived' reality of prison life was like for Muslim prisoners and what challenges, concerns or practical issues the Muslim prisoner population presented for staff. Prisoner respondents were encouraged to participate largely on altruistic grounds for the benefit of future prisoners. Some prisoners were motivated by wanting to 'get their story out' or to expose discrimination that they felt could perhaps be investigated by the researcher.

In order to facilitate the research I was based in the chaplaincy department of each prison and since my prisoner respondents were Muslim, I shadowed the imams in each institution. It was my concern that prisoners and staff would think I was a trainee imam. Officers often thought I was an imam, despite the absence of a beard. This was evidenced during a prison visit when, on entering the chapel, officers mistook me for the imam, who had not arrived, and signalled the release of prisoners from cells to the chapel building for Friday prayers (field notes, Prison 1, 3/8/2001).

I was particularly concerned about not disclosing the fact that I have a degree in law to the prisoners and made the imams aware of this. Unfortunately, regardless of our previous arrangement, the imam in one prison introduced me to the congregation as 'a lawyer'. Despite my immediate attempts to emphasise that I was an academic rather than a practitioner, the damage had been done and in many of my subsequent exchanges with prisoners, questions specifically relating to legal advice were raised. While such inquiries eventually subsided, it did consume valuable research time. Of course, the prospect of legal advice may have encouraged prisoners to sign up for interviews in the first place, and ethnography acknowledges this as an integral part of the fieldwork experience.

I was very careful not to establish any hierarchy between the Muslim prisoners who attended congregational prayers and myself. I specifically informed the imams in each prison that while I would willingly join the congregation to pray, I did not wish to lead the prayers, deliver sermons or anything that would risk presenting me in the perception of the prisoners in any supervisory role. Unfortunately, in one prison, one of the temporary imams spoke little English and asked me to translate part of his *khutbah* (sermon) for the congregation (field notes, Prison 1, Aug 2001).

Contrary to prior concerns about the prison communities greeting me with suspicion, my role became one of confidante, not only for prisoners, but for chaplains, imams and uniformed officers alike. In one prison, a chaplain agreed for a Pakistani prisoner to use the chaplaincy telephone providing I monitored what he was saying. I frequently accompanied chaplains to collect books, or sacks of stamps, or to speak with those with mental ill health on the hospital wings. In one prison, a female officer asked whether she could speak with me in 'confidence' about an incident regarding the provision of halal food (field notes, Prison 2, 12/02/02).

Being Muslim researching Muslim prisoners

As a practising Muslim my experiences of the facilities in prison provided an insight to the complaints of prisoners. When I entered an empty cell I was able to imagine how difficult it would be to perform ablution. When I actually did perform ablution in the chapel the experience contextualised the accounts relayed to me from prisoners.

> ... in the world faiths room.... With some difficulty I performed ablution in the toilets using the wash basin. There were no mats or provisions to conduct this adequately. I had to balance myself and wash my feet, and rest each foot on my shoe to avoid touching the toilet floor which is considered impure. (Field notes, Prison 1, 22/08/01)

In developing contact with Muslim prisoners I felt compelled to join them during Friday prayers since this was one of the rare occasions when they could meet in significant numbers. In one prison I was invited by the imam and prisoners to attend *Eid-al-Adha* (feast of sacrifice) prayers and the celebratory meal. This represented a sacrifice for me since *Eid* is normally spent with family, but I felt it was necessary to maintain rapport with my prisoner respondents. In the same prison there was no full-time imam and so I was in the curious position of pointing out to the management that they had the incorrect day scheduled for *Eid* and hence rapid logistical changes had to be made to accommodate the celebrations. Had it not been for my observation, it is debatable whether prisoners would have been able to celebrate on the correct date (field notes, Prison 3, 3/02/02).

Such biographical factors are essential to formulating the qualitative picture and lines of enquiry, tactics and interpretations of field data (Pogrebin, 2003).

In developing and maintaining rapport, the researcher perhaps seeks commonalities between himself/herself and respondents yet the relationship is based on factors of ethnicity, language, gender and class (Martin, 2002). In the present study, my personal biography connected with respondents on a number of conscious and unconscious levels. I shared similar ethnic origin, language and age group with many respondents. Where these differed, I emphasised common religious beliefs. Nevertheless, on deeper reflection, there remained significant differences between my prisoner respondents and myself. It was apparent that many of the prisoners spoke with regional dialects from London and the Midlands (I was from Manchester); the third prison was a dispersal prison and so the accents tended to be more varied. Also, I became aware that the vast majority did not hold further or higher education qualifications (I hold a law degree and was about to complete my doctorate). Furthermore, I am Urdu-speaking, therefore the Mirpuri and Punjabi spoken by many of the Pakistani prisoners was largely indecipherable to me. I was conscious all of these aspects would mark out my difference rather than similarity to the prisoners. However, as noted by ethnographers such as Mitchell Duneier, the difference of race rather than class or language is perhaps more significant in such research environments (Duneier, 2004).

My ethnicity and faith figured in two incidents in the same prison where I was subject to racist language and verbal abuse from prison officers. The first incident involved a prison officer who expressed irritation at the purpose of the research on Muslims and vented some xenophobic views about immigration and how he would never attend any race relations training (field notes, Prison 1, 1/08/01). In the second incident I was sitting in the reception area when three officers walked past me. One officer said "You have to watch out for all the fucking niggers on your way out!" while staring at me (field notes, Prison 1 24/09/01). These incidents left me feeling humiliated and powerless but I did not want to report them for the problems I perceived they would cause with regard to developing rapport with prison officers.

Conclusion

In summary we have observed that research on Muslim communities is an underdeveloped field within criminology but that the neglect is now beginning to be addressed. Any new research in the area will face the methodological challenges highlighted such as the complexities of classification within official criminal statistics. More importantly, researchers will be compelled to walk the tightrope between ascertaining the commonalities within Muslim communities while avoiding charges of essentialism. Issues of faith, spirituality and their impact on crime motivation and control require further study and clarification. Criminologists should not confuse the task of assessing the impact of spirituality and religious norms on offending with confirmation for the theological perspectives being articulated.

The interpretation, comprehension and articulation of *Sharia* provides a vexing challenge for scholars. While Muslim communities are aware of certain aspects of Islamic criminal law, other classifications are less understood. If criminologists wish to engage with Muslim communities they would benefit by including an assessment and awareness of *Sharia* and *fiqh* within their remit to interrogate the links between religiosity and deviance.

Researching Muslim prisoners has presented particular challenges in terms of access, and maintaining and developing rapport with prisoners while trying not to alienate staff. Few criminological studies exist on the influence of faith identity of researchers on the research process. Being a practising Muslim enabled me to evaluate religious provision in prison from an informed ethnographic perspective.

The discussion highlights the complexities of undertaking crime research but particularly in relation to a community subject to increased suspicion. The prison fieldwork was able to chart a shift towards increased scrutiny of the researcher as a Muslim and increased challenges to the legitimacy of a project which explored discrimination towards Muslim prisoners.

In negotiating a role it was apparent how those in prison constructed perceptions of the researcher as confidante, adviser or witness. The research demonstrated the degree to which a researcher may feel compelled to participate in the life of a prison, whether this involves attending congregational prayers, the burden of drawing keys or experiencing direct discrimination due to faith or ethnic identity.

Notes

[1] These are the *shahāda* (declaration of faith that 'There is no god but God; Muhammad is the Messenger of God'); *salāh* (obligatory prayers performed five times daily); *zakāt* (alms-giving or compulsory charity); *sawm* (fasting during the month of Ramadān) and *hajj* (annual pilgrimage at least once in a lifetime to Makkah in Saudi Arabia).

[2] SAW stands for the Arabic expression, *Salallahu 'Alayi wa Sallam*, meaning 'may the peace and blessings of Allah be upon him' – Islamic etiquette when mentioning the Prophet.

[3] See Quraishi (2007) for a fuller discussion of these issues.

References

Ahmed, A. (2002) *Discovering Islam: Making sense of Muslim history and society*, London and New York, NY: Routledge.

Alam, M.Y. and Husband, C. (2006) *British-Pakistani men from Bradford: Linking narratives to policy*, York: Joseph Rowntree Foundation.

Alexander, C. (2004) 'Writing race: ethnography and the imagination of The Asian Gang', in M. Bulmer and J. Solomos (eds) *Researching race and racism*, London and New York, NY: Routledge, chapter 9.

Baca Zinn, M. (1979) 'Field research in minority communities', *Social Problems*, vol 27, pp 209-19.

Baier, C.J. and Wright. B.R.E. (2001) 'If you love me keep my commandments: a meta-analysis of the effect of religion on crime', *Journal of Research in Crime and Delinquency*, vol 38, no 1, pp 3-21.

Beckford, J.A. (1989) *Religion and advanced industrial society*, London: Unwin/Hyman.

Beckford, J.A. and Gilliat, S. (1998) *Religion in prison: Equal rites in a multi-faith society*, Cambridge: Cambridge University Press.

Beckford, J.A., Joly, D. and Khosrokhavar, F. (2005) *Muslims in prison: Challenge and change in Britain and France*, Basingstoke: Palgrave Macmillan.

Blakey, H., Pearce, J. and Chesters, G. (2006) *Minorities within minorities: Beneath the surface of South Asian participation*, York: Joseph Rowntree Foundation.

Bowling, B. and Phillips, C. (2002) *Racism, crime and justice*, London: Longman/Pearson.

Clear, T.R. and Sumter, M.T. (2002) 'Prisoners, prison and religion: religion and adjustments to prison', *Journal of Offender Rehabilitation*, vol 35, nos 3/4, pp 127-59.

Coulson, N.J. (1964) *A history of Islamic law*, Edinburgh: Edinburgh University Press.

Cretacci, M. (2003) 'Religion and social control: an application of a modified social bond on violence', *Criminal Justice Review*, vol 28, no 2, pp 254-77.

De Andrade, L.L. (2000) 'Negotiations from the inside: constructing racial and ethnic identity in qualitative research', *Journal of Contemporary Ethnography*, vol 29, no 3, pp 268-90.

Duneier, M. (2004) 'Three rules I go by in my ethnographic research on race and racism', in M. Bulmer and J. Solomos (eds) *Researching race and racism*, London and New York, NY: Routledge, chapter 6.

Eade, J. (1994) 'Identity, nationality and religion: educated young Bangladeshi Muslims in London's East End', *International Sociology*, vol 9, no 3, pp 377-94.

Evans, T.D., Cullen, F.T., Dunaway, R.G. and Burton Jr, V.S. (1995) 'Religion and crime re-examined: the impact of religion, secular controls and social ecology on adult criminality', *Criminology*, vol 33, no 2, pp 195-217.

Fernander, A., Wilson, J.F., Staton, M. and Leukefeld, C. (2005) 'Exploring the type-of-crime hypothesis, religiosity, and spirituality in an adult male prison population', *International Journal of Offender Therapy and Comparative Criminology*, vol 49, no 6, pp 682-95.

Finkelstein, E. (1993) *Prison culture: An inside view*, Aldershot: Avebury.

Fitzgerald, M. (1997) 'Minorities, crime and criminal justice in Britain', in I. Marshall (ed) *Minorities, migrants and crime: Diversity and similarity across Europe and the United States*, Thousand Oaks, CA, and London: Sage Publications, Chapter 2.

Glynn, S. (2002) 'Bengali Muslims: the New East End radicals', *Ethnic and Racial Studies*, vol 25, no 6, pp 969-88.

Guessous, F., Hooper, N. and Moorthy, U. (2001) *Religion in prison 1999 and 2000*, Home Office National Statistics, London: Crown.

Home Office (2004) *2003 Home Office Citizenship Survey: People, families and communities*, Home Office Research Study 289, Research, Development and Statistics Directorate, London: Crown.

Home Office (2006) *Race and the criminal justice system: An overview to the complete statistics 2004–2005, Pursuant to Section 95 Criminal Justice Act 1991*, London: Home Office, Crown.

Joly, D. (1995) *Britannia's crescent*, Aldershot: Avebury.

Küçükcan, T. (1999) *Politics of ethnicity, identity and religion: Turkish Muslims in Britain*, Aldershot: Ashgate.

Lewis, P. (1994) *Islamic Britain: Religion, politics and identity among British Muslims*, London: IB Tauris & Co Ltd.

Macey, M. (1999) 'Class, gender and religious influences on changing patterns of Pakistani Muslim male violence in Bradford', *Ethnic and Racial Studies*, vol 22, no 5, September, pp 845-66.

Macey, M. (2002) 'Interpreting Islam: young Muslim men's involvement in criminal activity in Bradford', in B. Spalek, *Islam, crime and criminal justice*, London: Willan, Chapter 2.

Martin, C. (2002) 'Doing research in a prison setting', in V. Jupp, P. Davies and P. Francis (eds) *Doing criminological research*, London: Sage.

Mawby, B.I. and Batta, L.D. (1980) *Asians and crime: The Bradford experience*, Middlesex: Scope Communication.

Mehdi, R. (1994) *The Islamization of the law in Pakistan*, Richmond: Curzon.

Modood, T. (1996) *Not easy being British: Colour, culture and citizenship*, London: Runnymede Trust/Trentham.

Nelken, D. (ed) (1997) *Issues in comparative criminology*, Aldershot: Ashgate/Dartmouth.

Pogrebin, M.R. (ed) (2003) *Qualitative approaches to criminal justice: Perspectives from the field*, Thousand Oaks, CA: Sage Publications.

Quraishi, M. (2005) *Muslims and crime: A comparative study*, Aldershot: Ashgate.

Quraishi, M. (2007) 'Researching Muslim prisoners', *International Journal of Social Research Methodology: Theory & Practice*, online: DOI:10.1080/13645570701622199.

Reason, P. (1998) 'Political, epistemological, ecological and spiritual dimensions of participation', *Studies in Cultures, Organizations and Societies*, vol 4, no 2, pp 147-67.

Runnymede Trust (1997) 'Report on British Muslims and Islamophobia', The Runnymede Trust Commission, Professor Gordon Conway, Chair, Runnymede Trust.

Smiljanic, N. (2002) 'Human rights and Muslims in Britain', in B. Spalek (ed) *Islam, crime and criminal justice*, Cullompton: Willan.

Spalek, B. (2002) *Islam, crime and criminal justice*, London: Willan.

Spalek, B. (2004) 'Muslims in the UK and the criminal justice system', in Open Society Institute, *Muslims in the UK: Policies for engaged citizens*, OSI/EU Monitoring Programme, Hungary, Budapest and New York, NY, chapter 4.

Spalek, B. and Wilson, D. (2001) 'Not just "visitors" to prison: the experiences of Imams who work inside the penal system', *The Howard Journal*, vol 40, no 1, pp 3-13.

Stark, R. and Bainbridge, W.S. (1996) *Religion deviance and social control*, New York, NY and London: Routledge.

Sztompka, P. (1990) 'Conceptual frameworks in comparative enquiry: divergent or convergent', in M. Albrow and E. King (eds) *Globalisation: Knowledge and society*, London: Sage Publications.

Wardak, A. (2000) *Social control and deviance: A South Asian community in Scotland*, Aldershot: Ashgate.

Webster, C. (1997) 'The construction Of British Asian criminality', *International Journal of the Sociology of Law*, vol 25, pp 65-86.

Young, Jr, A. (2004) 'Experiences in ethnographic interviewing about race: the inside and outside of it', in M. Bulmer and J. Solomos (eds) *Researching race and racism*, London and New York, NY: Routledge, chapter 13.

FOURTEEN

Inadvertent offence: when 'a little knowledge is a dangerous thing'

Maree Gruppetta

Introduction

This chapter discusses the myriad ways the researcher/practitioner can inadvertently offend those with specific faith identities, which is based on experiences as both a researcher and practitioner working within the social sciences. When embarking on research involving faith communities there are few ethical guidelines one can access and only through sharing the experiences of others can such dilemmas be avoided and addressed. Many researchers and practitioners believe the issues arising from conflict within religious and spiritual beliefs are relatively easy to solve (Bouma, 2006). However, these assumptions can be misleading. Issues that are most likely to cause offence can be categorised as either a 'macro' issue or a 'micro' issue. Macro issues are formalised, standardised issues within faith traditions such as food/dietary requirements, dress codes and appropriate terminology. I argue that such issues are less likely to be at the heart of incidents of inadvertent offence because they are relatively easy to research in advance and there tends to be significant levels of publicly accessible knowledge about them. Instead, it is often 'micro' issues that acts of inadvertent offence centre on as these are what I term 'day-to-day' practices of religiosity and custom which frequently vary dramatically within faith traditions and are often not well documented. This chapter focuses on a number of examples of the micro issues that were at the centre of incidents of inadvertent offence.

At an individual level few religious observances and customs are standard. It is dangerous to assume all faith communities share exactly the same beliefs and practices (Bouma, 2006). The global beliefs concerning a particular religion may not apply to a specific faith community, or apply only in its broadest sense. Within each religious community there may be a variety of different branches, strands, groups and subgroups. Each of these can develop their own particular beliefs and practices in a similar manner to the development of cultural traits, and it is at this micro level that the researcher or practitioner encounters difficulty.

For instance, one particular manifestation of these difficulties was the need to respond sensitively to the contention by most of the participants in this particular study that their personal concept of religion or spirituality was *the* 'truth'. In part this required specialised methodological design. By using phenomenology, a theoretical perspective that permits the researcher to investigate the way the *participant* views the world, the researcher was able to accept *their* perspective as the 'truth', as *they* perceived it. The interview questions had to be carefully constructed to avoid cultural or religious weighting, and interactions were constantly negotiated to avoid and address situations of inadvertent offence during the course of the research. The influence of the individual participants and their faith communities on the researcher's methodological choices, and the ways these voices are presented in the research products, are examples of techniques respectfully incorporating faith perspectives within social science research in the context of multicultural Australia.

Multicultural Australia

The study of human culture necessitates a study of various religions and spirituality pathways. In ancient times religion was one of the strongest factors in cultural development:

> Because religion is not a separate entity, but an aspect of culture which grows out of ordinary life, shares the importance of story, ritual and belief with ordinary life, it is often difficult to know where ordinary life ends and "religion" begins. (Lovat et al, 2000, p 237)

Lives were influenced and shaped by religious beliefs and practices, and culture in turn shaped religion. As sea travel broadened migration prospects, other religious and cultural groups influenced basic religious concepts, and as a result most religions have more similarities than differences. Many religions can be traced to common ancestry and the slight differences are due to increased human migration in recent centuries. The most obvious examples are the changes to Japanese Shintoism due to the influence of Chinese Taoism, Confucianism, Buddhism (Clarke and Somers, 1994), and the development of Sikhism from Hindu and Islamic cultures (Sikh Missionary Center, 1990).

Australia since first settlement has been multicultural, and multireligious. Religious contact took place early in its history. The first Muslim contact took place in the 17th century when Macassarese fishing expeditions resulted in contact with the Australian Aboriginal people (Kabir, 2005, p 3). Among the various Christian faiths represented amongst the passengers of the first fleet were 16 Jewish individuals (Carey, 1996; Rutland, 2005), and it was estimated that about 800 Jewish convicts had arrived by 1845 (Rutland, 2005). The muster of 1802 'listed a number of Mohammedans, the term used for Muslims at the time' (Kabir, 2005, p 3), and 19 Muslims were registered in the 1928 Census (Carey, 1996).

Due to the distances involved, contacting religious authorities in one's country of origin was often difficult for religious minorities without access to their spiritual home. As a result, from European settlement in 1788, the various faith communities in the new colonies had to make their own theological decisions in the new country (Carey, 1996). Consequently, Australian religion was least organised between 1788 and 1840, as many immigrants were 'religiously inarticulate' (Bouma, 2006, p 39) due to either their own alienation from organised religion, or to the lack of spiritual leadership. At this time only some Church of England chaplains were present in Australia (Bouma, 2006). The arrival of Phillip Joseph Cohen in 1928 with authority from the Chief Rabbi to perform Jewish marriages consolidated the organisation of Judaism in Australia (Rutland, 2005, p 16). Due to the long periods without religious leadership there are documented instances that when religious leaders and authorities finally arrived in the colonies they were appalled to find significant cultural differences in religious practice (Carey, 1996). For instance, it was difficult to maintain a *kosher* bush hut or muster a *minyan*, the required 10 men needed for a valid religious ceremony (Falk, cited in Turnbull, 1999, p 11). and many married out of their faith due to the scarcity of women (Turnbull, 1999, p 11).

Although increased communication and travel opportunities have lessened this type of problem in recent times, cultural adaptation of religions to specific Australian conditions still occurs. For example, historically 'Islam was not only a religion, but the Shari provided a legal code for handling business and dealing with conflicts' (Manager, 1999, p 7). In contrast Australia has no religious law equivalent to secular law, and religious leaders have no legal status in Australia (Storer, 1985, p 183). Thus conflicts between faith practices and Australian law have influenced changes to religious practice within Australia over the past few decades. Australian legislation is 'alien' to many (Storer, 1985, p 188), especially in regard to the dissolution of marriage, child custody arrangements and inheritance laws (Storer, 1985, p 190). Acceptance of circumcision, a religious commandment in Judaism and Islam, also customary in some Coptic, Orthodox and Christian churches (Brasch, 1999), is changing and may affect the practices of these religious groups within Australia in the future.

As a researcher engaging with faith communities in Australia, it was advisable to investigate these macro issues, rather than assume that the religious beliefs are always those of the original religious source as practised overseas, because religion is not a 'static identity' (Manager, 1999, p 1). Religious practice is a 'dynamic' and 'lived' experience (Manager, 1999, p 2). 'The ability of Muslim culture to absorb, adapt, and transmit culture from neighbouring civilisations' (Eaton, 1990, p 17, cited in Manager, 1999, p 7) is part of their experience of being Muslim in their particular world, and the same is true for any religion. There are as 'many Islams as there are situations that sustain them' (Manager, 1999, p 17), and just as many types of Christianity, Judaism, Buddhism and Hindu. Religion is also a world-view, a perspective of living that is beyond mere politics or culture (Gruppetta, 2004b).

Researching across cultures/religions

As a researcher, I was already aware of the ease of offending inadvertently and the ethical and methodological basis for my doctoral research had to be carefully designed to support and include a range of cultural and religious viewpoints. The project involved in-depth narrative inquiry into the life stories of gifted adults within multicultural Australia. Participants were sought from a range of ethnicities and cultures, and involved critical scrutiny of recruitment procedures, methodology and ethical considerations. Due to the small number of participants required for an in-depth case study, 'snowball sampling', a type of 'chain-referral sampling' (Streeton et al, 2004) methodology was used to recruit subjects. Characteristic of this approach is the use of groups or individuals to gain access to the population sample (Faugier and Sergeant, 1997, cited in Streeton et al, 2004). Therefore, as the sample was to be drawn across cultures, religions and socioeconomic status, various religious and cultural groups were contacted and requested to nominate a 'gifted' individual to represent their particular group.

The religious and cultural groups contacted have been identified as representative of a wide range of cultures and religions. For instance: one Australian Islamic organisation represents Islamic groups from a wide range of ethnic/racial heritages including members from Arabia, Egypt, Indonesia, South Africa, Turkey and many other countries. Using organisations as nominating bodies generated a much richer possible pool of participants. These organisations became 'key informants' (Streeton et al, 2004, p 38) within the research study, by providing information on cultural sensitivities or expectations that were otherwise unknown to the researcher, and negotiating initial contact with the participants (Gruppetta, 2005a). 'The voice of the insider is assumed to be more "true" than that of the outsider in current debate' (Reed-Danahay, 1997, p 4), hence the need to locate a 'key-informant' (Gubrium and Holstein, 1997). As an outsider, the researcher is positioned as an external observer, which then raises the question of truth within their research.

Methodology

Phenomenology is the study of the lived experience from the unique perspective of the individual that is engaged in the experience (Thibodeau and MacRae, 1997). It is a theoretical perspective where the researcher is concerned with the way the participant views the world (van Manen, 2000) and their perceptions of it. The researcher assumes a subordinate position, channelling thoughts back through the participant to gather their essential lived experience (Shultz, 2002). To critically elicit participants' beliefs in this study a phenomenological approach was used as this method permitted the 'truth' of the individual participant to be presented within the research (Gruppetta, 2004a).

The goal of phenomenology is to provide 'voice' for the participant, not to interpret or subjugate meaning through the lenses of the researcher's perception (Shultz, 2002). Thus a phenomenological approach permits the researcher to perceive the participants' 'truth' rather than their own. The researcher must *interpret* the participants' experience, *as the participants see it*, rather than *infer* meaning through their own personal biases (Thomas and Pollio, 2002).

In positivist qualitative research, interviews are generally expected to keep their 'selves' out of the interview process as 'neutrality is the byword' (Gubrium and Holstein, 1997, p 31). Yet, behind every interpretive study stands the biographically, multiculturally situated researcher, 'who speaks from a particular class, racial, cultural, and ethnic community perspective' (Denzin and Lincoln, 1998, p 23). While some may avoid religious issues due to controversy (Clark and Hoover, 1997), some find religious issues difficult because they conflict with their own faith (Dart, 1997). It is therefore important for the researcher to reflect critically on the differences between the frameworks of themselves as researcher and the research participants, as research participants must be permitted to provide their own interpretations (Hunter, 2006). Yet all researchers interpret their data. We need to overcome ourselves, our own prior knowledge, when crossing the boundaries into qualitative research (Tolich and Davidson, 1999, p 183).

A 'double subjectivity' (Ellis and Berger, 2003) occurs in the act of interviewing, whereby the participant's feelings, thoughts and attitudes are affected by the relationship between the participant and the researcher. Consequently, the personal and social identities of the interviewer and the interviewee become important factors in shaping the relationship. Trust is imperative for accurate research when investigating sensitive issues and minority cultures. It is crucial to establish trust to be included in participants' religious observances. For instance, when entering a Hindu temple it is expected that menstruating women may not attend, nor anyone with a recent birth in the family, and one may not eat meat prior to attending the temple.[1] There is no real way to verify these practices; the researcher's compliance must simply be taken on trust. Any hint of deception would taint the establishment of trust in the relationship. If researchers are viewed with suspicion it becomes difficult to establish the participant trust necessary for effective research, which is essential in terms of investigating sensitive issues and minority cultures where trust is imperative for accurate research (Gruppetta, 2005b).

Religion is often related to participants' family and cultural experience and as such can be sectored into a private sphere of life where questioning about deeply held beliefs becomes an invasion of privacy (Blasi, 2002). Asking questions about specific practices or religious beliefs could cause concern for potential participants as the area of belief may be considered too personal (Lovat et al, 2000). The 'right to know' is a Western assumption (O'Riley, 2003, p 154). The researcher, student, academic world in general believes they have a 'right to know' all facets of the culture or individual being presented. O'Riley also speaks of the 'right of those who know not to share what they know' (2003, p 154). There are intimate knowledges within most cultures that are understood by the members of that culture. From habits to secrets, they are not easily explained to an outsider, and many are not intended to be shared beyond the circle of that specific culture. A participant's right to withhold or omit such information must be respected.

Cultural and religious practice when observed by outsiders can be misinterpreted and misrepresented (Gruppetta, 2004b), and participants from minority groups could be quite concerned with misrepresentation. Hanson (2000) investigated media presentation of Judaism, contending that singling out issues of Judaic observance reinforced the view that Jewish people are alien, and therefore not like the 'rest of America' (p 43). Misreporting strengthens prejudice, and any non-mainstream religion is presented as 'quasi-criminal' (Wah, 2001). The issue surrounding the misrepresentation of the 'other' is the reluctance of people, especially those with power and privilege, 'to perceive those different from themselves except through their own culturally clouded vision' (Delpit, 1995, p xiv).

Baumann (1994) argues that the sceptical and positivist assumptions of modern research are inhospitable to the spiritual beliefs of Christianity, Judaism or Islam. Yet society appears to condone the deliberate manipulation of information as morally justifiable and becomes indifferent to these forms of deception because, as Berry (2000) states, they are perceived as part of human nature. As a consequence of the perceived hostility of the media, and previous negative experiences with that medium, both Wilkes (1992) and Wosk (1995) found that members of religious communities have little reason for speaking to the press because so much of what they say is misinterpreted. This perception can also translate to a lack of trust in researchers, as many are fearful their beliefs will be misrepresented in some way.

Researchers are responsible not only to the ethical code of the university-based human research ethics committee but also to those being studied (Christians, 2000). Participants have the right to express their lived religiosity in a forum that respects their beliefs and practices, and will endeavour to portray their lived experience in a favourable rather than critical light.

Ethical considerations

The ethics of researching areas of religious and/or cultural sensitivity are ambiguous at best (Gruppetta, 2005b). In terms of this research there were no specific guidelines relating to asking questions surrounding a person's personal beliefs. Ivey and Ivey (2003) suggest that to be 'culturally competent' the interviewer needs to be culturally aware, ask culturally neutral, very open questions and be flexible in response to the answers in order to gather maximum information from the participant (Ivey and Ivey, 2003). Therefore questions were designed to be open to the individual's lived experience but not weighted to a particular religious or cultural viewpoint. For example, in investigating beliefs about what might occur to an individual after they die, the question was phrased as 'what do you believe will happen when *you* die?', specifically questioning their personal belief, rather than 'what happens when we go to heaven?', as this question is weighted toward Christian beliefs. According to Kameniar (2004), using the terms 'we believe' and 'they believe' positions all religions and cultures other than your own as the 'other', reinforcing the idea that all of society believes the same things, therefore marginalising all those who have different beliefs. It is preferable to ask 'what do *you* believe?' to ensure that language is consistent in presentation and does not 'other' the participant.

As previously discussed, researchers external to the culture being studied have the potential to detrimentally portray beliefs that conflict with their own (Delamont, 2002). Therefore any study involving individual belief, religious or otherwise, should be approached with caution. Any dilemmas arising throughout the research must be addressed through consultation with the participants and their cultural leaders in order to ensure cultural sensitivity. In terms of this research this involved negotiation with the organisations operating as key informants, and with individual participants, including questioning my own interaction with those involved.

Examples from the field

When I arrived for an interview with minute strands of dog hair on my clothing, two of the participants, one Muslim and one Hindu, took offence as both believed that dogs were 'unclean'. These beliefs do not necessarily reflect the beliefs of the whole of their faith communities, but initially affected my ability to establish a relationship with these particular participants.

Although I critically research aspects of correct attire, customs and conduct prior to initial meetings, when first meeting 'Zara', an Indonesian Muslim woman, she was obviously distressed and actually recoiled when approached. Zara explained: "according to Hadith, anything a dog touches must be washed seven times, the final time in dust". This aspect of Islamic belief was previously unknown to me, and had not been mentioned during arrangements with the Islamic agency referring the participant; however, it meant much negotiation was required before another interview could be scheduled. Therefore it was arranged that I would shower and change into 'dog-free' clothing prior to our next meeting and on arrival wash my hands the required seven times, the last time 'in dust', which meant I conducted the interview with filthy hands as Zara required full compliance. Taking the trouble to comply was crucial to establishing trust and worth the effort, as further interviews did not require this last restriction, provided no dog hair was evident on my clothing.

It should be noted that this belief concerning dogs is not common to all Muslims. Dogs are considered unclean according to some who study Islamic law, and contested by modern scholars of the Qur'an (El Fadl, 2006). When I enquired how Zara could be sure of keeping clean in public places, where a dog may have been, she replied that she washes quite thoroughly after negotiating any public area where a dog may have been, particularly before praying.

After further research into this area, at the next meeting reference to newspaper articles referring to Muslim taxi drivers refusing to carry guide dogs in their cars (Saleh, 2006) was also a cultural faux pas, as Zara explained that no access to newspaper or television reports was permitted during Ramadan. Other Muslim participants were not restricted from media forums during this time, therefore this restriction may have been specific to Zara's interpretation of her own religious practice. This perspective highlights the need for individual interpretation, as one Asian cannot speak for all Asians, one Aboriginal cannot speak for all Aboriginals, nor can one woman speak for all women (Denzin and Lincoln, 1998). Nevertheless, they provide an authoritative voice that permits an insightful glimpse of an otherwise hidden world. Zara's hidden world may not be one shared by all Muslims, but her interpretation is as valid as any other interpretation, because it is *her* 'lived experience' (Thibodeau and MacRae, 1997).

In another example, during the initial arrangements for interviewing Alex, a young man describing himself as a 'Fijian Indian' and a practising Hindu, we quickly established that my own premises, where my dogs were permitted access to the living areas, were completely out of the question. His explanation was as follows:

> 'I have to be excessively clean. If I touch the dog, I have to wash my hands. I don't touch my dog but I really care for my dog, I chuck it food. I will, like, come home and check whether he has been fed.... I have had numerous dogs, I used to touch the dog but then I got grossed [*sic*] out. If I touch the dog I can't just wash my hands, I have to have a whole shower.' (Alex, 2006)

The exchange highlights the difficulty of establishing a rapport between participant and researcher. After reassurance that his opinion of dogs was not offensive we moved on to discussion of other areas of the interview; however, initial conversations and interviews are exploratory until each is able to establish the level of conversation that they are comfortable to share. A certain amount of trust is necessary in order to share your life story, indeed yourself, with another person and these contradictions in micro perspectives impact on the establishment of a relationship.

Alex may have shared a similar sense of faith imperatives as Zara regarding any interaction with dogs, as cleanliness and hygiene are central to Hindu practices and beliefs. However, Alex also described himself as 'excessively clean', and noted that his parents and siblings were not as meticulous as he was, particularly with their interaction with the family pet. Alex also stated that despite his previous description of himself as a 'practising Hindu', he was not as religiously observant as his parents and often only worshipped to appease his mother. Therefore it is difficult to state empirically that Alex's beliefs were the sole basis for the inadvertent offence caused by this micro issue.

In contrast, another participant, Fred, also describing himself as a 'Fijian Indian' and practising Hindu, told me that dogs were revered because they 'could see "angels" (spirits) and would look up and howl just before a death because they could see the spirits hovering over a house waiting for the "soul" to depart'. When asked what he meant by 'angels', he replied that he had only used that word to describe the 'spirits' because he thought the biblical reference would be easier to understand, whereas he had no real way of explaining his belief in 'spirits' to a non-Hindu.

The broader implications of this belief are profound. Fred's description of his own beliefs were 'Christianised' in order to be shared with someone from another cultural viewpoint, as he believed that those external to his faith could not understand the concepts as readily unless described with Christian connotations. It is not only Fred's belief that he cannot convey elements of his own faith to a non-Hindu researcher, he has assumed that all information is measured through 'Christian' viewpoints, at least within Australia. This 'socially desirable response' (Guba and Lincoln, 1989, p 53) could mean the essence of Fred's truth was lost in the translation.

Conclusion

The chapter has looked at some of the ways the researcher/practitioner can inadvertently offend those within specific faith identities. As highlighted by these examples of inadvertent offence, these participants' viewpoints are already altered through their marginality and as such they are more sensitive to perceptions of a society weighted to mainstream viewpoints (Collins, 2004). Thus more intensive research to investigate the effect of mainstream societal expectations on participant interaction is required. Open discussions of beliefs, either cultural or religious, are paramount to the shared reality of our multicultural existence and integral to deeper research.

With few guidelines for research involving faith communities it is only through sharing the experiences of others that such dilemmas can be avoided and/or addressed. The dynamic lived experience of religiosity must be experienced firsthand. There is no other way to learn these micro facets of religious and cultural practice. Such experience must be literally lived and therefore researched as part of the participants' lived experiences. The lack of documentation of micro religious practices within the variety of faith traditions in Australia requires more intensive negotiation within the researcher–participant relationship in order to overcome the dangers of a little knowledge of macro issues causing inadvertent offence on micro levels.

Notes

[1] Personal communication with K. Sabanathan, Director of Educational Activities, Sydney Murugan Temple, Mays Hill.

[2] All participants in this study have been given psuedonyms to protect their anonymity.

References

Baumann, P. (1994) 'Epistemological muddles', *Commonweal*, vol 121, no 17, pp 4-6.

Berry, D. (2000) *Ethics and media culture: Practices and representations*, Oxford: Reed Educational.

Blasi, A.J. (2002) 'Marginality as a societal position of religion', *Sociology of Religion*, fall, vol 63, no 3, pp 267-90.

Bouma, G. (2006) *Australian soul: Religion and spirituality in the twenty-first century*, Port Melbourne: Cambridge University Press.

Brasch, R. (1999) *The Star of David: The story of Judaism, its teachings, philosophy and symbols*, New York, NY: HarperCollins Publishers.

Carey, H.M. (1996) *Believing in Australia: A cultural history of religions*, St Leonards, Australia: Allen & Unwin Pty Ltd.

Christians, C.G. (2000) 'Ethics and politics in qualitative research', in N.K. Denzin and Y. Lincoln (eds) *Handbook of qualitative research* (2nd edn), London: Sage Publications, pp 133-55.

Clark, L.S. and Hoover, S.M. (1997) 'At the intersection of media, culture and religion: a bibliographic essay', in S.M. Hoover and K. Lundby (eds) *Rethinking media, religion and culture*, Thousand Oaks, CA: Sage Publications, pp 15-36.

Clarke, P.B. and Somers, J. (eds) (1994) *Japanese new religions in the west*, Oxford: Bodleian Japanese Library.

Collins, P.H. (2004) 'Learning from the outsider within: the sociological significance of Black feminist thought', in S. Harding (ed) *The feminist standpoint theory reader: Intellectual and political controversies*, London: Routledge, pp 103-26.

Dart, J. (1997) 'The pull of faith: noxious, negligible or negotiable?', *The Nieman Reports*, vol 51, no 3, pp 5-8.

Delamont, S. (2002) 'Whose side are we on? Revisiting Becker's classic ethical question at the fin de siecle', in T. Welland and L. Pugsley (eds) *Ethical dilemmas in qualitative research*, Aldershot: Ashgate, pp 149-63.

Delpit, L. (1995) *Other people's children: Cultural conflict in the classroom*, New York, NY: New Press.

Denzin, N.K. and Lincoln, Y.S. (1998) *Collecting and interpreting qualitative materials*, London: Sage Publications.

El Fadl, K.A. (2006) *The search for beauty in Islam: A conference of the books*, Lanham, MD: Rowman & Littlefield Publishers Inc.

Ellis, C. and Berger, L. (2003) 'Their story/my story/our story: including the researcher's experience in interview research', in J.F. Gubrium and J.A. Holstein (eds) *Postmodern interviewing*, London: Sage Publications, pp 157-86.

Gruppetta, M. (2004a) *Autophenomenography? Alternative uses of autographically based research*, AARE: Australian Association for Research in Education, Annual Conference, Melbourne, 28 November-2 December (www.aare.edu.au/04pap/gru04228.pdf).

Gruppetta, M. (2004b) 'Media misrepresentation: misinformation, misconceptions and mythology that maintain mistrust', Proceedings of the 'Fear and Fascination: The Other in Religion' Conference, Sydney: University of Western Sydney.

Gruppetta, M. (2005a) '"Snowball recruiting": capitalising on the theoretical "six degrees of separation"', in B. Kozuh, T.N. Beran, A. Kowlowska and P. Bayliss (eds) *Measurement and assessment in educational and social research*, Krakow: Slovenian Research Agency, pp 151-60.

Gruppetta, M. (2005b) 'Ethical interviewing across cultures', Australian Government, National Health and Medical Research Council 'Ethics in Human Research' Conference, 12-13 May, Canberra (www.nhmrc.gov.au/news/events/_files/gruppetta.pdf).

Guba, E.G. and Lincoln, Y.S. (1989) *Fourth generation evaluation*, London: Sage Publications.

Gubrium, J.F. and Holstein, J.A. (1997) *The new language of qualitative method*, New York, NY: Oxford University Press.

Hanson, C. (2000) 'God and man on the campaign trail', *Columbia Journalism Review*, vol 39, no 4, pp 40-6.

Hunter, M.G. (2006) 'Experiences conducting cross-cultural research', *Journal of Global Information Management*, vol 14, no 2, pp 75-89, April-June.

Ivey, A.E. and Ivey, M.B. (2003) *Intentional interview and counselling: Facilitating client development in a multicultural society*, Australia: Thomson.

Kabir, N. (2005) *Muslims in Australia: Immigration, race relations, and cultural history*, London: Kegan Paul Limited.

Kameniar, B. (2004) 'Hosts and hostages in the religion education classroom', Paper presented at 'Fear and Fascination: The Other in Religion', Australian Association for the Study of Religions and the Affinity Intercultural Foundation Conference, UWS Bankstown, 16-18 July.

Lovat, T., Follers, J., Parnell, V. Hill, B. and Allard, G. (2000) *New society and culture* (2nd edn), Katoomba, Australia: Social Science Press.

Manager, L. (ed) (1999) *Muslim diversity: Local Islam in global contexts*, Richmond: Curzon Press.

O'Riley, P.A. (2003) *Technology, culture, and socioeconomics: A rhizoanalysis of educational discourses*, New York, NY: Peter Lang.

Reed-Danahay, D.E. (ed) (1997) *Auto/ethnography: Rewriting the social and the self*, New York, NY: Berg.

Rutland, S.D. (2005) *The Jews in Australia*, Port Melbourne: Cambridge University Press.

Saleh, L. (2006) 'Taxi driver clash of faith', *The Daily Telegraph*, 12 October, pp 1-2.

Shultz, R.A. (2002) 'Illuminating realities: a phenomenological view from two underachieving gifted learners', *Roeper Review*, vol 24, no 4, pp 203-13.

Sikh Missionary Center (1990) *Sikh religion*, Michigan, MI: Sikh Missionary Center.

Storer, D. (ed) (1985) *Ethnic family values in Australia*, Sydney: Prentice-Hall.

Streeton, R., Cooke, M. and Campbell, J. (2004) 'Researching the researchers: using a snowballing technique', *Nurse Researcher*, vol 12, no 1, pp 35-47.

Thibodeau, J. and MacRae, J. (1997) 'Breast cancer survival: a phenomenological inquiry', *Advances in Nursing Science*, vol 19, no 4, pp 65-75.

Thomas, S.P. and Pollio, H.R. (2002) *Listening to patients: A phenomenological approach to nursing research and practice*, New York, NY: Springer.

Tolich, M. and Davidson, C. (1999) *Starting fieldwork: An introduction to qualitative research in New Zealand*, Melbourne: Oxford University Press.

Turnbull, M. (1999) *Safe haven: Records of the Jewish experience in Australia*, Canberra: National Archives of Australia.

van Manen, M. (2000) 'Phenomenology online: glossary', University of Alberta, Edmonton, Canada (www.phenomenologyonline.com/glossary/glossary.html#phenemenology).

Wah, C.R. (2001) 'Jehovah's Witnesses and the responsibility of religious freedom: the European experience', *Journal of Church and State*, vol 43, no 3, pp 579-602.

Wilkes, P. (1992) 'Why people of God don't talk to the press', *Columbia Journalism Review*, vol 31, no 3, pp 54-6.

Wosk, Y. (1995) 'Judaism: 4,000 years of media attention', *Nieman Reports*, vol 49, no 3, pp 78-81.

Conclusion

Basia Spalek and Alia Imtoual

Introduction

Throughout this collection it has been argued that the social sciences are disciplines that have arisen out of an engagement with modernity. A number of contributions have argued that because of this, the values associated with Enlightenment philosophies in terms of secularism, rationalism and objectivity are hegemonic discourses. These hegemonic discourses have shaped not only social science theory but also many of the dominant social science research methodologies. Of particular interest to this volume has been the centrality of secularism within social science theory and research approaches. Many of the individual chapters have explicitly argued that secularism remains a powerful and largely invisible framework of understanding that has a profound effect on social science researchers engaging with questions of religion, faith and spirituality.

In a time where, despite the centrality of secularist attitudes, a growing number of individuals are claiming or reclaiming a religious or spiritual identity for themselves, we argue that social science researchers must engage with this seeming incompatibility if they are to conduct ethical, respectful and accurate research. In order for this to occur, social science researchers must engage with the implications of a religious/spiritual identity on social science methodologies that arise from a largely secularist intellectual tradition. All the contributors to this collection have engaged with these difficult issues in a variety of ways.

A number of factors appear to have led to a heightened focus on religious and spiritual matters within contemporary Western societies. In many parts of the world, even those experiencing modernisation, including Africa, Asia, European countries and the US, religion has been at the forefront of collective action, where it has constituted a form of identity politics. For example, according to Wilmore (1999), Black communities in the US have been bound together through biblical stories and the event of worship, and according to Appleyard (2006), right-wing religious evangelism constitutes a strong political force in the US. Religious group collective identities might be viewed from a Durkheimian perspective, whereby religion is conceptualised as a form of collective memory or collective consciousness, based on a community of past, present and future members, as well as tradition (Davie, 2002). At the same time, religion may also be highly individualised, reflecting the fragmentation, individualisation and fluidity of identities associated with conditions of contemporary Western society, so that individuals' (particularly young people's) beliefs become increasingly 'personal, detached and heterogeneous' (Davie, 2002, p 8). It has been claimed, for example, that increasing numbers of young Muslims in Britain are using the Qur'an and hadiths directly as a resource rather than accepting the traditional views passed on to them from their parents (Joly, 1995).

Although, traditionally, religious questions have been marginalised by academia, with, for example, sociologists assuming that religion is a declining phenomenon that requires little attention (Lyon, 1996), more recently, particularly since the 1990s, researchers have increasingly been including a spiritual/religious dimension in their work. Social theorists have turned a critical gaze towards contemporary Western society, highlighting that liberal democratic societies are marked by risk and uncertainty (Beck, 1992; Lyon, 1996; Young, 1999, Bauman, 2000). As a result of the demise of the so-called 'Golden Age' of postwar Europe and North America of full employment and rising affluence, and the emergence of insecurity and anxiety, there has been increased attention placed on the construction of social identities, and religion and/or spirituality might be viewed as constituting some of the material from which identities are built (Giddens, 1991; Beckford, 2003). Beckford (1996) links Ulrich Beck's work in *Risk society: Towards a new modernity* (1992) to spirituality, arguing that there are religious or spiritual overtones to Beck's claim that the risks accompanying modernisation in contemporary Western society are so severe that a new collective consciousness emerges, one which 'may even generate a solidarity of living things' (Beckford, 1996, p 39). And according to King (1993, p 215), although feminism might be viewed as being linked to the notion of secularism, the women's movement might also be seen as grounded in an act of faith for the possibility of a better society, so that the emergence of feminism 'points to new religious and spiritual developments which affirm the resacralisation of nature, the earth, the body, sexuality and the celebration of the bonds of community'.

At the same time, in a post 9/11 context the concept and practical aspects of religion and spirituality are taking on greater political significance, with attention being placed particularly, although not exclusively, on Muslim communities. Policy makers are grappling with notions of citizenship and individual rights in multi-ethnic and multireligious contemporary democratic societies, which inevitably lead to an increased focus on religious identities. Popular interest in these topics can also be seen, as evidenced by a number of television programmes like the BBC2 series in December 2005 'The Story of God', presented by Professor Robert Winston, and a Channel 4 programme, 'The Root of all Evil? The God Delusion?', presented by Professor Richard Dawkins. The box office popularity of films such as 'The Da Vinci Code' and 'The Passion of the Christ' are further examples of the interest that religious and spiritual issues are generating. In Australia, there has been a steady increase in the number of programmes devoted to issues of religion, faith and spirituality, such as the SBS series 'John Safran vs God' and 'Speaking in Tongues', and the ABC programme 'Compass' screening weekly on a variety of religion/spirituality-related issues.

Religion, spirituality and the social sciences reflects the heightened focus on the religious and the spiritual in popular culture and policy arenas as well as within the academy, comprising of three main parts. The first part examined the notion of secularism in relation to contemporary Western society. Secularism might be viewed as an ideology, the philosophical and historical underpinnings of which lie within the European Enlightenment, where scientific reasoning increasingly replaced theological frameworks of understanding. At the same time, the influence of religious institutions on civil society declined with the emergence of modern institutions and professional bodies that came to be separated out from their religious roots (Beckford, 1996; Jürgensmeyer, 2003). Importantly, secularism is a multilayered and complex notion, as different contexts will contain different dynamics that might be considered to comprise 'the secular'. As a result, the first part of this book consists of a collection of work from writers who engaged with, and examined, notions of secularism from within a wide range of settings, from a wide variety of subject disciplines and theoretical traditions.

Part 1 also included a focus on secularisation, which might be viewed as a process, as comprising of a widespread alienation from organised churches and religious institutions (Berger, 1999; Davie, 2002). Similar to secularism, the notion of secularisation has generated much controversy. For instance, Berger (1999) has argued that secularisation on a societal level does not necessarily mean secularisation at the level of individual consciousness. According to Davie (2002, p 162), the number of young people in Northern Europe who believe in life after death and in a 'god within' is growing. Luckmann (1996) has argued that although institutional forms of religion have declined in late modernity, new social forms of religion have emerged, at the core of which is the construction of meaning through the construction of the self. Beckford (1996) argues that, despite the effects of the Enlightenment, religion continues to be used as a cultural resource, and many writers maintain that religion has undergone a resurgence in contemporary Western society, as evidenced by the rising numbers of people joining new religious movements, or practising 'New Age' forms of spirituality (Lyon, 1996; Heelas and Woodhead, 2005; Heelas, 2006).

Part 2 considered the emergence of social scientific disciplines within the context of modernity and Enlightenment philosophy, exploring how the values underpinning social scientific enquiry might serve to marginalise religion and spirituality. For example, in relation to criminology, Morrison (1995, p 5) has argued that this subject was 'born with the death of God', suggesting that religious and spiritual beliefs and experiences are not open, or indeed relevant, to criminological investigation. It seems that values associated with Enlightenment philosophies in terms of secularism, rationalism and objectivity predominate, despite challenges from critical approaches. Such narrowing of the lens of analysis is unhelpful in the expansion of the field of research. The sidelining of religion and spirituality has occurred in many social science disciplines and can be identified in a range of aspects: from the definition of key concepts through to the topics and methods of empirical research that have been used, as well as the construction of models and theory. Part 2 highlighted that although critical perspectives challenge normative structures in society that can serve to oppress, and which can impose borders on knowledge, in relation to racism, feminism, heteronormativity, ageism, ablebodiedness and class, critical perspectives have tended to overlook the notion of secularism as a powerful, if invisible, normative structure and framework of understanding. This part of the book consists of a body of work from writers who are asking critical questions about the theoretical underpinnings of social science disciplines and the challenges that are posed by religious and spiritual questions.

Part 3 consists of a series of reflections on social science research methodologies when researching religion and spirituality. This part included the work of researchers who raised significant questions about how social science research methods/methodologies reflected the deep importance of religion and spirituality to significant numbers of individuals. As such this part builds on a growing body of research. For example, critical Black feminists have introduced the notion of 'spirit injury' as constituting an important aspect of the process of victimisation (Davis, 1997; Williams, 1997), victimologists have examined spiritual aspects to the process of victimisation (Kennedy et al, 1998; Ganzevoort, 2007), and work involving Muslim communities has highlighted the importance of religion in individuals' lives. If religious identity is an important aspect of research participants' self-identity, then secularist frameworks of understanding that focus solely on the role of societal and cultural traditions in religion may be inappropriate, since it might be argued that these ignore the centrality of faith (Roald, 2001; Bullock, 2002; Spalek, 2005). Further to this, a researcher who holds little theological knowledge of a particular religion will encounter significant difficulties when trying to understand individuals' interpretations of their religion and their belief systems. At the same time, the complexity and fluidity of a term such as 'spiritual', and the difficulty of applying scientific techniques to its measurement and exploration, pose some difficult research questions. Part 3 included reflections about how researchers have begun to engage with religion/spirituality in their work, raising questions about how new methodologies might be developed so as to capture these aspects of individuals' lives.

Concluding thoughts

This volume set out to explore the current theoretical underpinnings of various social science disciplines, to link these to the development of research approaches and the resultant ways in which religion and spirituality have been marginalised from these approaches. In providing a space for the engagement with issues of religion and spirituality in research we aimed to explore the ways in which researchers contend with structural and cultural borders around knowledge and methodologies and how they are creating ways to conduct social science research that acknowledge and respect the importance of belief and faith identities. In doing so, we also wanted to break down the borders between 'quantitative' and 'qualitative' research, as this volume is more concerned with research approaches than data collection procedures. This collection has also provided a space to explore some of the complexities for researchers who are negotiating with the voices of faith communities and how social science research frameworks can respectfully and critically work with these communities, particularly around issues of identity, difference and representation. As many of the chapters attest to, committed and ethical researchers are looking for ways that are more inclusive of religion, spirituality and faith identities to transform existing social science approaches. We are confident that these approaches will become more widespread, and these voices more often heard.

References

Appleyard, B. (2006) 'Is it time to take God out of the State?', *The Sunday Times*, 22 October, pp 14-15.

Bauman, Z. (2000) *Liquid modernity*, Cambridge: Polity Press.

Beck, U. (1992) *Risk society: Towards a new modernity*, London: Sage Publications.

Beckford, J. (1996) 'Postmodernity, high modernity and new modernity: three concepts in search of religion', in K. Flanagan and P. Jupp (eds) *Postmodernity, sociology and religion*, Basingstoke: Macmillan, pp 30-47.

Beckford, J. (2003) *Social theory and religion*, Cambridge: Cambridge University Press.

Berger, P. (ed) (1999) *The desecularization of the world: Resurgent religion and world politics*, Grand Rapids, MI: William B. Eerdmans Publishing.

Bullock, K. (2002) *Rethinking Muslim women and the veil: Challenging historical and modern stereotypes*, London: International Institute of Islamic Thought.

Davie, G. (2002) *Europe: The exceptional case*, London: Darton, Longman and Todd.

Davis, D. (1997) 'The harm that has no name: street harassment, embodiment and African American women', in A. Wing (ed) *Critical race feminism: A reader*, New York, NY: New York University Press, pp 192-202.

Ganzevoort, R. (2007) 'Coping with tragedy and malice', in L.J. Minnema and P.E. van Doorn-Harder (eds) *Coping with evil in religion and culture: Case studies*, Amsterdam: Rodopi, pp 247-60.

Giddens, A. (1991) *Modernity and self identity*, Cambridge: Polity Press.

Heelas, P. (2006) 'Challenging secularization theory: the growth of New Age spiritualities of life', *Hedgehog Review. Critical Reflections on Contemporary Culture* (issue on after secularisation), vol 8, nos 1 and 2, pp 46-58.

Heelas, P. and Woodhead, L. (2005) *The spiritual revolution: Why religion is giving way to spirituality*, Oxford: Blackwell.

Joly, D. (1995) *Britannia's crescent: Making a place for Muslims in British society*, Aldershot: Avebury.

Jürgensmeyer, M. (2003) *Terror in the mind of God*, London: University of California Press.

Kennedy, J., Davis, R. and Taylor, B. (1998) 'Changes in spirituality and well-being among victims of sexual assault', *Journal of the Scientific Study of Religion*, vol 37, no 2, pp 322-8.

King, U. (1993) *Women and spirituality* (2nd edn), London: Macmillan.

Luckmann, T. (1996) 'The privatization of religion and morality', in P. Heelas, S. Lash and P. Morris (eds) *Detraditionalization: Critical reflections on authority and identity*, Oxford: Blackwell, pp 72-86.

Lyon, D. (1996) 'Religion and the post-modern: old problems, new prospects', in K. Flanagan and P. Jupp (eds) *Postmodernity, sociology and religion*, Basingstoke: Macmillan, pp 14-29.

Morrison, W. (1995) *Theoretical criminology: From modernity to post-modernism*, London: Cavendish Publishing.

Roald, A.S. (2001) *Women in Islam: The Western experience*, London and New York, NY: Routledge.

Spalek, B. (2005) 'Researching Black Muslim women's lives: a critical reflection', *The International Journal of Social Research Methodology*, vol 8, no 5, pp 1-14.

Williams, P. (1997) 'Spirit-murdering the messenger: the discourse of finger pointing as the law's response to racism', in A. Wing (ed) *Critical race feminism: A reader*, New York, NY: New York University Press, pp 229-36.

Wilmore, G. (1999) *Black religion and black radicalism* (3rd edn), New York, NY: Orbis Books.

Young, J. (1999) *The exclusive society*, London: Sage Publications.

Index